I Need to Know

answers to

questions

about God

I Need to Know

FAMILY CHRISTIAN STORES

www.FamilyChristian.com

Scripture quotations marked (NIV) are taken from the Holy Bible,
New International Version®. NIV®. Copyright © 1973, 1978, 1984 by
International Bible Society. Used by permission of Zondervan
Publishing House. All rights reserved. Scripture quotations marked
(NKJV) are taken from the New King James Version of the Bible.
Copyright © 1979, 1980, 1982, Thomas Nelson, Inc. Publishers.
Scripture quotations marked (KJV) are taken from the King James
Version. Scripture quotations marked (NASB or NAS) are taken
from NEW AMERICAN STANDARD BIBLE® (NASB) Copyright ©
1960, 1977, 1995 by the Lockman Foundation. Used by permission.

Published by Family Christian Stores, 5300 Patterson Avenue SE,
Grand Rapids, Michigan 49530.

ISBN 159391035 5

1 2 3 4 5 6 7 8 9 10

Dear Valued Guest,

At some point we all ask "Is there a God?," "Who is Jesus?," "What is being saved?" If this is where you are at this time, this book is for you! At a later point, maybe we are walking a smooth path in our journey of faith when the road suddenly takes a sharp curve or we stumble into some deep holes we didn't anticipate. A job is lost. A spouse or child becomes ill. A relationship turns sour. We're sent reeling and while it may appear we're holding it together on the outside, we're asking questions on the inside. "Why did you let this happen, God?" "Where are you in the midst of this pain?" "You're supposed to be good – so why did You allow this to happen?" And a part of us may feel that asking hard questions like these means that our faith isn't strong, adding to the pain and confusion. Again, this book is for you!

It's important to understand that our questions don't frighten God and that in fact, questions are a part of faith. Read through the Psalms and you'll find David – someone described as a man's after God's own heart – asking tough questions. Thumb through the book of Job and find a man who's had his life turned upside down, with questions that may mirror yours. You're not alone.

The book you hold in your hands explores some of the questions we'll all face at some point in our lives. You may not find easy answers, but my prayer is that you find some peace in the midst of the storm.

Answering the call to help strengthen
the hearts, minds & souls of our guests,

Dave Browne
President/CEO
Family Christian Stores

Questions

Foreword
by Ted Dekker

I'll never forget the day I lost my faith. That ill-fated morning will be forever stamped upon my mind. I'd gone to sleep on a ship moored in a peaceful cove of understanding, and awoke to find that the anchor line had been severed.

I lay motionless in bed for an hour, staring at the ceiling, but try as I did, the old familiar confidence of my origin and my purpose on this floating globe we call Earth, refused to return to me. I was adrift in a sea of meaninglessness without the slightest notion of where my ship was heading.

I was twenty-one years old, and for the first time in my life, I was truly and hopelessly lost. Don't get me wrong, I'd questioned my faith many a time in my formative years, and during the previous two years I'd tangled with an onslaught of questions while studying religion and philosophy at Evangel University in Springfield Missouri. I'd come through unscathed. Or so I'd thought.

Clearly my descent into this abyss of uncertainty couldn't have been an overnight journey, but the sudden realization that I no longer knew whether or not God even existed, much less cared about me, felt abrupt and jarring. If I found any solace during that time it was in discovering that I was not alone. In fact, being adrift is common place today. The only challenge greater than guiding my ship back onto its true course was avoiding all the other ships crowding that foggy sea.

Many drift into the waters of apathy when confronted by their own uncertainties. Others lock their minds in denial by turning away from the questions altogether. A few panic.

I panicked.

There were a number of good explanations for my strong reaction. For starters, having studied philosophy, I was convinced that the only plausible alternative to believing in a Creator who had purpose was Existentialism, which ultimately delivers a life of utter hopelessness. I had neither the desire nor the patience for this alternative.

Another reason for my strong reaction was the fact that I'd grown up not only in the Church, but as the son of Christian missionaries in the jungles of Indonesia. My entire life had revolved around the fundamental belief that God existed and that he'd made a way for me to have a relationship with Him. Life was nothing less than a love affair between the Creator and me.

Now I was suddenly faced with the prospect that the Creator might not be interested in a relationship with me after all. Worse, He might not even exist!

My experience was tantamount to that of Arnold Schwarzenegger in the movie *Total Recall*, in which he awakens to discover that everything about his life, including his wife, are based on planted memories. Falsehoods.

Whether you're Muslim, Hindu, Christian, agnostic, atheist— whatever beliefs you've grown up with, your world view is bound to be challenged at some point. It took me months to examine my faith and rebuild my world view after that morning crash, but I can stand before you today, two decades later, and say with utmost confidence, that the journey I embarked upon that day was perhaps the most important of my life. Certainly the most satisfying.

The course was also quite harrowing. I won't pretend it was a picnic. As a writer with over a dozen novels in print, I have learned how to deliver high drama, and I promise you spiritual discovery is an adventure unequaled by any movie or novel.

But the journey was also surprisingly reasonable. Truth, it turns out, is not a thin, wispy cloud that the faithful grasp at to find meaning. True, all world views begin with presuppositions which are anchored in faith. But all questions of life, even the most difficult, are surrounded by sound reason and the conclusions which follow any diligent examination is fairly straightforward.

There's no doubt in my mind that if I would have had this book as a resource that morning twenty years ago, my journey of discovery would have been a much shorter journey. Not since C.S. Lewis penned his book, *Mere Christianity*, has a single book so adequately examined Christianity in such a practical and accessible way.

This is no sermon preached to the faithful. Neither is it an apologetic determined to sway the feeble-minded. This book is a fresh, honest examination of life's most important questions at a time in history when those questions are most misunderstood.

If you're anything like me, you believe whatever makes most sense to you, period. Intellectual suicide is not an activity you relish. If someone suggests something that makes no sense to you, regardless of whom that someone is, it goes in the mental bin reserved for deliberations in a time of either complete boredom or a time of crises. Let me assure you that neither boredom, nor desperation are prerequisites for this book. It will engage you from beginning to end in a way that all humans are meant to be engaged.

We were all born with minds for good reason, it's time we use them. Read the book, draw your own conclusions. Whatever you decide, the journey may very well be the most important one you take.

Bon Voyage.

Author's Bio Ted Dekker is known for novels that combine adrenaline-laced plot twists with the supernatural and the surreal. His books have created quite a stir among fiction readers. Ted grew up as a missionary kid in the jungles of Indonesia and now lives with his family in the mountains of Colorado. His upbringing had a definite influence on his writing. To learn more you can visit his web site at www.teddekker.com

Does God Exist?

by Steve Kumar

Chapter:
Does God Exist?

Book:
Christianity for Skeptics

Look for your coupons for this and other featured titles in the back of this book.

Author's Bio

Dr. Steve Kumar is an international lecturer on apologetics and the director of New Zealand's Apologetics Society. He has also written *Think What You Believe* and *Answering the Counterfeit*. Dr. Kumar makes his home in New Zealand.

Does God Exist?
by Steve Kumar

Is it reasonable to believe in God? Can God's existence be logically proven without appealing to religious experience or a leap of faith? Is God merely a psychological projection, a primitive myth? How could anyone be sure there is a God? What evidence supports God's existence?

Our secular culture may dismiss God as irrelevant to our existence and give the seductive impression that God is on a long vacation. This popular myth may provide some humans with a sense of freedom and autonomy, but it has not delivered us from boredom, anxiety, suicide, stress, drugs, crime, addiction to entertainment, and other neuroses. After diagnosing the human predicament, psychiatrist Victor Frankl observes, "More people today have the means to live, but no meaning to live for" According to Erich Fromm, one of the leading specialists in human behavior, the majority of those who visit psychiatrists suffer from "an inner deadness. They live in the midst of plenty and are joyless."

In the light of our social and spiritual crisis it is not beyond reason to propose that the missing element in our recipe for existence is the reality of God. History has repeatedly confirmed the tragic truth that when people ignore the Transcendent they descend into the abyss of nihilism. Where God is abandoned, human life becomes, in the words of Thomas Hubb, "nasty, brutish and short." There is no song of hope but only the cry of despair.

THE RELEVANCE OF GOD

The reality of God's existence has serious consequences to human existence. No other issue touches our lives as does this subject. It has a profound philosophical implication on all matters of reality.

It is vital to reflect on the relevance of God before we demonstrate the reality of God. The existence of God plays a significant role in our lives. Superficially many may not acknowledge this reality, but upon deeper reflection, the relevance of God is inescapable.

Some time ago a New York police officer observed a man standing on a bridge, apparently thinking of committing suicide. The policeman approached him and said, "Let me make a deal with you. Give me ten minutes to tell you why I think life is worth living, then you take ten minutes and tell me why you think life is not worth living. If I am unable to convince you, I will let you jump." According to the story, after twenty minutes they joined hands and both jumped off the bridge.

The story poses serious questions. Is life really worth living? If there is no God, what is the reason for our being? What is the logical ground for our values, morality, rationality, dignity, and personality? If there is no God, we are, in the words of philosopher William James, like dogs in a library observing the volumes but unable to read the print. Are we just an accidental by-product of matter evolved mindlessly on an infinitesimal speck of dust called Planet Earth? How could we find meaning in a meaningless universe? Reason in an irrational world? Value in a material universe and purpose in a random existence? The absence of God in reality is the absence of goodness, truth, value, meaning, reason, life, and joy. Many of our brilliant minds have understood only too well the truth that the rejection of God logically implies the rejection of all reality that is fundamental to God.

Although the subject of God may appear to be simple on the surface, it is an extremely profound matter. God is not a secondary issue but an ultimate factor. The very nature of God demands an approach that transcends the normal and the contingent. One should not attempt to prove God the way we try to prove apples and atoms. The reality of God is in a category that is radically trans-natural—that which is beyond and above nature. God is transcendent. One must not commit the categorical mistake of equating God with the phenomena which he has made.

If God is the cause of the universe, he must be beyond and greater than the physical dimension. Therefore we may discover the effects or evidence of God in the universe but not necessarily observe the essence of God within the universe, for the profound reason that he transcends the categories of space, time, and matter. The skeptic who says, "Show me your God!" and demands a scientific proof, is extremely simplistic.

The story of the man who went fishing illustrates an important truth. Every time he caught a big fish he kept throwing it back into the lake, and each time he caught a small one, he kept it. A mystified bystander, observing his peculiar process of selection, asked him what on earth he was doing. With a smile the man replied, "I only have an eight inch frying pan and so the larger fish won't fit." The trouble is, many a skeptic rejects God because God won't fit into their naturalistic philosophical frying pan. The truth is, there are realities which go beyond our limited paradigm, but to reject them because they do not fit our limited scientific category is to become a poor metaphysical fisherman. The trouble with our naturalistic metaphysical frying pan is that it is not big enough to include all of reality.

The question of God's existence is a perennial issue which presses upon all of us and demands a rational response. To go through life without examining ultimate questions is to miss the central point of human existence. The meaning of life is to find the meaning for life, and the purpose of existence is to discover the purpose worth living for. A sensible existence is possible only when we try to make sense of our lives and the universe.

Since the concept of God's existence is the greatest issue confronting humanity, it deserves our most thoughtful attention. Evangelical philosopher C. Stephen Evans affirms, "Belief in God is genuinely coherent with all we know about ourselves and our universe. It contradicts no known facts and it makes sense of many things that would otherwise be inexplicable."

Time magazine, in an interesting article, "Modernizing the Case for God," reports, "In a quiet revolution in thought and argument that hardly anyone could have foreseen only two decades ago, God is making a comeback." A generation ago there were few intellectuals in academic circles providing logical arguments for the existence of God, but today the situation has altered. As *Time* suggests, "Now it is more respectable among philosophers than it has been for a generation to talk about the possibility of God's existence."

Great thinkers who affirm the existence of God have left a legacy of arguments for us to reflect upon. We will examine several of them. These arguments have been reinforced by recent developments in contemporary logic, philosophical arguments, and a number of scientific data. They are valuable in supporting our confidence in the reality of God.

I. CONCLUSIVE COSMOLOGICAL EVIDENCE

In the opinion of many Christian philosophers, one of the most forceful arguments for the existence of God is the cosmic evidence. The existence of the universe is an undeniable reality. The fact of existence is indeed a mystery which staggers the mind. Sophists may deny the reality of the universe, but such an attempt is futile, for the Sophist must exist in order to deny it, therefore it is self-refuting. A good case in point is the example of a student at New York University who troubled his professor with a contradictory question, "Sir, how do I know that I exist?" The professor paused for a while, lowered his glasses, gazed at the student and demanded, "And whom shall I say is asking?" The notion that existence is an illusion is logically incoherent and factually meaningless.

The most profound philosophical question that has caused many debates and much discussion among philosophers is, "Why is there something, rather than nothing?" The reality of the universe demands a verdict. There is hardly a philosopher worth a grain of salt who has not struggled over this question. Every thinking person at some point confronts the problem. Philosopher John Hick writes:

> When we try to think about this infinitely fascinating universe in which we live we find that we are faced in the end with the mystery of existence, of why there is a universe at all.

Philosopher and theologian H. D. Lewis from London University notes, "The question 'Why is there something rather than nothing?' is regarded even by some skeptical philosophers as a significant one." This question caused considerable philosophical speculation for the German philosopher Gottfried Wilhelm Leibniz, who finally came to the conclusion that, "The first question which should rightly be asked is: Why is there something rather than nothing?"

Indeed, the fact is that we are existing rather than that we are not. Existential theologian Paul Tillich admits that "the riddle of all riddles" is the mystery that there is anything at all. The question of Being, as Martin Heidegger pointed out, is the most significant of all questions and deserves every energy of our intellectual effort.

Edward Sillem insists, "Man cannot find the ultimate explanation of his own being anywhere but in God Himself." In the same vein, philosopher Fredrick Copleston asserts, "What we call the world is intrinsically unintelligible, apart from the existence of God." It is no wonder that Voltaire echoed the obvious maxim, "If God did not exist it would be necessary to invent him." Speaking about the universe, Colin Brown, the British theologian, writes, "Are we to regard it as the product of pure chance, and believe that everything happens at random without rhyme or reason?" No! This would be mental suicide. Even a radical skeptic such as David Hume admitted the force of this argument when he wrote, "I never asserted so absurd a proposition as that anything might arise without a cause."

The weight of the cosmological argument is further strengthened by the confirmation of the majority of scientists today. Dr. Robert Gange, a research scientist, in his excellent book, *Origins and Destiny*, provides ample scientific evidence for the beginning of the universe. In the past scientists believed that the First Law of Thermodynamics led to a "steady state" theory of the universe: that the universe and everything in it has existed in one form or other forever. However, Dr. Gange notes, "Today, there's a problem with this idea *because the beginning of the universe has actually been measured*. Although the measurement is indirect, it nonetheless teaches that there actually was a beginning!"

Dr. Jastrow, who claims to be an agnostic, argues that the evidence from astronomy demonstrates that the universe had a beginning at a certain moment in time. He declares, "Now we see how the astronomical evidence leads to a biblical view of the origin of the world." He notes, "The details differ, but the essential elements in the astronomical and biblical accounts of Genesis are the same: the chain of events leading to man commenced suddenly and sharply at a definite moment in time, in a flash of light and energy." His brilliant conclusion is worth reflection:

> For the scientist who has lived by his faith in the power of reason, the story ends like a bad dream. He has scaled the mountains of ignorance; he is about to conquer the highest peak; as he pulls himself over the final rock, he is greeted by a band of theologians who have been sitting there for centuries.

The apostle Paul speaking to the Greek philosophers of his day argued that the existence of the universe provided good and sufficient reason to trust in the existence of God:

> The God who made the world and everything in it is the Lord of heaven and earth and does not live in temples built by hands. And he is not served by human hands, as if he needed anything, because he himself gives all men life and breath and everything else. "For in him we live and move and have our being"
> (ACTS 17:24, 25, 28 NIV).

The universe is a remarkable evidence of an infinite Creator. Its very existence points to the reality of a powerful God. The Psalmist understood this truth when he wrote, "The heavens declare the glory of God; the skies proclaim the work of his hands. Day after day they pour forth speech; night after night they display knowledge" (PSALM 19:1, 2 NIV).

II. COMPELLING TELEOLOGICAL EVIDENCE

The wonder and the beauty of our universe are amazing sights to observe. In every realm we observe compelling evidence of design, purpose, beauty, complexity, and order. This amazing evidence convinced Albert Einstein to make the eloquent remark, "I cannot believe that God plays dice with the cosmos." Astrophysicists declare that our planet is incredibly unique in its position, function and existence. It is the right distance from the sun for human life to exist. If it were any closer it would be too hot, if further away it would be too cold. As philosopher J. P. Moreland suggests, "In the formation of the universe, the balance of matter to antimatter had to be accurate to one part in ten billion for the universe to even arise. Had it been larger or greater by one part in ten billion, no universe would have arisen."

For many scientists, exposure to the order of the universe, as well as its beauty and complexity, is an occasion of wonder and reverence. Philosopher of science Stanley L. Jaki, referring to the splendor of our universe, observes, "It has supreme coherence from the very small to the very large. It is a consistent unity free of debilitating paradoxes. It is beautifully proportioned into layers or dimensions and yet all of them are in perfect interaction." Even the skeptic David Hume, a renowned critic of the proofs for God's existence, was so impressed by the force of the evidence that he wrote, "A purpose, an intention, or design strikes everywhere the most careless, the most stupid thinker; and no man can be so hardened in absurd systems, as at all times to reject it." One of the greatest minds of science, if not the greatest scientist, Sir Isaac Newton, whose scientific achievements still boggle the modern mind, was a firm believer in the argument from design.

The evidence of intricate order and complexity in the universe confirmed his confidence in the existence of an intelligent Designer.

He declares, "When I look at the solar system, I see the earth at the right distance from the sun to receive the proper amounts of heat and light. This did not happen by chance."

The evidence from design commonly regarded as the teleological argument is one of the most popular arguments employed by philosophers. The great philosopher Plato observed there are two things that lead people to believe in God: the evidence from the experience of the soul and "from the order of the motion of the stars, and of all things under the dominion of the mind which ordered the universe." Even the great logician Aristotle, who gave us the laws of logic and proposed that philosophy begins with the sense of wonder, was impressed by the wonder of the cosmos. The elegance of this argument is evident in its impact on numerous scientists today. This argument, notes philosopher William Craig, is "the oldest and most popular of all the arguments for the existence of God." Referring to this evidence, the German philosopher Immanuel Kant in his famous work, *Critique of Pure Reason* insists that the argument "always deserves to be mentioned with respect."

Recent scientific observation is providing supporting evidence in the light of what scientists presently call the "anthropic principle" in cosmology. Astrophysicists suggest that life in our universe would not be possible if the early condition of the universe had varied even slightly. The universe appears to be designed for life. In other words, it is "fine-tuned" for our existence. The brilliant scientist Stephen W. Hawking observes, "If the rate of expansion one second after the big bang had been smaller by even one part in a hundred thousand million million, the universe would have re-collapsed before it even reached its present size." Philosopher John Leslie argues that the anthropic principle provides an excellent defense for the design argument. In his work, *The Probability of God*, Hugh Montefiore offers compelling evidence of a designed universe, including the anthropic principle. He claims that chance and natural selection do not offer adequate explanation for the reality of life. God is, notes Montefiore, "by far the most probable explanation."

After returning from his unforgettable flight around the moon Apollo 8, astronaut Frank Borman was questioned by a reporter. The reporter pointed out that the Soviet cosmonaut who recently returned from space flight said that he did not see God or angels on his flight. "Did you see God?" questioned the reporter. To this complex question Frank Borman gave a brilliant response, "No, I did not see him either, but I saw his evidence."

David correctly states, "In the beginning you laid the foundations of the earth, and the heavens are the work of your hands" (PSALM 102:25 NIV).

III. CONSCIOUS MORAL EVIDENCE

A compelling evidence that points to the existence of God is our moral experience. Morality is an essential part of our human fabric. At the conclusion of his famous work, *Critique of Practical Reason*, Immanuel Kant proposed a new argument for the existence of God called "the moral argument." Kant declares, "Two things fill the mind with ever new and increasing admiration and awe ... the starry heavens above me and the moral law within me." Plato long before Kant argued that the concept of goodness makes good sense only in relation to the greater or the ultimate good.

If God exists, it would be natural to expect his created beings to experience moral convictions. No human existence is possible without subscribing to moral values. Every day we observe politicians, doctors, lawyers, psychologists, judges, sociologists, editors, police, and citizens arguing for justice, fairness, equality, tolerance, honesty, responsibility, duty, accountability, civil rights, human rights, women's rights, etc. We believe it is right to treat all people with equal right. We condemn racism, rape, violence, child abuse, war, corruption, murder, treason, betrayal, abortion, and other behavior as evil and wrong. The reality of our moral commitment and conscience is unavoidable: we live in a moral universe.

Every individual appeals to a moral law by which he/she makes moral judgements. Our moral standards provide a basis for our thinking and behavior. But what about the relativist who insists there are no absolutes and argues everything is relative? Those who reject absolute moral law and advocate relativism engage in promoting a belief which is logically self-contradictory, subjective, and arbitrary. The rejection of absolutes in an important sense is the death of morals, where the individual becomes morally paralyzed and unable to make a distinction between good and evil, right and wrong. The suggestion that there are no absolutes is in fact an absolute position. It is self-contradictory for someone to say, "I am absolutely sure that there are no absolutes!" It does not remove absolutes but seductively substitutes itself as the guiding principle. Like the statements: There are no rules; Trust no authority; Everything is relative; All beliefs are false, each affirmation becomes an absolute in itself, which is what the person wishes to deny. Hence it is not only self-refuting but arbitrary and meaningless. This type of thinking can be seen in the ancient Greek saying, "Every statement is a lie!" and the Zen Buddhist aphorism, "All statements are absurd!" To reject moral absolutes is in essence to affirm that there are no real differences between Mother Teresa and Hitler.

Relativism may appear impressive on the surface, but it is philosophically false. It is logically contradictory, morally inadequate, and existentially unlivable. Consider the true story of a philosophy student who wrote an ethics paper arguing that there are no absolutes and everything is relative. Judged by the research, documentation, and scholarship, the paper deserved an "A". The professor, however, gave it an "F" with a note explaining, "I do not like blue covers!" When the student received his paper, he was so upset that he stormed into the professor's office protesting, "This is not fair! This is not just! I shouldn't be graded on the color of the cover but on the content of my paper."

The professor looked the student in the eye and asked, "Was this the paper which argued that there are no objective moral principles such as fairness and justice and everything is relative to one's taste?"

"Yes! Yes! That's the one," replied the student.

"Well then," said the professor. "I do not like blue covers. The grade will remain an 'F'!" Suddenly the young man understood that moral absolutes are unavoidable, that in fact he believed in moral principles such as fairness and justice, and that furthermore he was expecting them to be applied in his case.

The Cambridge scholar C. S. Lewis writes, "If no set of moral ideas were truer or better than any other, there would be no sense in preferring civilised morality to savage morality, or Christian morality to Nazi morality." Thus he says:

> The moment you say that one set of moral ideas can be better than another, you are, in fact, measuring them both by a standard, saying that one of them conforms to that standard more nearly than the other.

The reality of this universal law is very much part of our human fabric. We are not merely mechanical beings. Our moral convictions are essential to our existence; without them we would hardly qualify to be human, as Henry M. Morris plainly explains:

> Each individual, however benighted, recognises something in him that tells him that he ought to do the thing that is right morally and ought to shun the wrong—even though individual standards as to what constitutes right and wrong seem to vary somewhat with time and place.

An interesting episode at an eastern United States university illustrates this truth remarkably. A professor informed his students, before their exam, to sit one seat apart so that they may avoid all appearance of evil "as the Good Book says."

"What if we don't believe in the Good Book?" asked a skeptical student.

"Then you put two seats between you," replied the professor. Point well made. Without morals life is unlivable.

Our moral reality provides a crucial clue to the meaning of the universe. In the words of the famous New York scholar Peter Berger, our moral factors are "*signals of transcendence* within the … human condition." The apostle Paul, writing to the Christians in Rome, confirms the reality of the moral evidence, "Since they show that the requirements of the law are written on their hearts, their consciences also bearing witness, and their thoughts now accusing, now even defending them" (ROMANS 2:15 NIV).

IV. CONCRETE CHRISTOLOGICAL EVIDENCE

I. The Empty Tomb

One significant evidence for the resurrection is the empty tomb. The disciples of Jesus observed that the tomb was empty after the resurrection. The Gospels affirm that at least six of Christ's followers saw the empty tomb:

Mary Magdalene (MATTHEW 28:1-10); Mary (the mother of James) and Salome (MARK 16:1-8); Joanna (LUKE 24:10); Peter and John (JOHN 20:2-8). The Roman guards also saw the empty tomb (MATTHEW 28:2,11-15). The Jews never denied it and Peter proclaimed the resurrection to 3,000 people who could have refuted it. It is difficult to dismiss the evidence for the empty tomb.

According to D. H. Van Daalen, "It is extremely difficult to object to the empty tomb on historical grounds; those who deny it do so on the basis of theological or philosophical assumptions"[76] There are more than fifty reputable scholars who accept the evidence for the empty tomb.

2. The Appearances of Christ

Luke writes, "He showed himself to these men and gave many convincing proofs that he was alive. He appeared to them over a period of forty days and spoke about the kingdom of God" (ACTS 1:3 NIV). The belief in the resurrection is based not simply on an empty tomb but rather on a living encounter with a risen Lord. The disciples of Christ persisted in their remarkable claim that they saw the living Christ, even under persecution, torture, and death. We cannot dismiss the resurrection experience on the basis of vision or hallucination, for they are insufficient to explain the disciples' revolutionary transformation. This significant fact is vital to the case for the resurrection. Their unique testimony is powerful evidence that their message is trustworthy.

The facts demonstrate that on several occasions different individuals and groups saw Jesus alive after his death. He was seen not only by believers but also by skeptics, unbelievers, and even enemies. Dr. Yandall Woodfin offers an insightful note:

> If the early followers had made up the stories, they had
> little to gain but outward persecution and a lifelong
> battle with guilt. It seems more reasonable to believe,
> rather, that hypocrites do not become good martyrs and
> that the resurrection happened.

The questions which we must face if we reject their testimony
are, why would the disciples lie and what would they gain by lying
about the event? This would be a greater miracle indeed.

3. The Origin of Faith

The origin of the church proves the resurrection. What gave
birth to the church? Why and how did the church come into being?
What persuaded the early Jewish believers to put their faith in
Jesus Christ? Scholars agree that Christianity came into being
because the disciples believed that God had raised Jesus from the
dead. Something dramatic took place in Jerusalem which has
altered human history. What caused the disciples to believe and
preach the resurrection? It was the fact of the resurrection. (ACTS
2:32, 36; 13:26-39; 17:22-34; ROMANS 1:4; 14:9; I THESSALONIANS 4:14). All the
above evidences confirm that God really exists and that there is
enough evidence for a man who wants to believe, but there is no
evidence for a man who refuses to believe. The conclusion of
Pascal is most appropriate, "The evidence of God's existence and
His gift is more than compelling, but those who insist that they have
no need of Him or it will always find ways to discount the offer."

A teacher once told her students to produce a painting. Nearly
all the pictures were vaguely human except the one produced by
a boy named Tommy. "What's that?" inquired the teacher, observing
a peculiar mass of color.

"It's God!" replied the youngster.

"But no one knows what God is like," said the teacher.

The boy looked up with an air of confidence and a sense of
triumph, "Now they do!" This is precisely what the disciples said
about Jesus Christ. "No one has ever seen God, but God the One
and Only, who is at the Father's side, has made him known" (JOHN
1:18 NIV). By the light of the sun we see the world, but by the

brilliance of Christ we see God. In the ocean of darkness, Christ shines as a beacon of light. The apostle Paul understood this truth when he wrote, "For God, who said, 'Let light shine out of darkness' made his light shine in our hearts to give us the light of the knowledge of the glory of God in the face of Christ" (2 CORINTHIANS 4:6 NIV). ❖

Is Jesus God?

by Lee Strobel

Chapter:
The Fingerprint Evidence

Book:
The Case for Christ

Look for your coupons for this and other
featured titles in the back of this book.

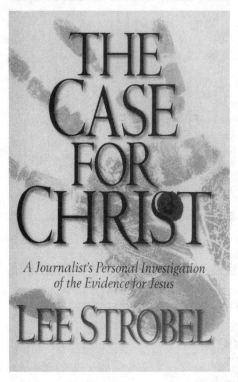

Author's Bio

Lee Strobel, a former atheist, holds
a Master of Studies in Law degree from
Yale Law School, was the award-winning
legal editor of the *Chicago Tribune*. He is
the author of numerous books, including
the Gold Medallion winners *The Case for
Christ* and *Inside the Mind of Unchurched
Harry and Mary*.

Is Jesus God?
by Lee Strobel

Did Jesus—and Jesus Alone—Match the Identity of the Messiah?

It was an uneventful Saturday at the Hiller home in Chicago. Clarence Hiller spent the afternoon painting the trim on the outside of his two-story house on West 104th Street. By early evening he and his family had retired to bed. However, what happened next would change criminal law in America forever.

The Hillers woke in the early morning hours of September 19, 1910, and became suspicious that a gaslight near their daughter's bedroom had gone out. Clarence went to investigate. His wife heard a quick succession of sounds: a scuffle, two men tumbling down the stairs, two gunshots, and the slamming of the front door. She emerged to find Clarence dead at the foot of the stairs.

Police arrested Thomas Jennings, a convicted burglar, less than a mile away. There was blood on his clothes and his left arm had been injured—both, he said, from falling on a streetcar. In his pocket they found the same kind of gun that had been used to shoot Clarence Hiller, but they couldn't determine if it was the murder weapon.

Knowing they needed more to convict Jennings, detectives scoured the inside of Hiller's home in a search for additional clues. One fact soon became obvious: the killer had entered through a rear kitchen window. Detectives went outside—and there, next to that window, forever imprinted in the white paint that the murder victim himself had so carefully applied to a railing only hours before his death, they found four clear fingerprints from someone's left hand.

Fingerprint evidence was a new concept at the time, having been recently introduced at an international police exhibition in St. Louis. So far, fingerprints had never been used to convict anyone of murder in the United States.

Despite strong objections by defense attorneys that such evidence was unscientific and inadmissible, four officers testified that the fingerprints in the paint perfectly matched those of Thomas Jennings—and him alone. The jury found Jennings guilty, the Illinois Supreme Court upheld his conviction in a historic ruling, and he was later hanged.[1]

The premise behind fingerprint evidence is simple: each individual has unique ridges on his or her fingers. When a print found on an object matches the pattern of ridges on a person's finger, investigators can conclude with scientific certainty that this specific individual has touched that object.

In many criminal cases, fingerprint identification is the pivotal evidence. I remember covering a trial in which a single thumbprint found on the cellophane wrapper of a cigarette package was the determining factor in convicting a twenty-year-old burglar of murdering a college coed.[2] That's how conclusive fingerprint evidence can be.

OK, but what has this got to do with Jesus Christ? Simply this: There is another kind of evidence that's analogous to fingerprints and establishes to an astounding degree of certainty that Jesus is indeed the Messiah of Israel and the world.

In the Jewish Scriptures, which Christians call the Old Testament, there are several dozen major prophecies about the coming of the Messiah, who would be sent by God to redeem his people. In effect, these predictions formed a figurative fingerprint that only the Anointed One would be able to match. This way, the Israelites could rule out any impostors and validate the credentials of the authentic Messiah.

The Greek word for "Messiah" is *Christ*. But was Jesus really the Christ? Did he miraculously fulfill these predictions that were written hundreds of years before he was born? And how do we know he was the only individual throughout history who fit the prophetic fingerprint?

There are plenty of scholars with long strings of initials after their names whom I could have asked about this topic. However, I wanted to interview someone for whom this was more than just an abstract academic exercise, and that took me to a very unlikely setting in southern California.

THE NINTH INTERVIEW:
LOUIS S. LAPIDES, M.DIV., TH.M.

Usually a church would be a natural location in which to question someone about a biblical issue. But there was something different about sitting down with Pastor Louis Lapides in the sanctuary of his congregation on the morning after Sunday worship services. This setting of pews and stained glass was not where you would expect to find a nice Jewish boy from Newark, New Jersey.

Yet that's Lapides' background. For someone with his heritage, the question of whether Jesus is the long-anticipated Messiah goes beyond theory. It's intensely personal, and I had sought out Lapides so I could hear the story of his own investigation of this critical issue.

Lapides earned a bachelor's degree in theology from Dallas Baptist University as well as a master of divinity and a master of theology degree in Old Testament and Semitics from Talbot Theological Seminary. He served for a decade with Chosen People Ministries, talking about Jesus to Jewish college students. He has taught in the Bible department of Biola University and worked for seven years as an instructor for Walk Through the Bible seminars. He is also the former president of a national network of fifteen messianic congregations.

Slender and bespectacled, Lapides is soft-spoken but has a quick smile and ready laugh. He was upbeat and polite as he ushered me to a chair near the front of Beth Ariel Fellowship in Sherman Oaks, California. I didn't want to begin by debating biblical nuances; instead I started by inviting Lapides to tell me the story of his spiritual journey.

He folded his hands in his lap, looked at the dark wood walls for a moment as he decided where to start, and then began unfolding an extraordinary tale that took us from Newark to Greenwich Village to Vietnam to Los Angeles, from skepticism to faith, from Judaism to Christianity, from Jesus as irrelevant to Jesus as Messiah.

"As you know, I came from a Jewish family," he began. "I attended a conservative Jewish synagogue for seven years in preparation for bar mitzvah. Although we considered those studies to be very important, our family's faith didn't affect our everyday life very much. We didn't stop work on the Sabbath; we didn't have a kosher home."

He smiled. "However, on the High Holy Days we attended the stricter Orthodox synagogue, because somehow my dad felt that's where you went if you really wanted to get serious with God!"

When I interjected to ask what his parents had taught him about the Messiah, Lapides' answer was crisp. "It never came up," he said matter-of-factly.

I was incredulous. In fact, I thought I had misunderstood him. "You're saying it wasn't even discussed?" I asked.

"Never," he reiterated. "I don't even remember it being an issue in Hebrew school."

This was amazing to me. "How about Jesus?" I asked. "Was he ever talked about? Was his name used?"

"Only derogatorily!" Lapides quipped. "Basically, he was never discussed. My impressions of Jesus came from seeing Catholic churches: there was the cross, the crown of thorns, the pierced side, the blood coming from his head. It didn't make any sense to me. Why would you worship a man on a cross with nails in his hands and his feet? I never once thought Jesus had any connection to the Jewish people. I just thought he was a god of the Gentiles."

I suspected that Lapides' attitudes toward Christians had gone beyond mere confusion over their beliefs. "Did you believe Christians were at the root of anti-Semitism?" I asked.

"Gentiles were looked upon as synonymous with Christians, and we were taught to be cautious because there could be anti-Semitism among the Gentiles," he said, sounding a bit diplomatic.

I pursued the issue further. "Would you say you developed some negative attitudes toward Christians?"

This time he didn't mince words. "Yes, actually I did," he said. "In fact, later when the New Testament was first presented to me, I sincerely thought it was going to basically be a handbook on anti-Semitism: how to hate Jews, how to kill Jews, how to massacre them. I thought the American Nazi Party would have been very comfortable using it as a guidebook."

I shook my head, saddened at the thought of how many other Jewish children have grown up thinking of Christians as their enemies.

A SPIRITUAL QUEST BEGINS

Lapides said several incidents dimmed his allegiance to Judaism as he was growing up. Curious about the details, I asked him to elaborate, and he immediately turned to what was clearly the most heartrending episode of his life.

"My parents got divorced when I was seventeen," he said—and surprisingly, even after all these years I could still detect hurt in his voice. "That really put a stake in any religious heart I may have had. I wondered, Where does God come in? Why didn't they go to a rabbi for counseling? What good is religion if it can't help people in a practical way? It sure couldn't keep my parents together. When they split up, part of me split as well.

"On top of that, in Judaism I didn't feel as if I had a personal relationship with God. I had a lot of beautiful ceremonies and traditions, but he was the distant and detached God of Mount Sinai who said, 'Here are the rules—you live by them, you'll be OK; I'll see you later.' And there I was, an adolescent with raging hormones, wondering, Does God relate to my struggles? Does he care about me as an individual? Well, not in any way I could see."

The divorce prompted an era of rebellion. Consumed with music and influenced by the writings of Jack Kerouac and Timothy Leary, he spent too much time in Greenwich Village coffeehouses to go to college—making him vulnerable to the draft. By 1967 he found himself on the other side of the world in a cargo boat whose volatile freight—ammunition, bombs, rockets, and other high explosives—made it a tempting target for the Vietcong.

"I remember being told at our orientation in Vietnam, 'Twenty percent of you will probably get killed, and the other eighty percent will probably get a venereal disease or become alcoholics or get hooked on drugs.' I thought, I don't even have a one percent chance of coming out normal!

"It was a very dark period. I witnessed suffering. I saw body bags; I saw the devastation from war. And I encountered anti-Semitism among some of the GIs. A few of them from the South even burned a cross one night. I probably wanted to distance myself from my Jewish identity—maybe that's why I began delving into Eastern religions."

Lapides read books on Eastern philosophies and visited Buddhist temples while in Japan. "I was extremely bothered by the evil I had seen, and I was trying to figure out how faith can deal with it," he told me. "I used to say, 'If there's a God, I don't care if I find him on Mount Sinai or Mount Fuji. I'll take him either way.'"

He survived Vietnam, returning home with a newfound taste for marijuana and plans to become a Buddhist priest. He tried to live an ascetic lifestyle of self-denial in an effort to work off the bad karma for the misdeeds of his past, but soon he realized he'd never be able to make up for all his wrongs.

Lapides was quiet for a moment. "I got depressed," he said. "I remember getting on the subway and thinking, Maybe jumping onto the tracks is the answer. I could free myself from this body and just merge with God. I was very confused. To make matters worse, I started experimenting with LSD."

Looking for a new start, he decided to move to California, where his spiritual quest continued. "I went to Buddhist meetings, but that was empty," he said. "Chinese Buddhism was atheistic, Japanese Buddhism worshiped statues of Buddha, Zen Buddhism was too elusive. I went to Scientology meetings, but they were too manipulative and controlling. Hinduism believed in all these crazy orgies that the gods would have and in gods who were blue elephants. None of it made sense; none of it was satisfying."

He even accompanied friends to meetings that had Satanic undercurrents. "I would watch and think, Something is going on here, but it's not good," he said. "In the midst of my drug-crazed world, I told my friends I believed there's a power of evil that's beyond me, that can work in me, that exists as an entity. I had seen enough evil in my life to believe that."

He looked at me with an ironic smile. "I guess I accepted Satan's existence," he said, "before I accepted God's."

"I CAN'T BELIEVE IN JESUS"

It was 1969. Lapides' curiosity prompted him to visit Sunset Strip to gawk at an evangelist who had chained himself to an eight-foot cross to protest the way local tavern owners had managed to get him evicted from his storefront ministry. There on the sidewalk Lapides encountered some Christians who engaged him in an impromptu spiritual debate.

A bit cocky, he started throwing Eastern philosophy at them. "There is no God out there," he said, gesturing toward the heavens. "We're God. I'm God. You're God. You just have to realize it."

"Well, if you're God, why don't you create a rock?" one person replied. "Just make something appear. That's what God does."

In his drug-addled mind Lapides imagined he was holding a rock. "Yeah, well, here's a rock," he said, extending his empty hand.

The Christian scoffed. "That's the difference between you and the true God," he said. "When God creates something, everyone can see it. It's objective, not subjective."

That registered with Lapides. After thinking about it for a while, he said to himself, If I find God, he's got to be objective. I'm through with this Eastern philosophy that says it's all in my mind and that I can create my own reality. God has to be an objective reality if he's going to have any meaning beyond my own imagination.

When one of the Christians brought up the name of Jesus, Lapides tried to fend him off with his stock answer. "I'm Jewish," he said. "I can't believe in Jesus."

A pastor spoke up. "Do you know of the prophecies about the Messiah?" he asked.

Lapides was taken off guard. "Prophecies?" he said. "I've never heard of them."

The minister startled Lapides by referring to some of the Old Testament predictions. Wait a minute! Lapides thought. Those are my Jewish Scriptures he's quoting! How could Jesus be in there?

When the pastor offered him a Bible, Lapides was skeptical. "Is the New Testament in there?" he asked. The pastor nodded. "OK, I'll read the Old Testament, but I'm not going to open up the other one," Lapides told him.

He was taken aback by the minister's response. "Fine," said the pastor. "Just read the Old Testament and ask the God of Abraham, Isaac, and Jacob—the God of Israel—to show you if Jesus is the Messiah. Because he is your Messiah. He came to the Jewish people initially, and then he was also the Savior of the world."

To Lapides, this was new information. Intriguing information. Astonishing information. So he went back to his apartment, opened the Old Testament to its first book, Genesis, and went hunting for Jesus among words that had been written hundreds of years before the carpenter of Nazareth had ever been born.

"PIERCED FOR OUR TRANSGRESSIONS"

"Pretty soon," Lapides told me, "I was reading the Old Testament every day and seeing one prophecy after another. For instance, Deuteronomy talked about a prophet greater than Moses who will come and whom we should listen to. I thought, Who can be greater than Moses? It sounded like the Messiah—someone as great and as respected as Moses but a greater teacher and a greater authority. I grabbed ahold of that and went searching for him."

As Lapides progressed through the Scriptures, he was stopped cold by Isaiah 53. With clarity and specificity, in a haunting prediction wrapped in exquisite poetry, here was the picture of a Messiah who would suffer and die for the sins of Israel and the world—all written more than seven hundred years before Jesus walked the earth.

> He was despised and rejected by men,
> a man of sorrows, and familiar with suffering.

Like one from whom men hide their faces
he was despised, and we esteemed him not.

Surely he took up our infirmities
and carried our sorrows,
yet we considered him stricken by God,
smitten by him, and afflicted.

But he was pierced for our transgressions,
he was crushed for our iniquities;
the punishment that brought us peace was upon him,
and by his wounds we are healed.

We all, like sheep, have gone astray,
each of us has turned to his own way;
and the LORD has laid on him the iniquity of us all.

He was oppressed and afflicted,
yet he did not open his mouth;
he was led like a lamb to the slaughter,
and as a sheep before her shearers is silent,
so he did not open his mouth.
By oppression and judgment he was taken away.
And who can speak of his descendants?
For he was cut off from the land of the living;
for the transgression of my people he was stricken.
He was assigned a grave with the wicked,
and with the rich in his death,
though he had done no violence,
nor was any deceit in his mouth....

For he bore the sin of many,
and made intercession for the transgressors.
(ISAIAH 53:3–9, 12)

Instantly Lapides recognized the portrait: this was Jesus of
Nazareth! Now he was beginning to understand the paintings he
had seen in the Catholic churches he had passed as a child: the
suffering Jesus, the crucified Jesus, the Jesus who he now realized
had been "pierced for our transgressions" as he "bore the sin of many."

As Jews in the Old Testament sought to atone for their sins
through a system of animal sacrifices, here was Jesus, the ultimate

sacrificial lamb of God, who paid for sin once and for all. Here was the personification of God's plan of redemption.

So breathtaking was this discovery that Lapides could only come to one conclusion: it was a fraud! He believed that Christians had rewritten the Old Testament and twisted Isaiah's words to make it sound as if the prophet had been foreshadowing Jesus.

Lapides set out to expose the deception. "I asked my stepmother to send me a Jewish Bible so I could check it out myself," he told me. "She did, and guess what? I found that it said the same thing! Now I really had to deal with it."

THE JEWISHNESS OF JESUS

Over and over Lapides would come upon prophecies in the Old Testament—more than four dozen major predictions in all. Isaiah revealed the manner of the Messiah's birth (of a virgin); Micah pinpointed the place of his birth (Bethlehem); Genesis and Jeremiah specified his ancestry (a descendent of Abraham, Isaac, and Jacob, from the tribe of Judah, the house of David); the Psalms foretold his betrayal, his accusation by false witnesses, his manner of death (pierced in the hands and feet, although crucifixion hadn't been invented yet), and his resurrection (he would not decay but would ascend on high); and on and on.[3] Each one chipped away at Lapides' skepticism until he was finally willing to take a drastic step.

"I decided to open the New Testament and just read the first page," he said. "With trepidation I slowly turned to Matthew as I looked up to heaven, waiting for the lightning bolt to strike!"

Matthew's initial words leaped off the page: "A record of the genealogy of Jesus Christ the son of David, the son of Abraham …"

Lapides' eyes widened as he recalled the moment he first read that sentence. "I thought, Wow! Son of Abraham, son of David—it was all fitting together! I went to the birth narratives and thought, Look at this! Matthew is quoting from Isaiah 7:14: 'The virgin will be with child and will give birth to a son.' And then I saw him quoting from the prophet Jeremiah. I sat there thinking, You know, this is about Jewish people. Where do the Gentiles come in? What's going on here?

"I couldn't put it down. I read through the rest of the gospels, and I realized this wasn't a handbook for the American Nazi Party; it was an interaction between Jesus and the Jewish community. I got to the book of Acts and—this was incredible!— they were trying to figure out how the Jews could bring the story of Jesus to the Gentiles. Talk about role reversal!"

So convincing were the fulfilled prophecies that Lapides started telling people that he thought Jesus was the Messiah. At the time, this was merely an intellectual possibility to him, yet its implications were deeply troubling.

"I realized that if I were to accept Jesus into my life, there would have to be some significant changes in the way I was living," he explained. "I'd have to deal with the drugs, the sex, and so forth. I didn't understand that God would help me make those changes; I thought I had to clean up my life on my own."

EPIPHANY IN THE DESERT

Lapides and some friends headed into the Mojave Desert for a getaway. Spiritually he was feeling conflicted. He had been unsettled by nightmares of being torn apart by dogs pulling at him from opposite directions. Sitting among the desert scrub, he recalled the words someone had spoken to him on Sunset Strip: "You're either on God's side or on Satan's side."

He believed in the embodiment of evil—and that's not whose side he wanted to be on. So Lapides prayed, "God, I've got to come to the end of this struggle. I have to know beyond a shadow of a doubt that Jesus is the Messiah. I need to know that you, as the God of Israel, want me to believe this."

As he related the story to me, Lapides hesitated, unsure how to put into words what happened next. A few moments passed. Then he told me, "The best I can put together out of that experience is that God objectively spoke to my heart. He convinced me, experientially, that he exists. And at that point, out in the desert,

in my heart I said, 'God, I accept Jesus into my life. I don't understand what I'm supposed to do with him, but I want him. I've
pretty much made a mess of my life; I need you to change me.'"

And God began to do that in a process that continues to
this day. "My friends knew my life had changed, and they couldn't
understand it," he said. "They'd say, 'Something happened to you in
the desert. You don't want to do drugs anymore. There's something
different about you.'

"I would say, 'Well, I can't explain what happened. All I know is
that there's someone in my life, and it's someone who's holy, who's
righteous, who's a source of positive thoughts about life—and I just
feel whole.'"

That last word, it seemed, said everything. "*Whole*," he
emphasized to me, "in a way I had never felt before."

Despite the positive changes, he was concerned about breaking
the news to his parents. When he finally did, reaction was mixed.
"At first they were joyful because they could tell I was no longer
dependent on drugs and I sounded much better emotionally," he
recalled. "But that began to unravel when they understood the
source of all the changes. They winced, as if to say, 'Why does it
have to be Jesus? Why can't it be something else?' They didn't
know what to do with it."

With a trace of sadness in his voice, he added, "I'm still not
sure they really do."

Through a remarkable string of circumstances, Lapides' prayer
for a wife was answered when he met Deborah, who was also
Jewish and a follower of Jesus. She took him to her church—the
same one, it turned out, that was pastored by the minister who
many months earlier on Sunset Strip had challenged Lapides to
read the Old Testament.

Lapides laughed. "I'll tell you what—his jaw dropped open
when he saw me walk into the church!"

That congregation was filled with ex-bikers, ex-hippies, and
ex-addicts from the Strip, along with a spattering of transplanted
Southerners. For a young Jewish man from Newark who was
relationally gun-shy with people who were different from him,

because of the anti-Semitism he feared he would encounter, it was healing to learn to call such a diverse crowd "brothers and sisters."

Lapides married Deborah a year after they met. Since then she has given birth to two sons. And together they've given birth to Beth Ariel Fellowship, a home for Jews and Gentiles who also are finding wholeness in Christ.

RESPONDING TO OBJECTIONS

Lapides finished his story and relaxed in his chair. I let the moment linger. The sanctuary was peaceful; the stained glass was glowing red and yellow and blue from the California sun. I sat musing over the power of one person's story of a faith found. I marveled at this saga of war and drugs, of Greenwich Village and Sunset Strip and a barren desert, none of which I ever would have associated with the pleasant, well-adjusted minister sitting in front of me.

But I didn't want to ignore the obvious questions that his story raised. With Lapides' permission I started by asking the one that was foremost on my mind: "If the prophecies were so obvious to you and pointed so unquestionably toward Jesus, why don't more Jews accept him as their Messiah?"

It was a question Lapides has asked himself a lot during the three decades since he was challenged by a Christian to investigate the Jewish Scriptures. "In my case, I took the time to read them," he replied. "Oddly enough, even though the Jewish people are known for having high intellects, in this area there's a lot of ignorance.

"Plus you have countermissionary organizations that hold seminars in synagogues to try to disprove the messianic prophecies. Jewish people hear them and use them as an excuse for not exploring the prophecies personally. They'll say, 'The rabbi told me there's nothing to this.'

"I'll ask them, 'Do you think the rabbi just brought up an objection that Christianity has never heard before? I mean, scholars have been working on this for hundreds of years! There's great literature out there and powerful Christian answers to those challenges.' If they're interested, I help them go further."

I wondered about the ostracism a Jewish person faces if he or she becomes a Christian. "That's definitely a factor," he said. "Some people won't let the messianic prophecies grab them, because they're afraid of the repercussions—potential rejection by their family and the Jewish community. That's not easy to face. Believe me, I know."

Even so, some of the challenges to the prophecies sound pretty convincing when a person first hears them. So one by one I posed the most common objections to Lapides to see how he would respond.

1. The Coincidence Argument

First, I asked Lapides whether it's possible that Jesus merely fulfilled the prophecies by accident. Maybe he's just one of many throughout history who have coincidentally fit the prophetic fingerprint.

"Not a chance," came his response. "The odds are so astronomical that they rule that out. Someone did the math and figured out that the probability of just eight prophecies being fulfilled is one chance in one hundred million billion. That number is millions of times greater than the total number of people who've ever walked the planet!

"He calculated that if you took this number of silver dollars, they would cover the state of Texas to a depth of two feet. If you marked one silver dollar among them and then had a blindfolded person wander the whole state and bend down to pick up one coin, what would be the odds he'd choose the one that had been marked?"

With that he answered his own question: "The same odds that anybody in history could have fulfilled just eight of the prophecies."

I had studied this same statistical analysis by mathematician Peter W. Stoner when I was investigating the messianic prophecies for myself. Stoner also computed that the probability of fulfilling forty-eight prophecies was one chance in a trillion, trillion, trillion,

trillion, trillion, trillion, trillion, trillion, trillion, trillion, trillion, trillion, trillion![4]

Our minds can't comprehend a number that big. This is a staggering statistic that's equal to the number of minuscule atoms in a trillion, trillion, trillion, trillion, billion universes the size of our universe!

"The odds alone say it would be impossible for anyone to fulfill the Old Testament prophecies," Lapides concluded. "Yet Jesus—and only Jesus throughout all of history—managed to do it."

The words of the apostle Peter popped into my head: "But the things which God announced beforehand by the mouth of all the prophets, that His Christ should suffer, He has thus fulfilled" (ACTS 3:18 NASB).

2. The Altered Gospel Argument

I painted another scenario for Lapides, asking, "Isn't it possible that the gospel writers fabricated details to make it appear that Jesus fulfilled the prophecies?

"For example," I said, "the prophecies say the Messiah's bones would remain unbroken, so maybe John invented the story about the Romans breaking the legs of the two thieves being crucified with Jesus, and not breaking his legs. And the prophecies talk about betrayal for thirty pieces of silver, so maybe Matthew played fast and loose with the facts and said, yeah, Judas sold out Jesus for that same amount."

But that objection didn't fly any further than the previous one. "In God's wisdom, he created checks and balances both inside and outside the Christian community," Lapides explained. "When the gospels were being circulated, there were people living who had been around when all these things happened. Someone would have said to Matthew, 'You know it didn't happen that way. We're trying to communicate a life of righteousness and truth, so don't taint it with a lie.'"

Besides, he added, why would Matthew have fabricated fulfilled prophecies and then willingly allowed himself to be put to death for following someone who he secretly knew was really not the Messiah? That wouldn't make any sense.

What's more, the Jewish community would have jumped on any opportunity to discredit the gospels by pointing out falsehoods. "They would have said, 'I was there, and Jesus' bones *were* broken by the Romans during the Crucifixion,'" Lapides said. "But even though the Jewish Talmud refers to Jesus in derogatory ways, it never once makes the claim that the fulfillment of prophecies was falsified. Not one time."

3. The Intentional Fulfillment Argument

Some skeptics have asserted that Jesus merely maneuvered his life in a way to fulfill the prophecies. "Couldn't he have read in Zechariah that the Messiah would ride a donkey into Jerusalem, and then arrange to do exactly that?" I asked.

Lapides made a small concession. "For a few of the prophecies, yes, that's certainly conceivable," he said. "But there are many others for which this just wouldn't have been possible.

"For instance, how would he control the fact that the Sanhedrin offered Judas thirty pieces of silver to betray him? How could he arrange for his ancestry, or the place of his birth, or his method of execution, or that soldiers gambled for his clothing, or that his legs remained unbroken on the cross? How would he arrange to perform miracles in front of skeptics? How would he arrange for his resurrection? And how would he arrange to be born when he was?"

That last comment piqued my curiosity. "What do you mean by when he was born?" I asked.

"When you interpret Daniel 9:24–26, it foretells that the Messiah would appear a certain length of time after King Artaxerxes I issued a decree for the Jewish people to go from Persia to rebuild the walls in Jerusalem," Lapides replied.

He leaned forward to deliver the clincher: "That puts the anticipated appearance of the Messiah at the exact moment in history when Jesus showed up," he said. "Certainly that's nothing he could have prearranged."[5]

4. The Context Argument

One other objection needed to be addressed: were the passages that Christians identify as messianic prophecies really intended to point to the coming of the Anointed One, or do Christians rip them out of context and misinterpret them?

Lapides sighed. "You know, I go through the books that people write to try to tear down what we believe. That's not fun to do, but I spend the time to look at each objection individually and then to research the context and the wording in the original language," he said. "And every single time, the prophecies have stood up and shown themselves to be true.

"So here's my challenge to skeptics: don't accept my word for it, but don't accept your rabbi's either. Spend the time to research it yourself. Today nobody can say, 'There's no information.' There are plenty of books out there to help you.

"And one more thing: sincerely ask God to show you whether or not Jesus is the Messiah. That's what I did—and without any coaching it became clear to me who fit the fingerprint of the Messiah."

"EVERYTHING MUST BE FULFILLED ..."

I appreciated the way Lapides had responded to the objections, but ultimately it was the story of his spiritual journey that kept replaying in my mind as I flew back to Chicago late that night. I reflected on how many times I had encountered similar stories, especially among successful and thoughtful Jewish people who had specifically set out to refute Jesus' messianic claims.

I thought about Stan Telchin, the East Coast businessman who had embarked on a quest to expose the "cult" of Christianity after his daughter went away to college and received Y'shua (Jesus) as her Messiah. He was astonished to find that his investigation led him—and his wife and second daughter—to the same Messiah. He later became a Christian minister, and his book that recounts his story, Betrayed!, has been translated into more than twenty languages.[6]

There was Jack Sternberg, a prominent cancer physician in Little Rock, Arkansas, who was so alarmed at what he found in the Old Testament that he challenged three rabbis to disprove that Jesus was the Messiah. They couldn't, and he too has claimed to have found wholeness in Christ.[7]

And there was Peter Greenspan, an obstetrician-gynecologist who practices in the Kansas City area and is a clinical assistant professor at the University of Missouri–Kansas City School of Medicine. Like Lapides, he had been challenged to look for Jesus in Judaism. What he found troubled him, so he went to the Torah and Talmud, seeking to discredit Jesus' messianic credentials. Instead he concluded that Jesus did miraculously fulfill the prophecies.

For him, the more he read books by those trying to undermine the evidence for Jesus as the Messiah, the more he saw the flaws in their arguments. Ironically, concluded Greenspan, "I think I actually came to faith in Y'shua by reading what detractors wrote."[8]

He found, as have Lapides and others, that Jesus' words in the gospel of Luke have proved true: "Everything must be fulfilled that is written about me in the Law of Moses, the Prophets and the Psalms" (LUKE 24:44). It was fulfilled, and only in Jesus—the sole individual in history who has matched the prophetic fingerprint of God's anointed one. ❖

DELIBERATIONS—Questions for Reflection or Group Study

1. Even if you're not Jewish, is there an aspect of Lapides' spiritual journey that is similar to your own? Were there any lessons you learned from Lapides about how you should proceed?

2. Lapides considered his Jewish heritage and unbiblical lifestyle impediments to becoming a follower of Jesus. Is there anything in your life that would make it difficult to become a Christian? Do you see any costs that you might incur if you became a Christian? How might they compare with the benefits?

3. Lapides thought Christians were anti-Semitic. In a recent word-association exercise at an East Coast university, the word most often associated with Christian was intolerant. Do you have negative perceptions of Christians? What do they stem from? How might this influence your receptivity to the evidence about Jesus?

FOR FURTHER EVIDENCE—More Resources on This Topic

Fruchtenbaum, Arnold. *Jesus Was a Jew*. Tustin, Calif.: Ariel Ministries, 1981.

Frydland, Rachmiel. *What the Rabbis Know about the Messiah*. Cincinnati: Messianic, 1993.

Kaiser, Walter C., Jr. *The Messiah in the Old Testament*. Grand Rapids: Zondervan, 1995.

Rosen, Moishe. *Y'shua, the Jewish Way to Say Jesus*. Chicago: Moody Press, 1982.

Rosen, Ruth, ed. *Jewish Doctors Meet the Great Physician*. San Francisco: Purple Pomegranate, 1997.

Telchin, Stan. *Betrayed!* Grand Rapids: Chosen, 1982.

CHAPTER NOTES

1. Evans, *The Casebook of Forensic Detection*, 98–100.

2. Lee Strobel, "'Textbook' Thumbprint Aids Conviction in Coed's Killing," *Chicago Tribune* (June 29, 1976).

3. For basic details on fulfilled prophecies, see McDowell, *Evidence That Demands a Verdict*, 141–77.

4. Peter W. Stoner, *Science Speaks* (Chicago: Moody Press, 1969), 109.

5. For a discussion of the Daniel prophecy, see Robert C. Newman, "Fulfilled Prophecy As Miracle," in R. Douglas Geivett and Gary R. Habermas, eds., *In Defense of Miracles* (Downers Grove, Ill.: InterVarsity Press, 1997), 214–25.

6. Stan Telchin, *Betrayed!* (Grand Rapids: Chosen, 1982).

7. Ruth Rosen, ed., *Jewish Doctors Meet the Great Physician* (San Francisco: Purple Pomegranate, 1997), 9–23.

8. Ibid., 34–35.

Is Jesus the Only Way to Salvation?

by Lee Strobel

Chapter:
**It's Offensive to Claim Jesus
is the Only Way to God**

Book:
The Case for Faith

Look for your coupons for this and other
featured titles in the back of this book.

THE
CASE
FOR
faith

*A Journalist Investigates the
Toughest Objections to Christianity*
LEE STROBEL
Author of *The Case for Christ*

Author's Bio

Lee Strobel, a former atheist, holds
a Master of Studies in Law degree from
Yale Law School, was the award-winning
legal editor of the *Chicago Tribune*. He is
the author of numerous books, including
the Gold Medallion winners *The Case for
Christ* and *Inside the Mind of Unchurched
Harry and Mary*.

Is Jesus the Only Way to Salavation?

by Lee Strobel

> *I am absolutely against any religion that says that one faith*
> *is superior to another. I don't see how that is anything*
> *different than spiritual racism. It's a way of saying that we*
> *are closer to God than you, and that's what leads to hatred.*
> —Rabbi Schmuley Boteach[1]

> *Moses could mediate on the law; Muhammad could brandish*
> *a sword; Buddha could give personal counsel; Confucius could*
> *offer wise sayings; but none of these men was qualified to*
> *offer an atonement for the sins of the world.... Christ alone is*
> *worthy of unlimited devotion and service.*
> —Theologian R. C. Sproul[2]

Walter Chaplinsky had strong opinions about religion and wasn't shy about expressing them. In 1940 he caused a ruckus in Rochester, New Hampshire, by loudly denouncing organized religion as being "a racket" and condemning several Christian denominations by name. The result: he found himself arrested and convicted under a state law making it a crime to speak "any offensive, derisive or annoying word to any person who is lawfully in any street or other public place."

Believing that his free-speech rights were being violated, Chaplinsky appealed his case all the way to the United States Supreme Court. However, in 1942 the justices unanimously affirmed his conviction, saying that "fighting words" like the ones he shouted fall outside the protection of the First Amendment.[3] Thirty years later, the high court clarified its definition of "fighting words" by calling them "personally abusive epithets" that are "inherently likely to provoke violent action."[4]

"Fighting words" arouse a visceral response in people, making their guts churn and their hands ball into fists. This offensive language strikes deep inside by attacking their most cherished beliefs, virtually taunting them to lash out in retaliation. To some people, such are the outrageous words of Jesus Christ: "I am the way and the truth and the life. No one comes to the Father except through me."[5]

Many people consider it arrogant, narrow-minded, and bigoted for Christians to contend that the only path to God must go through Jesus of Nazareth. In a day of religious pluralism and tolerance, this exclusivity claim is politically incorrect, a verbal slap in the face of other belief systems. Pluralist Rosemary Radford Ruether labeled it "absurd religious chauvinism,"[6] while one Jewish rabbi called it a "spiritual dictatorship" that fosters the kind of smug and superior attitude that can lead to hatred and violence toward people who believe differently.[7]

Certainly an approach like the one expressed by Indian philosopher Swami Vivekenanda is much more acceptable today: "We [Hindus] accept all religions to be true," he told the World Parliament of Religions in 1893. The real sin, he said, is to call someone else a sinner.[8]

That kind of open-mindedness and liberality fits well with our current culture of relativism, where no "fact" is considered universally true at all times, at all places, for all people, and in all cultures. Indeed, fully two-thirds of Americans now deny there's any such thing as truth.[9]

When I was an atheist, I bristled at assertions by Christians that they held a monopoly on the only correct approach to religion. "Who do they think they are?" I'd grouse. "Who are they to judge everyone else? Where's the love of Jesus in that?"

Charles Templeton called it "insufferable presumption"[10] for the Bible to claim that besides Jesus there is "no other name under heaven ... by which we must be saved."[11] Templeton added:

> Christians are a small minority in the world.
> Approximately four out of every five people on the face
> of the earth believe in gods other than the Christian
> God. The more than five billion people who live on
> earth revere or worship more than three hundred gods.
> If one includes the animist or tribal religions, the
> number rises to more than three thousand. *Are we to
> believe that only Christians are right?*[12]

Despite Templeton's woeful undercounting of the number of gods worshiped in the world, his point remains. The exclusivity claim of Jesus is among the biggest obstacles to spiritual seekers today. With a subject this volatile, I knew I needed to talk with an expert who has a crisp, analytical mind, a sound philosophical background, and extensive experience with a wide range of different world religions. Those criteria led me to a suburb of Atlanta, Georgia, and the office of Ravi Zacharias, who was born and raised in India.

THE FIFTH INTERVIEW: RAVI ZACHARIAS, D.D., LL.D.

"There's an old Indian saying that says there are two ways to get to your nose," Ravi Zacharias told me as he removed his black suit coat and sat down at a round wooden table in his office.

"There's this way," he said, pointing directly to his nose. Then he reached around the back of his head and touched his nose from the far side. "And there's *this* way," he said with a smile.

In other words, Indians sometimes prefer to take a long and circuitous route to an answer rather than getting to the point too quickly. And sometimes that's true of Zacharias, who has earned a reputation as being among the world's most astute and articulate defenders of Christianity.

Gentle-spirited but with a razor-sharp intellect, Zacharias has been called "a man of great spiritual perception and intellectual integrity" by Billy Graham.[13] He has spoken about Christianity, philosophy, world religions, and cults in fifty countries and numerous universities. His books include the award-winning *Can Man Live Without God*, partly based on a series of penetrating lectures he delivered at Harvard University; *A Shattered Visage: The Real Face of Atheism; Deliver Us From Evil; Cries of the Heart;* and *Jesus Among Other Gods*. His first children's book, *The Merchant and the Thief*, was released in 1999.

Zacharias was educated at Trinity Evangelical Divinity School, where he earned a master's of divinity degree, and he has been a visiting scholar at Cambridge University. He has been honored by the conferring of Doctor of Divinity degrees from Houghton College and Tyndale College and Seminary, as well as a Doctor of Laws degree from Asbury College. He is the former chair of evangelism and contemporary thought at Alliance Theological Seminary.

Currently, Zacharias heads Ravi Zacharias International Ministries, with offices in the United States, Canada, India, and England. He and his wife, Margaret, have three children.

Zacharias is an imposing figure with a boyish smile. His medium bronze skin contrasts with hair that's so white it's almost luminous. He speaks in a soft, husky voice with a distinctive Indian accent and cadence. Unfailingly polite and hospitable, he was generous with his time and completely focused on our interview, even though behind the scenes his staff was feverishly making preparations for another international trip on which he was about to embark.

I had come to question him about Jesus' claim that he is the sole path to God, an assertion he had made to his disciple Thomas. According to tradition, the once-doubting Thomas, his faith bolstered by his encounter with the resurrected Christ, later ventured deep into India to communicate the Christian message, finally being murdered near Madras. Zacharias was born a scant six miles from the memorial erected to his martyrdom.

In a sense, Zacharias' spiritual journey is reminiscent of Thomas's. After spending his early years as a Christian in name only, Zacharias found a tentative kind of faith at age seventeen after hearing an American evangelist speak at a rally. Later he ended up in the hospital after attempting to kill himself over the meaninglessness of life, an experience through which he became a radically devoted follower of Jesus and a missionary from India to places around the world.

I knew his experience in that multicultural, multireligious environment, where he grew up among Muslims, Hindus, and Sikhs, would enrich his perspective on this troubling question of Christ's exclusivity. As he sipped hot tea, I pulled my notes out of my briefcase and immediately zeroed in on the topic at hand.

THE ARROGANCE OF CHRISTIANITY

"Forgive me for being blunt," I said in prefacing my question, "but isn't it grossly arrogant for Christians to claim Jesus is the one and only way to God? Why do Christians think they're justified in asserting that they're right and that everybody else in the world is wrong?"

While Zacharias' accent and conservative business attire— a starched white shirt and muted tie—gave him an air of formality, he was invariably enthusiastic, warm, and engaging in his answers.

"Lee, I hear that question so much, especially in the East," he said, his voice animated and his eyes looking sincere and concerned. "The first thing I do is try to deal with the misinformation that is inherent in it."

"Misinformation?" I asked. "Like what?"

"First," he said, "it's important to understand that Christianity is not the only religion that claims exclusivity. For instance, Muslims radically claim exclusivity—not just theologically, but also linguistically. Muslims believe that the sole, sufficient, and consummate miracle of Islam is the Koran. They say, however, it's only recognizable in Arabic, and that any translation desacralizes it. And it's not just a basic understanding of Arabic that's required, but a sophisticated knowledge of the language.

"As for Buddhism, it was born when Gautama Buddha rejected two fundamental assertions of Hinduism—the ultimate authority of the Vedas, which are their scriptures, and the caste system. Hinduism itself is absolutely uncompromising on two or three issues: the law of karma, which is the law of moral cause and effect, so that every birth is a rebirth that makes recompense for the previous life; the authority of the Vedas; and reincarnation."

I interrupted. "But I've heard Hindus say quite nobly that Hinduism is a very tolerant faith," I said, thinking of statements like the one made by Swami Vivekenanda near the beginning of this chapter.

He smiled. "Whenever you hear that statement, don't take it at face value," he said. "What it really means is that Hinduism allows you to practice your religion so long as it buys into their notion of truth, which is syncretistic," he said. Syncretism is the attempt to blend together different or even opposing beliefs.

"As for Sikhism," he continued, "it came as a challenge to both Hinduism and Buddhism. Then there are the atheists—they reject the viewpoints of those who believe in God. And even Baha'ism, which claims to be a cosmic embrace of all religions, ends up excluding the exclusivists! Therefore, the statement that Christians are arrogant by claiming exclusivity ignores the reality that every other major religion does as well. So when people talk of arrogance, this cannot be a logical attack they are making."

I started to formulate my next question, but Zacharias anticipated where it was headed and jumped in to complete my sentence.

"You believe that all truth—" I began.

"Is, by definition, exclusive," he said. "Yes, yes, I do. If truth does not exclude, then no assertion of a truth claim is being made; it's just an opinion that is being stated. Any time you make a truth claim, you mean something contrary to it is false. Truth excludes its opposite."

"There are those who deny that," I observed.

"Yes, but think about this: to deny the exclusive nature of truth is to make a truth claim, and is that person then not arrogant too? That's the boomerang effect that the condemner often doesn't pause to consider. The clear implications of Jesus saying he's the way, the truth, and the life are that, first, truth is absolute, and second, truth is knowable. His claim of exclusivity means categorically that anything that contradicts what he says is by definition false."

"It's one thing for Christians to believe that," I said. "It's another thing to communicate it without sounding smug or superior. But Christians often come off that way."

Zacharias sighed. It was a charge he had heard all too often. "Yes, if truth is not undergirded by love, it makes the possessor of that truth obnoxious and the truth repulsive," he said. "Having been raised in India and having all Hindu, Muslim, Buddhist, and

Sikh friends growing up, I can appreciate some of their criticisms of Christians. Christianity's history has some explaining to do with its methodology. Violence, antagonism, and hostility are contrary to the love of Christ. One cannot communicate the love of Christ in non-loving terms.

"In India we have a proverb that says once you cut off a person's nose, there's no point in giving him a rose to smell," he continued. "And if a Christian's arrogance turns off somebody, that person won't be receptive to the Christian message. Mahatma Gandhi said, 'I like their Christ, I don't like their Christians.' Friedrich Nietzshe said, 'I will believe in the Redeemer when the Christian looks a little more redeemed.' Their points need to be taken.

"However," he added, "it is possible to lovingly claim exclusive truth, just as a scientist can very gently say, 'This is the second law of thermodynamics' without adding, 'Now, can we vote on how many of us can cooperate with it or not?'"

"So the criticism of Christians is often valid?"

"Yes, sometimes we have run afoul of cultural sensitivities. At the same time, however, Eastern religions have a lot of soul-searching to do in this regard today. Clannish and political conflicts aside, I know of no Christianized country where your life is in danger because you are from another faith. But today there are many countries in the world—such as Pakistan, Saudia Arabia, and Iran—where to become a follower of Christ is to put your life and your family at risk."

I had read enough newspaper accounts in recent years to know that was accurate, including in Zacharias' native land, where several Christians have been killed by militant Hindus in recent years. But sometimes it's not the manner in which the Christians try to spread their faith that's offensive. Sometimes people are simply reacting to the message itself.

"Even the one whose life was most perfectly lived ended up on a cross," Zacharias noted. "Resistance to truth can be so strong that it can still engender violence and hate even when the person has done absolutely nothing wrong."

ORIGIN, MEANING, MORALITY, DESTINY

Anyone can claim to be the only path to God. In fact, quite a few crackpots have made that assertion throughout history. The real issue is why anybody should believe Jesus was telling the truth when he said it.

"On what basis do you believe this claim by Jesus is true?" I asked Zacharias.

"Ah, yes, that is the heart of the question," he replied, his head nodding. "On one hand, you can say that the resurrection of Jesus established him as being the son of God. If that's true, then all other faith systems cannot be true, because they each assert something contrary to his divinity. And of course, the historical record concerning the Resurrection is extremely compelling.

"On the other hand, you can approach this issue by looking at the four fundamental questions that every religion seeks to answer: Origin, meaning, morality, and destiny. I believe that only the answers of Jesus Christ correspond to reality. There is a coherence among his answers unlike those of any other religion."

That was a bold statement. "Can you back that up with examples of how other faiths fail those tests?"

"Consider Buddhism," he replied. "Buddha's answer on the question of morality does not cohere with his answer concerning origins. You see, Buddhism is technically nontheistic, if not athe-istic. But if there was no Creator, from where does one arrive at a moral law? Or consider the Hindu version of reincarnation. If every birth is a rebirth, and if every life pays for the previous life, then what were you paying for in your first birth? You see— incoherence dominates."

He was quick to add that he was not trying to denigrate those religions. "Great scholars will tell you there is incoherence," he said. "Even Gandhi said that if he had his way he would expunge some of the scriptures from Hinduism, because they are so contradictory with each other. By contrast, Jesus provides answers to these four fundamental questions of life in a way that corresponds with reality and has internal consistency, unlike any other faith system."

That statement invited challenge. "Go through each one," I said, "and tell me how."

"Fair enough," he replied. "Concerning origins, the Bible says we are not identical with God—contrary to the Hindu claim—but we are distinct from him. In other words, we didn't bring ourselves into being, but we are a creation of God. Since we were created in his image, this accounts for human beings having a moral point of reference. No system is able to explain this except the monotheistic ones. Even naturalists have no explanation for humanity's moral framework. However, this moral framework corresponds to the reality of human experience.

"Also, Christianity says we rejected the divine will. The tempter in the garden said if you eat this fruit, you will become as gods, knowing good and evil. The implication is that you become the definer of good and evil. Humanism was born right there; man became the measure of all things. This willful rebellion and rejection of God corresponds to reality. As Malcolm Muggeridge said, human depravity is at once the most empirically verifiable reality but also the most philosophically resistant.

"Next, the issue of meaning. Here again, the Christian faith stands without parallel. The simplest way to describe it is that God does not call us to meaning by asking us to be good people. He does not call us to meaning just by telling us to love one another. It is only in the experience of worship that meaning comes to be. Only something greater than pleasure can provide meaning, and that is the perpetual novelty of God himself in worship. The Bible tells us to love the Lord our God with all our heart, soul, and mind, and only when we've done that can we begin to love our neighbors as ourselves. This also corresponds to experience.

"Next, Christianity says morality is not culturally based, but instead it grows out of the very character of God. Otherwise, you end up with the dilemma from philosophy of old: is the moral law over and above you, or is a moral law subject to you? If it is over and above you, where do you find its root, then? The only way to explain that is to find it in an eternal, moral, omnipotent, infinite God who is inseparable from his character. Thus, Christianity explains morality in a coherent manner.

"Finally, destiny is based on the resurrection of Jesus Christ, the historical event that proved his divinity and that opened the door to heaven for everyone who will follow him. Where else do you have anything that comes close to claiming this?

"Billy Graham once told of meeting Konrad Adenauer, the mayor of Cologne who was imprisoned by Hitler for opposing the Nazi regime and who later became the highly regarded chancellor of West Germany from 1949 to 1963. Adenauer looked Graham in the eyes and asked, 'Do you believe in the resurrection of Jesus Christ from the dead?' Graham said, 'Of course I do.' To which Adenauer replied: 'Mr. Graham, outside of the resurrection of Jesus, I do not know of any other hope for this world.'

"He was right. Because the Resurrection is an actual historical event, we can be forgiven, we can be reconciled with God, we can spend eternity with him, and we can trust Jesus' teachings as being from God.

"One of my friends was a Muslim convert who was later martyred. I remember visiting him in the hospital after his legs had been blown off, and he said: 'The more I understand of what others have claimed and taught, the more beautiful Jesus Christ looks to me.' I've never forgotten that, and I believe that to be absolutely true.

"No man spoke like Jesus. No one ever answered the questions the way he answered them, not only propositionally but also in his person. Existentially, we can test it out. Empirically, we can test it out. The Bible is not just a book of mysticism or spirituality; it is a book that also gives geographical truths and historical truths. If you're an honest skeptic, it's not just calling you to a feeling; it's calling you to a real Person. That's why the apostle Peter said, 'We did not follow cleverly invented stories when we told you about the power and coming of our Lord Jesus Christ, but we were eyewitnesses of his majesty.'[14]

"He's saying, 'This is true. This is reality. This can be trusted.' And, yes, this truth excludes that which is contrary."

OF ELEPHANTS AND FAITH

Even if Zacharias was right about Christianity, however, does this necessarily mean that all other religions are false? Perhaps they're all teaching the same fundamental truths at their core, using different language, diverse images, and various traditions to communicate basically identical beliefs.

"Some people say that when you strip away everything, all the world religions are essentially teaching the universal fatherhood of God and the universal brotherhood of humankind," I said. "That would mean that all the world's faith systems are equally valid."

Zacharias shook his head, his face registering dismay. "Only someone who doesn't understand the world religions would claim they basically teach the same thing," he said.

"What do they mean by the universal fatherhood of God when Buddhism doesn't even claim that there is a God? What do we mean by the fatherhood of God when Shankara, one of the most respected Hindu philosophers, said theism is only a child's way to ultimately get to the top, where you find out God is not distinct from you? What then does the fatherhood of God mean? It's an illusion. This fatherhood of God is not a trans-religious doctrine.

"Secondly, the brotherhood of humanity—yes, we are brothers and sisters as fellow human beings, but the only reason we are is because we have been fashioned by God. Once you take that foundation away," he said with a chuckle, "then brotherhood ends up with more hoods than brothers! In sum, Islam, Buddhism, Hinduism, and Christianity are not saying the same thing. They are distinct and mutually exclusive religious doctrines. They all cannot be true at the same time."

Still, I wasn't through attempting to harmonize them. "Maybe the various religions each have a slice of the truth," I suggested. "Theologian John Hick said the world religions are different culturally conditioned responses to the ultimately 'Real,' or God.[15] Isn't this like the old story of the three blind men feeling the elephant—each religion is a sincere but inadequate attempt to explain the mystery of God, and so each one is valid in its own way?"

Zacharias started with a bit of philosophical judo. "Either Hick is the product of his own culture or he has transcended his culture in making that statement," he countered. "And if he has transcended his culture, why hasn't anyone else transcended culture? It sounds very academically sophisticated, but it has too many problems at its heart."

"Like what?" I asked.

"For instance, does the atheist have a piece of the truth, or is the atheist marginalized here? If the atheist does have a piece of the truth, which piece is it, since the fundamental tenet of atheism is the denial of God's very existence?"

He paused, letting the question answer itself. Then he added: "I will say this: there are aspects of truth in virtually all of the major religions. They contain some great thoughts and ideas. Reading the notable Eastern philosophers is very, very stimulating. But it's not like we are blind people exploring the elephant, with one person feeling the leg and thinking it's a tree; the other person feeling the trunk and thinking it's a rope; and the third feeling the ear and thinking it's a fan.

"The point is," he said, his voice rising for emphasis, "the parable has already given away the fact that this, indeed, is an elephant! The blind man may tell you it's a tree, but he's wrong. It is not a tree or a rope or a fan. The seeing man knows this is an elephant. He knows the truth; his sight has revealed it to him. And Jesus Christ has made it clear that the eternal truths of God may be known. Jesus Christ is the centerpiece of the gospel—in him, all of truth came together. So while there may be aspects of truth elsewhere, the sum total of truth is in Christ.

"Hick's explanation ignores the possibility that God would reveal himself, and that therefore we can have knowledge of who he is. Instead, Hick has made culture and intuition supreme. But the Bible says God *did* reveal himself: 'In the beginning was the Word, and the Word was with God, and the Word was God.... The Word became flesh and made his dwelling among us. We have seen his glory, the glory of the One and Only, who came from the Father, full of grace and truth.'"[16]

REDEMPTION, RIGHTEOUSNESS, WORSHIP

Comedian Quentin Crisp once said: "When I told the people of Northern Ireland that I was an atheist, a woman in the audience stood up and said, 'Yes, but is it the God of the Catholics or the God of the Protestants in whom you don't believe?'"

His humor was actually a sad commentary on the depth of sectarian strife in that land. Through the centuries, the world has seen plenty of acrimony and violence over differences in the way people view God. Disgusted by religious bickering, some people have thrown up their hands and said the world would be a much better place if people simply stopped arguing over doctrinal disputes and instead focused on living in peace with each other.

"There are moral-living Muslims, Jews, Christians, Mormons, and Hindus," I pointed out to Zacharias. "Isn't how a person lives and treats his neighbor more important than what he believes theologically?"

"How a person lives and how he treats his neighbor is very important," came his reply. "But it is not more important than what he believes, because the way he lives is reflective of what he believes. Regardless of whether he has ever signed a doctrinal statement, what he really and truly believes is what he will ultimately live out. But this question makes the assumption that morality is what life is all about."

"If life isn't about being moral," I said, "then what is it about?"

"Jesus Christ didn't come into this world to make bad people good," he said. "He came into this world to make dead people live. He came so that those who are dead to God can come alive to God. If this life were only about morality, then how you live would be the most important thing, although it would still be connected to what you believe. But that misunderstands the Christian concept, which is no matter how well we live, we cannot live up to the standard and character of God.

"The word 'sin' means missing the mark. And if that is a correct definition, then the grace of God becomes the most important truth. Apart from him, we cannot even believe what is right, let alone live the right way.

"So, yes, living kindly and morally good lives is important, if purely for survival. But philosophers from Socrates, Plato, and Aristotle, all the way to the Enlightenment thinkers like Immanuel Kant were unable to even define what morality is. Ultimately, they could only give us what morality did for society.

"When I did a study of options by which people can live good lives, I came down to six or seven of them, such as Joseph Fletcher's situation ethics, Ayn Rand's egocentric humanism, Kant's idea of duty, and so forth. But they contradicted one another pretty heavily, and the reason is that there was no transcendent, compelling moral reason. It was all reduced to mere survival. So I believe goodness or badness is the wrong starting point; life and death, spiritually, is where you begin."

"But as you conceded, it is important how people live," I said. "People say Gandhi lived a more virtuous life than most Christians. Why should he be sent to hell just because he wasn't a follower of Jesus?"

"That's a tough issue. When I get that question before big audiences, that's the time I want to take a break!" he said with a smile. "But the Bible does give us some guidance in answering this.

"First and foremost, it's important to know that no human being consigns anybody to heaven or hell. In fact, God himself does not send anybody to heaven or to hell; the person chooses to respond to the grace of God or to reject the grace of God, although even that decision is enabled by his grace.

"Second, Abraham asked God in the case of Sodom and Gomorrah whether he was going to let the righteous die with the unrighteous, and it was wonderful how Abraham answered his own question. He said, 'Will not the Judge of all the earth do right?'[17] This means we can be absolutely confident that whatever God does in the case of Gandhi or any other person, he will do what is right.

"Now, think about this: the Bible says anyone spending eternity with God in heaven is there because of the grace and provision of Jesus Christ, which the person has trusted and received. If the person has rejected that grace, then was he a good man or a bad man? That's an interesting question, because Scripture tells us nobody is really good until he or she is first redeemed."

"Elaborate on that," I said.

"The pattern in Exodus is threefold: God brought the people out of Egypt, he gave them the moral law, and then he gave them the tabernacle. In other words, redemption, righteousness, worship. You can never violate that sequence. Unless you are redeemed, you cannot be righteous. Unless you are redeemed and righteous, you cannot worship, 'for who shall ascend unto the hill of the Lord,' says the Bible, 'but he who has clean hands and a pure heart?'[18]

"So redemption is the most important step toward righteousness. If I try to work myself toward goodness, I am essentially saying I don't need to be redeemed by God. I am my own redeemer. Any person, good or bad in our eyes, who says that is in violation of a fundamental principle of God's revelation, which is that redemption is the first step."

SO WHAT ABOUT GANDHI?

Still, my mind was on Gandhi. "He didn't follow Jesus," I said, "so I suppose you would say he was not redeemed."

"That is something that will be determined by God," Zacharias replied. "However, what is it Gandhi believed? He summarized it in one statement: 'God is truth and truth is God.' My question to him would be, 'What does that mean?' We are sitting in a room; that is a true statement. What has this got to do with whether this room is god or not? It doesn't. It only conforms to a statement I have just made. God exists—is that a true statement? If that is a true statement, who is this God?"

I interrupted. "Yet here you have a person like Gandhi, who in the eyes of most people lived a good life, whereas a serial killer like David Berkowitz, the Son of Sam, murdered several innocent people and now says he's prayed a prayer to become a Christian. Christians would say Berkowitz is going to heaven but Gandhi isn't. Where's the equity in that?"

"Because we are moral human beings, we want to see equity. But when we reduce equity to issues of who behaved in what way during a given span of time, we miss the whole concept of equity. We are judging this from the point of view of our system. If God were to truly give what every one of us deserved, none of us would get to heaven.

"There's the joke about two brothers who lived scandalous lives, and when one of them suddenly died, the surviving brother went to a minister and asked if he would preach at his brother's funeral. He said, 'I just have one request: that you refer to my brother as a saint.' The pastor said he would do his best to accommodate him.

"The funeral came and the minister was eulogizing the deceased. 'I want you to know this man was a swindler, a liar, a cheater, and a thief,' he said. 'But compared to his brother, he was a saint!'

"Now, there is a sharp edge to that story. We try desperately to claim goodness by comparing ourselves to others. David Berkowitz can say, 'Wait a minute; I'm not Hitler! I didn't kill millions, I just killed a few.' Or 'I wasn't Jeffrey Dahmer; I didn't eat my victims.' We tend to do the kind of comparisons by which we always emerge better than someone else, and so we think we're good. But by the perfect moral standard of God, we all fail. We all need God's forgiveness and grace.

"Admittedly, what David Berkowitz did was violent and evil. There's no question about that. However, we have to look at this in the whole scheme of God's plan. You see, there are worse things than death or murder."

"Like what?" I asked.

"Though it's hard to comprehend," he said, "the worst thing is to say to God that you don't need him. Why? Because a dead person can be restored to life by God; a bereaved person can find peace from God; a person who has been violated can find God's sustenance and strength and even see God conquer through the dark mystery of evil. In other words, there is recourse through these atrocities and tragedies. But to a person who says he or she doesn't need God, what is the recourse? There is none.

"So the question is not whether I'm a David Berkowitz,

a Mahatma Gandhi, an Adolph Hitler, or a Mother Teresa. The question is, 'Have I come to the realization that I've fallen short of God's perfect standard and, therefore, apart from the grace of God, I have no possibility of being with him in heaven?'

"Frankly, if I have lived a life that I think is so good that I don't need God, then ironically Berkowitz will have found the ultimate truth to which my own arrogance and confidence have blinded me. What is hell but the absence of God? And for me to live my life with the absence of God is to already be on the road to hell."

"But," I protested, "is it fair for a killer like Berkowitz to get off scot-free?"

"I'm not sure he has," Zacharias said. "Yes, God has forgiven him if he has confessed and repented and sought God's mercy. But the more he is in tune with who Christ is, the deeper will be his pain for what he has done.

"Let me give you an example. Suppose you're driving and your mind wanders for a moment. Suddenly, a child runs in front of you and you hit that child. The closer you are in touch with the tragedy, the greater will be your burden for the rest of your life. You will never be able to look into the face of another child without thinking, 'What did I do? What did I do?'

"We may think Berkowitz got away in the sense that he didn't go to the gallows, but there is such a thing as the gallows of the heart. Your heart can be very attuned to the hell that you unleashed. I do not believe that a truly converted person would sit in his prison cell and think, 'Well, I've come to know Christ and so I'm off the hook on that.' No. Sometimes the hell of an inner heart may be very deep and painful.

"I believe there is a hell to a delayed salvation because the tears that flow are tears of what was lost before you came to know God. Does he forgive your past? Yes, but sometimes you cannot forget it."

Having said that, Zacharias paused and leaned back in his chair. When he resumed, he said: "Any time grace is misunderstood, it will always lead to comparison and jealousy or discontent and the charge of inequity. Interestingly enough, Jesus addresses this very issue.

"In one of his parables, the workers who labored all day were distressed that those who had come in at the last moment had also received the grace of the landlord.[19] One of the most staggering truths of the Scriptures is to understand that we do not earn our way to heaven. Also, we read in the Bible the story of the woman of ill repute who Jesus received. The Pharisee looked down his merit-formed nose and sneered at the mercy of God.[20] Works have a place—but as a demonstration of having received God's forgiveness, not as a badge of merit of having earned it."

WHAT OF THOSE WHO HAVEN'T HEARD?

Serial killer David Berkowitz was fortunate. He lives in a country where people freely talk about Christianity. Someone told him about Christ's offer of forgiveness, and he says he has confessed his offenses and put his faith in Jesus. But what about people who live in places where the gospel isn't routinely discussed or where its dissemination is actually outlawed?

"Isn't it unfair to condemn them when they never heard about Jesus and merely followed the religious traditions of their parents?" I asked.

Zacharias reached over to pick up his Bible. As he opened it and flipped to Acts, I caught a glimpse of the many places where he had highlighted key verses in yellow.

"The Bible says first of all that nobody will be in the presence of God apart from the fact that the person and work of Christ made it possible. That's the price it took: Christ's death on the cross as our substitute, paying the penalty we deserved to pay. Now, some people are born into one culture or another, but the apostle Paul said something very interesting about that when he was speaking to the Athenians."

Zacharias lifted his reading glasses out of his pocket and slipped them on so that they perched on his nose. Then he read part of a passage where Paul was debating some Greek philosophers:

> From one man he made every nation of men, that they should inhabit the whole earth; and he determined the

times set for them and the exact places where they
should live. God did this so that men would seek him
and perhaps reach out for him and find him, though he
is not far from each one of us.[21]

Removing his glasses, Zacharias looked up at me. "This
is important," he said, "because he's pointing out that there's
a sovereign plan in creation, where each person is assigned a place
of birth. God knows where we will be born and raised, and he puts
us in a position where we might seek him. We are clearly told that
wherever we live—in whatever culture, in whatever nation—he is
within reach of every one of us. There is always the possibility of
a person crying out on their knees, 'God, help me,' and if that
happens there are ways in which God can minister to them that
are beyond our understanding."

"For example?"

"For example, he might send someone to share the gospel with
them. Or let me tell you what happened in the case of a Muslim
woman who worked for a very well-known institution in her
country. She told me how she was leaving her office at the end of
her day's work and was very unhappy in her heart. As she was
walking, she muttered, 'I don't know why I am so empty,' and after
that, out of the blue, she said, 'Jesus, can you help me?' She
stopped on the sidewalk and said to herself, 'Why did I name him?'
Well, that woman ended up becoming a Christian.

"In her case, I think God saw a heart that hungered for him
but did not know how to reach him in the cloister of her existence.
I think this was God breaking past the barriers of her environment
because she was already breaking through the barriers of her inner
life, seeking after him. Thus, God can reach into any cultural
situation in response to anyone who wants to know him.

"Another way of looking at this issue comes from Romans,
where Paul says God's infinite power and deity are revealed to
everyone through creation.[22] Then Paul says God put the law in our
hearts and our consciences that we might seek after him.[23] And he
talks about the word of Christ that is necessary for a person to
come to know him.[24] I think more and more that this word of

Christ comes within the framework of different cultures.

"What do I mean by that?

"I have spoken in many Islamic countries, where it's tough to talk about Jesus. Virtually every Muslim who has come to follow Christ has done so, first, because of the love of Christ expressed through a Christian, or second, because of a vision, a dream, or some other supernatural intervention. Now, no religion has a more intricate doctrine of angels and visions than Islam, and I think it's extraordinary that God uses that sensitivity to the supernatural world in which he speaks in visions and dreams and reveals himself.

"One of India's greatest converts was a Sikh, Sundar Singh, who came to know Christ through an appearance of Christ in his room in a dream one night. It had a tremendous impact on his life and he became a Christian. So there are ways that God can reveal himself that go far beyond our own understanding.

"Now, if God is able to give the word of Christ in various settings in ways we can't even understand—if he's not far from us wherever we are, if he is able to speak through the general revelation of creation and through our conscience—then we have to accept the fact that we are without excuse. Every human being will know enough truth so that if they respond to that known truth, God will reveal more to them. Does that mean they have to have as much of a volume of truth as someone in another setting does? I don't believe so."

I tried to summarize his point. "You're saying that regardless of where a person lives in the world, regardless of the culture in which they live, anyone who responds to the understanding that they do have and sincerely seeks God will in some way be given an opportunity to respond to him?"

As I spoke, Zacharias was weighing my words with care. "I believe so," he replied. "We have to be very careful here, but I believe that if a person genuinely and sincerely seeks after him, there will be some way God makes available for that person to hear of him. If that person would not have responded to God under any circumstance, then perhaps he will not hear of him. But all people know enough to condemn them; they do not need to hear John 3:16 in order to be lost. They are lost because they've already rejected what God has spoken to them through creation, their conscience, and other ways. Because of that, we will all stand accountable before him."

"So sincerity is important?

"Sincerity is not salvation," came his response. "But I think sincerity brings about the possibility of God revealing himself to you. Some may seem sincere and when Christ is presented to them, they reject him. They fail the test of truth."

I said, "You believe, then, that the amount of information a person needs to have concerning Christ can vary widely?"

"Yes, I believe so. The danger of a Western perspective is thinking that if something isn't neatly packaged, it's no good. And unfortunately, some Western Christians think that unless a person says the creed just like they do, they don't know God.

"Yet what does an infant know of his mother? He knows she nourishes him, she changes him, she embraces him, she kisses him—she must be a friend. That child doesn't know his mother as well as he will when he's eighteen. But he knows her enough to love her. I believe that as God reveals himself there are levels of understanding that are bound to vary."

WHY NOT JESUS?

If Jesus is the truth, why do so many people reject him? If Christianity is true, shouldn't it ultimately triumph? That's not what the statistics show, however. Christianity is making relatively little progress in winning converts from other major world religions. Basically, people around the globe tend to adopt the religion of their parents.

I asked Zacharias about this, and he said these issues trouble him as a defender of Christianity. There are, though, some explanations, he said.

"To look at this from a different perspective, why is Buddhism so popular in America today?" he asked. "My answer is simple:

because you can be good without having God. If you can have a nice little dose of spirituality from three to five in the afternoon and then dichotomize your life once again and go live it any way you please—well, why not? A religion like that would have a lot of attraction.

"Why is Islam attractive to some? Because of geopolitical considerations. What is it about the Hindu faith that's attractive? It is rich in philosophy, and its tenet of treating the earth with reverence has some appeal today."

"Why not Christ?" I asked.

"Because he calls you to die to yourself," he replied. "Any time truth involves a total commitment in which you bring yourself to complete humility, to the surrender of the will, you will always have resistance. Christ violates our power and autonomy. He challenges us in areas of purity. John the Baptist came giving the law. People did not like it. Jesus came giving the message of grace and they said, 'Why don't you give us the firmness of the law?' Whatever Jesus brings into culture, culture will want to change it. At the heart of the rejection is resistance to the claim of who he is.

"Buddhism and other religious systems basically tell people how to pull themselves up by their ethical bootstraps. I have never had a problem knowing what is right and wrong in most situations; what I have lacked is the will to do what is right. That's where Christ comes in. He says if you'll bring all of yourself to him, he will not only give you eternal life, but he will change what you want to do in this life."

Given the level of commitment required by Christianity, I was curious about what prompted Zacharias to respond positively to the message of Jesus. "Tell me a bit of your story," I said.

He looked down for a moment, brushing a crumb off his shirt sleeve. Then he reached over to his cup of tea and took a sip before answering.

"In India, you are what you are born into," he began. "My father and mother were nominal Christians; in fact, the reason they were Christians was simply because they were not Buddhists, Muslims, or Hindus. I don't recall ever hearing the gospel preached at my church, which was very liberal-minded.

"Just prior to my coming to Christ, my sisters were exposed to the gospel and made their commitment. I came to believe in Jesus in two stages. The first stage was when I heard the gospel publicly proclaimed in an auditorium when I was seventeen. I said to myself, 'Something about this is true and I want it.' I went forward and was counseled, but I did not really understand. The baggage was too much.

"At the time, I was under a lot of pressure in a culture where academic performance was of supreme importance. If you're not at the top of the class, then you're not going to succeed. I couldn't cope with it. I also had a very strict father, and I struggled with that. I took a lot of punishment physically.

"So a few months later, I decided to end my own life. I was not depressed; my friends would have been shocked to hear suicide was on my mind. But for me, life had no meaning or purpose. I went to school one day and used the keys to the science lab to check out some poisons. I put them into a glass of water, gobbled it up, and collapsed on my knees."

I stared in disbelief. With Zacharias being as sophisticated, as erudite, as articulate, and as influential as he is today, it was impossible for me to visualize him as a confused and hope-starved teenager crumbling to his knees and gasping for breath as self-administered toxins coursed through his veins.

"My servant in the house rushed me to the hospital; if he were not there, I would be dead," he continued. "They emptied all of the poisons out of me. As I lay in bed, a friend walked in with a New Testament and showed me John chapter 14. I couldn't hold the book; my body was too dehydrated. My mother had to read it to me.

"There she was, reading where Jesus was talking to Thomas and saying, 'I am the way, the truth, and the life. No one comes to the Father except through me.' Then she came to verse 18, where Jesus tells his disciples, 'Because I live, you also will live.'

"That verse touched my soul. I said in a prayer, 'Jesus, I don't know much about who you are, but you are telling me you're the author of true life.' I didn't understand the concept of sin. In that culture, I couldn't have. But what I did understand was that he was offering himself to me to give me life.

"So I said, 'If you take me out of this hospital room, I will leave no stone unturned in my pursuit of truth.' And I walked out of that room five days later an absolutely brand new man. I began to study the Bible, and it dramatically changed my life. My brothers then came to follow Jesus, as did my parents before they died.

"But it was in that hospital room where Christ told me—through nobody explaining it to me—that he could give me what life was really meant to be. And I've never looked back. Years of study have only confirmed my decision to follow him. I took some philosophy courses at Cambridge under a renowned atheist, and I remember thinking in astonishment, 'These are the best arguments atheists have?' It merely confirmed the truth of Scripture."

"You deal with a lot of spiritual seekers now," I said. "What do you tell them?"

"The Bible says, 'You will seek me and find me when you seek me with all your heart.'[25] Think about that—that's an amazing promise. I encourage them to bring their heart and mind into a receptive mode and to not spare their intellect in testing the truth of the Bible. For any genuine person who brings an unprejudiced view, I don't see how he or she can walk away except saying there is nothing like this on the face of the earth.

"I have traveled the world. I have searched high and low. I have found nothing that satisfies my mind, my heart, and the deepest longings of my soul like Jesus does. He is not only the way, the truth, and the life; he is personal to me. He is my way, and my truth, and my life—just as he can be for anyone who reaches out to him.

"Because remember what Paul told the Athenians: 'He is not far,' he said, 'from each one of us.'" ❖

DELIBERATIONS—QUESTIONS FOR REFLECTION OR GROUP STUDY

◆ What was your emotional reaction the first time you heard the claim that Jesus is the only path to God? Has your viewpoint changed since reading Ravi Zacharias' interview? If so, how?

◆ Zacharias said: "The clear implications of Jesus saying he's the way, the truth, and the life are that, first, truth is absolute, and, second, truth is knowable." Do you believe those two assertions about truth? Why or why not?

◆ How well do you believe Christianity deals with the four fundamental issues of life: Origin, meaning, morality, and destiny? Does the Bible's teaching on those topics correspond to your experience?

◆ Have you personally considered any other world religion? If so, what did you find attractive about it? What aspects of Christianity attract you and which ones repel you?

◆ The Bible says about God, "You will seek me and find me when you seek me with all your heart." What three practical suggestions would you give to a friend who wants to know how he or she can seek God that way? Have you taken those steps yourself? What has been the result so far?

FOR FURTHER EVIDENCE—MORE RESOURCES ON THIS TOPIC

Ravi Zacharias. *Jesus Among Other Gods*. Nashville: Word, 2000.

Paul Copan. *True for You, But Not for Me*. Minneapolis: Bethany House, 1998.

Frank Beckwith and Gregory Koukl. *Relativism: Feet Firmly Planted in Mid-Air*. Grand Rapids, Mich.: Baker, 1998.

Millard J. Erickson. *How Shall They Be Saved?* Grand Rapids, Mich.: Baker, 1996.

CHAPTER NOTES

1. Available at: http://cnn.com/Transcripts/0001/12/lkl.00.html [2000. January 13].

2. R. C. Sproul, *Reason to Believe* (Grand Rapids, Mich.: Lamplighter Books, 1982), 44–45.

3. See: Robert J. Wagman, *The First Amendment Book* (New York: Pharos Books, 1991), 106. Also see: Chapkinsky v. New Hampshire, 315 U.S. 568 (1942).

4. See: Cohen v California, 403 U.S. 15 (1971).

5. John 14:6

6. See: John Hick and Paul F. Knitter, eds., *The Myth of Christian Uniqueness* (London: SCM Press, 1987), 141, quoted in: Paul Copan, *True for You, But Not for Me* (Minneapolis, Minn.: Bethany House, 1998), 78.

7. Available at: http://cnn.com/Transcripts/0001/12/lkl.00.html [2000. January 13].

8. Quoted in: Paul Copan, *True for You, But Not for Me*, 34.

9. Ravi Zacharias, *Can Man Live Without God* (Nashville, Tenn.: Word, 1994), from introduction by Charles Colson, ix.

10. Charles Templeton, *Farewell to God*, 27.

11. Acts 4:12

12. Charles Templeton, *Farewell to God*, 27, emphasis added.

13. Quoted in: Ravi Zacharias, *Can Man Live Without God*, back cover.

14. 2 Peter 1:16.

15. See: "The Exclusivism of Religious Pluralism," in Paul Copan, *True For You, But Not For Me*, 71–77.

16. John 1:1, 14.

17. Genesis 18:25c.

18. See: Psalm 24:3–4.

19. See: Matthew 20:1–16.

20. See: Luke 7:36–50.

21. Acts 17:26–27.

22. Romans 1:20.

23. Romans 2:14–15.

24. Romans 10:14–15.

25. Jeremiah 29:13.

Don't All Good People Go To Heaven?

by Andy Stanley

Look for your coupons for this and other
featured titles in the back of this book.

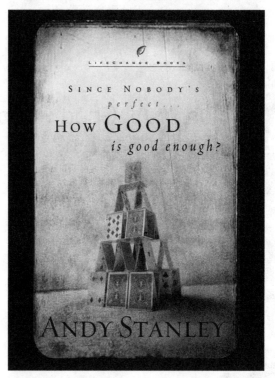

Author's Bio

Andy Stanley is a graduate of Dallas Theological
Seminary and the pastor of North Point
Community Church in Atlanta, Georgia. He
carries on a tradition of excellence in ministry
with a youthful congregation of over 12,000.
Andy is the author of *The Next Generation
Leader* and the 1998 Foreward Book of the
Year finalist *Visioneering*. He and his wife,
Sandra, have two sons, Andrew and Garrett,
and a daughter, Allison.

Don't All Good People Go To Heaven?

by Andy Stanley

One particular incident brought eye-popping clarity to what Jesus believed about good people and heaven.

Following his arrest and perfunctory trial, Jesus was beaten and forced to drag his cross toward the place of execution. Luke reports that at some point along the way the Roman guards conscripted a passerby named Simon to carry Jesus' cross for him, the implication being that he was too weak from loss of blood to drag it himself.

Once Jesus was nailed to the cross, Luke records an exchange that took place between Jesus and the men being crucified on either side of him. Before we listen in on their conversation, there are a couple of things about crucifixion you ought to know. In that day, it was considered the most shameful and painful form of execution. A man sentenced to crucifixion was stripped naked before being either tied or nailed to the wooden timbers, and he could hang for days in agony before finally succumbing to death.

Now with that in mind, let's look at what the men crucified beside Jesus said once they recognized who it was that hung between them:

> One of the criminals who hung there hurled insults at him: "Aren't you the Christ? Save yourself and us!"
>
> But the other criminal rebuked him. "Don't you fear God," he said, "since you are under the same sentence? We are punished justly, for we are getting what our deeds deserve. But this man has done nothing wrong."
> (LUKE 23:39–41)

Notice anything about what the second criminal said that is particularly relevant to our discussion? As horrible a death as crucifixion was, the second criminal readily admitted that his life was so horrible that he was actually getting what he deserved.

"We are getting what our *deeds* deserve." In other words, "Stack our deeds up and you won't find a good one in there anywhere."

Then the convicted criminal did the unthinkable: He asked Jesus for a favor. He asked Jesus to have mercy on him in spite of his worthless life. "Jesus," he said, "remember me when you come into your kingdom" *(LUKE 23:42)*.

Keep in mind, this man was in no position to bargain. There was no "from now on," no turning over a new leaf. The opportunity for doing good had come and gone. This was a dead man talking. He had come to the end of his miserable life and there was no chance to make up for lost time. He had lived his life exactly the way he wanted, with no concern for doing the right thing, and now, hours from the end, he suddenly gets religion and asks for mercy.

Now if Jesus, like most people, believed that good people go to heaven and bad people don't, what would you expect him to say to a guy who, by his own admission, had lived a life worthy of such a death?

What would *you* have told him? What if he had raped your sister or murdered your brother? What if you had been maimed for life because of this man's reckless behavior?

None of that mattered to Jesus. Pushing up on the nail that pierced his foot, for leverage, he managed to utter these words: "I tell you the truth, today you will be with me in paradise" *(LUKE 23:43)*.

Do you realize what that means? It means that Jesus not only didn't believe that good people go to heaven, but he believed that bad people *do*! One of his last acts before dying was to promise a criminal a spot in paradise!

Imagine if you had come out to see this man die because of what he had done to you or your family. Imagine how you might have felt as he hung there suffering. Finally, justice is served. Now imagine how irritated you would be to hear this self-proclaimed messiah announce that this filth of a human being would leave this world only to find himself in paradise.

Did Jesus know *nothing* of justice?

Clearly, he did not believe that good people go to heaven.

He was operating off some other premise unknown to this world. It is no wonder many refused to take his teachings seriously. He promised people precisely what they didn't deserve. Whatever God he came to represent, it was not the God worshiped by the majority. It was not the God of the "good people."

JESUS DOESN'T BLEND WELL

The reason I've gone on and on about Jesus is that everyone I have ever met that believes good people go to heaven has good things to say about Jesus. Somehow they are able to blend his teachings and his life with their *good people go* theology. But the two don't really mix.

That's why the religious leaders got rid of him. Jesus was teaching an entirely different message. His contemporaries understood exactly what he was saying. He wasn't offering yet another version of *the good guys win*. He was here to establish a new order. So they crucified him. "They" being men who believed with all their hearts that good people—lawkeepers, not lawbreakers—go to heaven.

And yet just about everybody has good things to say about Jesus. Every major cult has adopted parts of his teachings. Even Muhammad, the founder of Islam, had great respect for Jesus—he believed that Jesus was, in fact, a true prophet of God. But Jesus never claimed prophet status. He claimed far more. In fact, he claimed that all the prophets before his time were commissioned to prepare the world for his arrival.

Quite an ego, huh?

Unless, of course, he was right.

But Jesus could not possibly have been right, because his teachings about heaven contradicted everybody else's, before and since.

So if you embrace the notion that good people go to heaven, you can't embrace the teachings or person of Christ. At least, you can't if you are going to be intellectually honest.

I know it feels good to keep Jesus within reach. There *is* something special about him.... But he refuses to be blended with all the other religions which, frankly, are easy to blend. After all, they have a common denominator: Good people make it.

Jesus, on the other hand, said things like, "I am the way and the truth and the life. No one comes to the Father except through me" (JOHN 14:6).

Try blending *that*!

He didn't claim to be *a* way to God—he claimed to be *the* way. Contrast that with the wisdom of Muhammad:

> Surely those who believe, and those who are Jews, and the Christians, and the Sabians, whoever believes in Allah and the Last day *and does good*, they shall have their reward from their Lord, and there is no fear for them, nor shall they grieve. (THE COW 2.62, ITALICS MINE)

Jesus claimed otherwise. Embrace his teachings if you choose, but do so at your own risk. To side with Jesus is to embrace a completely different paradigm from what most world religions are teaching.

If there are many roads to God, as many suggest, Jesus' way is worlds apart from the rest.

Recapping

The *good people go to heaven* view has several seemingly insurmountable problems:

1. We don't know exactly what good is. Even our religious leaders can't agree on the subject.
2. Our internal moral gauges aren't much help. They don't line up cross-culturally (or even across the street, for that matter). And as time passes, our definitions of right and wrong tend to change.
3. We have no clear indication from God how the scoring system for good deeds works.
4. It is difficult to reconcile the notion of a good God with a system that is so unclear and seemingly unfair. This is especially true in light of what's at stake.
5. We can't use the Bible as a gauge to measure how close we are to getting in. The Bible doesn't claim to offer a way to heaven

through good works. Besides, the catalog of good works listed in the Old Testament is culturally irrelevant and physically impossible to keep.

6. Jesus assured the most religious people of his day that they weren't good enough to enter God's kingdom, while promising criminals and prostitutes that God would gladly welcome them.

Now you may be able to come up with some "What about...?" questions that breathe enough life into the *good people go* view to keep it alive a while longer. But still you are left to wonder and, as time marches on, to worry.

By the way, do you know where the *good people go* view originated? Not with God. It is a view that is as old as creation itself. Ancient men and women believed in multiple gods who, when angry, had to be appeased by their subjects. For millennia, people have been trying to find a successful formula for keeping the gods (or God) mollified and happy. This is a belief that will not go away, despite the fact that it really doesn't make any sense.

But why? Why do we persist in pursuing the favor of a deity who doesn't have the decency to speak clearly? Why do we persist in this charade?

Simple. There are no other good options. Other than abandoning belief in God altogether, there seems to be no other approach.

But all is not as it seems.

There is another way. ❖

Why Should I Follow Christ?

by Joseph Stowell

Chapter:
Simply Jesus

Book:
Experiencing Jesus

Look for your coupons for this and other
featured titles in the back of this book.

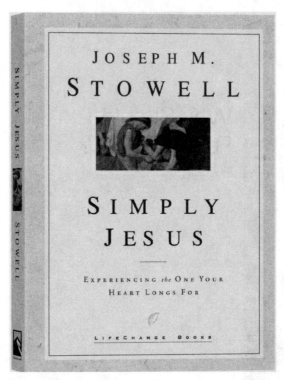

Author's Bio

Joseph M. Stowell became the seventh president
of Chicago's Moody Bible Institute in 1987. He is
a graduate of Cedarville College and Dallas
Theological Seminary and has written numerous
books, including *Eternity, Following Christ*, and
Strength for the Journey.

Why Should I Follow Christ?
by Joseph Stowell

Paul said that it was the throbbing ambition of his life to experience Jesus ... Is it yours?

When my secretary told me I'd been invited to the White House, my heart picked up a little speed.

I wonder if I'll get to meet the president.

Like everyone else, I'd read a lot about him and seen him countless times in pictures and on TV. I'd followed his political career with more than a little interest. In fact, I had voted for him. If someone had asked if I knew much about him, I could have launched into a rather extensive description—his background, his political philosophy, and his policies.

But this was different.

Now I was going to meet him.

I was on the verge of actually experiencing him. Personally.

Wearing my best navy pin-striped suit, a starched white shirt, and a "presidential" tie, I stopped long enough at the airport to get my shoes professionally shined. I could hardly keep myself from telling the man bent over my feet that these shoes were headed for the White House.

I felt sobered as I walked into the grand foyer of our president's home. *These truly are the halls of power*, I said to myself. *Behind closed doors in this very house wars have been declared—history made.*

I found myself seated on the front row of the East Room. The small gathering hushed as a commanding voice announced, "Ladies and gentlemen, the president of the United States." We stood as he walked in briskly and took his place on the low platform. I couldn't take my eyes off of him. I was in his presence and found myself intrigued by his every move. Later, in a very brief conversation, I was surprised at how engaged he seemed. With all this man had on his mind, he took time for me. If only for a moment, he looked into my eyes and gave me his attention.

Frankly, having experienced the reality of his presence, I will never view our president in the same way again. Having met him, I went away wishing I could know him better.

It's like that in your relationship with Jesus: You can be satisfied to just know about Him, or you can enter into an experience with Jesus. Only you can make the choice. And this choice determines the difference between religion as usual or the satisfaction of connecting with Jesus, the One we were created to enjoy.

MORE THAN MERE KNOWLEDGE

We all know who Jesus is. Right?

In the last two thousand years, no other individual has commanded such respect, such honor. Our entire western civilization—from its laws to its ethics—has been marked and molded by His teaching. For over two millennia, history's greatest works of art have centered on His life, death, and resurrection. Enduring musical masterpieces have celebrated His worth and glory. But for those who have personally embraced the liberating reality of His forgiveness of sin and hope of eternity, He is so much more.

Or … at least, He should be.

We preach and teach about His will and His ways; tell His stories by heart; celebrate Him in worship; and serve Him with enthusiasm. Yet underneath it all (if we are truly candid), there is a gnawing sense that there should be something … well, more to this relationship.

Why is it that He often feels so far away? So historical? So church related? So other? The distance between knowing Him and knowing about Him is vast. And the space between these two experiences separates the spectators from intimate participants.

Think carefully. It's a pretty safe bet that if you are reading this book you know at least something about Him. You know something about Him biographically and historically. In your more lucid moments, you might even be able to talk a little theology. But as impressive as your knowledge about Jesus may be, the unfortunate reality is that most of us stop there. Seemingly satisfied that knowing about Him is enough, we have no clue that there is more.

And there is more.

The thought of a deep richness waiting for those who get beyond knowing about Him to actually experiencing Him has either escaped us or—worse yet—exiled our pursuit to the vague regions of religious wishful thinking.

If that's your story, get ready.

The best is yet to come.

Jesus intends for you to experience the pleasure and reassuring peace of His presence at the core of your life. He wants to be more than just another volume in your encyclopedia of biblical facts. He didn't die for you to simply strike a deal guaranteeing heaven. He died for you to make you His own and to grant you the unspeakable privilege of experiencing Him personally.

As Paul wrote to early followers of Jesus…

> "He [God] is the one who invited you into this wonderful friendship with his Son, Jesus Christ." *(1 Corinthians 1:9, NLT)*

And think of this invitation that Jesus extends to all of us who will respond…

> "'Look! Here I stand at the door and knock. If you hear me calling and open the door, I will come in, and we will share a meal as friends.'" *(Revelation 3:20, NLT)*

This is incomparably better than an invitation to the White House. The eternal God of the universe has called us into fellowship—friendship, companionship, close contact—with His Son. Jesus never intended to connect only with your head; He lives to connect with the entire you. In fact, He sent us the Holy Spirit to make the total connection possible, and gave us His Word to show the way. And, regardless of who you are or how you have chosen to live your life, you can know the pleasure of His presence.

Up close and personal.

Forgive a trip down memory lane, but I long again to experience Jesus in my grandmother's quavery voice as she sang the words of her favorite hymn:

> I come to the garden alone
> While the dew is still on the roses,
> And the voice I hear falling on my ear
> The Son of God discloses.
> And He walks with me and He talks with me
> and He tells me I am His own.
> And the joy we share as we tarry there,
> None other has ever known.

Knowing my grandmother, I have little doubt that she had moved well beyond simply "knowing about Him" into the joy of experiencing Him.

And just in case you think that a closer relationship with Jesus is about some kind of rigid morning routine, some tedious-but-essential religious exercise, think again. While regular Bible study and cultivating a life of prayer are indispensable, there is far more to a personal experience with Jesus.

◆ It's about a deep and abiding sense of His nearness on the journey.

◆ It's about an unshakable confidence that only His abiding presence can give.

◆ It's about courage in the face of previously intimidating encounters.

◆ It's about a closeness that enables your spirit to commune with Him, anywhere, anytime, regardless.

◆ It's about meeting Him in places you may have never dreamed of … in the most heated of seductions, in the midst of suffering, and in acts of unflinching surrender.

There is a marvelously mystical aspect to all this. You can't wrap words around it. You can't put it in a box and tie it up with a red ribbon. When you try to fully define it, you degrade it.

Jesus is never predictable. Just totally available. He doesn't play hide-and-seek. In fact, He consistently rewards anyone who diligently seeks Him *(Hebrews 11:6)*. But to many of us, tasting of that reward seems so illusive. Could it be we simply don't know how to seek Him or where to find Him?

I'll never forget the frustrating experience early one Sunday morning when I was supposed to pick up an elderly relative who had come into Chicago on the train from Milwaukee. The whole purpose of the exercise was to find her and get her safely to our house. I showed up on time, but where was she? Certainly not where I thought she would be. I checked the monitor and the train was already in. With a sinking feeling in the pit of my stomach, I scoured the early morning loneliness of Union Station ... to no avail.

I was about ready to leave when I happened to glance down a hallway toward the baggage area. There she was, luggage at her feet, patiently waiting for me to arrive. She'd been there all the time. And to my chagrin, she was right where she should have been! I had been looking in all the wrong places.

The great news is that Jesus is there, patiently waiting for you. In fact, He not only waits, but is also at this very moment busily pursuing you. The fact that you are reading this book is no accident, no coincidence. It's just another one of the countless ways He hopes to get your attention.

It's time to connect.

YOU CAN'T GET ENOUGH OF HIM

The following lines of Scripture have captured my heart in recent days. Don't skip over them. Don't let your mind wander. If you really want to experience Jesus, you must read these words slowly and thoughtfully ... until they have gripped your heart.

> I once thought all these things were so very important,
> but now I consider them worthless because of what
> Christ has done. Yes, everything else is worthless when
> compared with the priceless gain of knowing Christ
> Jesus my Lord. I have discarded everything else,
> counting it all as garbage, so that I may have Christ and
> become one with him. I no longer count on my own
> goodness or my ability to obey God's law, but I trust

Christ to save me. For God's way of making us right with himself depends on faith. *As a result, I can really know Christ and experience the mighty power that raised him from the dead.* I can learn what it means to suffer with him, sharing in this death, so that, somehow, I can experience the resurrection from the dead! (*PHILIPPIANS 3:7–11, NLT, EMPHASIS ADDED*).

More than any other writer, Paul spoke most passionately about knowing Jesus. It was his singular quest in life. Everything else became peripheral—rubbish—compared to knowing God's Son. And in this text, when he speaks of giving everything up to know Jesus, he uses the Greek word that means to *know by experience*.

But here's the thought that sets me back on my heels. Paul had already experienced Jesus in far more dramatic ways than anyone before or since. On the Damascus highway, Jesus appeared to Paul in a bolt of white fire and spoke to him in person. Sometime later, Paul found himself swept up into the "third heaven," where he had an extended season of personal experience with Jesus.

Yet what did Paul want with all his heart?

He wanted more.

He was still so taken with Jesus that the entire focus of his life was to experience more of Him. Which only proves that once you get a taste, you can never get enough of Him. Having experienced Jesus makes even the brightest treasures of life look pallid by comparison.

Do you wonder if this is for you? Wonder no longer! He is at the door of your heart, wanting to come in for some serious fellowship. ❖

What is Grace?

by Brennan Manning

Chapter:
Something is Radically Wrong

Book:
The Ragamuffin Gospel

Look for your coupons for this and other featured titles in the back of this book.

Author's Bio

Since 1982, Brennan Manning has made his home in Louisiana, from where he continues to travel and speak on God's unconditional love through Willie Juan Ministries.

What is Grace?
by Brennan Manning

On a blustery October night in a church outside Minneapolis,
several hundred believers had gathered for a three-day seminar.
I began with a one-hour presentation on the gospel of grace and
the reality of salvation. Using Scripture, story, symbolism, and
personal experience, I focused on the total sufficiency of the
redeeming work of Jesus Christ on Calvary. The service ended with
a song and a prayer. Leaving the church by a side door, the pastor
turned to his associate and fumed.

"Humph, that airhead didn't say one thing about what we have
to do to earn our salvation!"

Something is radically wrong.

The bending of the mind by the powers of this world has
twisted the gospel of grace into religious bondage and distorted the
image of God into an eternal, small-minded bookkeeper. The
Christian community resembles a Wall Street exchange of works
wherein the elite are honored and the ordinary ignored. Love is
stifled, freedom shackled, and self-righteousness fastened. The
institutional church has become a wounder of the healers rather
than a healer of the wounded.

Put bluntly: the American Church today accepts grace
in theory but denies it in practice. We say we believe that the
fundamental structure of reality is grace, not works—but our lives
refute our faith. By and large, the gospel of grace is neither
proclaimed, understood, nor lived. Too many Christians are living
in the house of fear and not in the house of love.

Our culture has made the word *grace* impossible to understand.
We resonate to slogans such as:

"There's no free lunch."

"You get what you deserve."

"You want money? Work for it."

"You want love? Earn it."

"You want mercy? Show you deserve it."

"Do unto others before they do it unto you."

"Watch out for welfare lines, the shiftless street people, free hot dogs at school, affluent students with federal loans; it's a con game."

"By all means give others what they deserve—but not one penny more."

My editor at Revell told me she overheard a pastor say to a child: "God loves good little boys." As I listen to sermons with their pointed emphasis on personal effort—no pain, no gain—I get the impression that a "do-it-yourself" spirituality is the American fashion.

Though the Scriptures insist on God's initiative in the work of salvation—that by grace we are saved, that the Tremendous Lover has taken to the chase—our spirituality often starts with self, not God. Personal responsibility has replaced personal response. We talk about acquiring virtue as if it were a skill that can be attained like good handwriting or a well-grooved golf swing. In the penitential seasons we focus on overcoming our weaknesses, getting rid of our hang-ups, and reaching Christian maturity. We sweat through various spiritual exercises as if they were designed to produce a Christian Charles Atlas.

Though lip service is paid to the gospel of grace, many Christians live as if it is only personal discipline and self-denial that will mold the perfect me. The emphasis is on what I do rather than on what God is doing. In this curious process God is a benign old spectator in the bleachers who cheers when I show up for morning quiet time. We transfer the Horatio Alger legend of the self-made man into our relationship with God. As we read Psalm 123, "As the eyes of the servant are on the hands of his master, as the eyes of a maid are on the hands of her mistress," we experience a vague sense of existential guilt. Our eyes are not on God. At heart we are practicing Pelagians. We believe that we can pull ourselves up by our bootstraps—indeed, we can do it ourselves.

Sooner or later we are confronted with the painful truth of our inadequacy and insufficiency. Our security is shattered and our bootstraps are cut. Once the fervor has passed, weakness and infidelity appear. We discover our inability to add even a single inch to our spiritual stature. There begins a long winter of discontent that eventually flowers into gloom, pessimism, and a subtle despair: subtle because it goes unrecognized, unnoticed, and therefore unchallenged. It takes the form of boredom, drudgery. We are overcome by the ordinariness of life, by daily duties done over and over again. We secretly admit that the call of Jesus is too demanding, that surrender to the Spirit is beyond our reach. We start acting like everyone else. Life takes on a joyless, empty quality. We begin to resemble the leading character in Eugene O'Neill's play *The Great God Brown*: "Why am I afraid to dance, I who love music and rhythm and grace and song and laughter? Why am I afraid to live, I who love life and the beauty of flesh and the living colors of the earth and sky and sea? Why am I afraid to love, I who love love?"

Something is radically wrong.

Our huffing and puffing to impress God, our scrambling for brownie points, our thrashing about trying to fix ourselves while hiding our pettiness and wallowing in guilt are nauseating to God and are a flat denial of the gospel of grace.

Our approach to the Christian life is as absurd as the enthusiastic young man who had just received his plumber's license and was taken to see Niagara Falls. He studied it for a minute and then said, "I think I can fix this."[1]

The word itself, *grace*, has become trite and debased through misuse and overuse. It does not move us the way it moved our early Christian ancestors. In some European countries certain high ecclesiastical officials are still called "Your Grace." Sportswriters speak of Michael Jordan's "easy grace" and entrepreneur Donald Trump has been described as "lacking in grace." A new perfume appears with the label "grace" and a child's report card is called a "disgrace." The word has lost its raw, imaginative power.

Fyodor Dostoyevsky caught the shock and scandal of the gospel of grace when he wrote: "At the last Judgment Christ will say to us, 'Come, you also! Come, drunkards! Come, weaklings! Come, children of shame!' And he will say to us: 'Vile beings, you who are in the image of the beast and bear his mark, but come all the same, you as well.' And the wise and prudent will say, 'Lord, why do you welcome them?' And he will say: 'If I welcome them, you wise men, if I welcome them, you prudent men, it is because not one of them has ever been judged worthy.' And he will stretch out his arms, and we will fall at his feet, and we will cry out sobbing, and then we will understand all, we will understand the Gospel of grace! Lord, your Kingdom come!"[2]

I believe the Reformation actually began the day Martin Luther was praying over the meaning of Paul's words in Romans 1:17. "In the gospel this is what reveals the righteousness of God to us ... it shows how faith leads to faith, or as Scripture says: the righteous shall find life through faith." Like many Christians today, Luther wrestled through the night with the core question: how could the gospel of Christ be truly called "Good News" if God is a righteous judge rewarding the good and punishing the evil? Did Jesus really have to come to reveal that terrifying message? How could the revelation of God in Christ Jesus be accurately called "news" since the Old Testament carried the same theme, or "good" with the threat of punishment hanging like a dark cloud over the valley of history?

But as Jaroslav Pelikan notes, "Luther suddenly broke through to the insight that the 'righteousness of God' that Paul spoke of in this passage was not the righteousness by which God was righteous in himself (that would be passive righteousness,) but the righteousness by which, for the sake of Jesus Christ, God made sinners righteous (that is, active righteousness) through the forgiveness of sins in justification. When he discovered that, Luther said it was as though the very gates of Paradise had been opened to him."[3]

What a stunning truth!

"Justification by grace through faith" is the theologian's learned phrase for what Chesterton once called "the furious love of God." He is not moody or capricious; He knows no seasons of change. He has a single relentless stance toward us: He loves us. He is the only God man has ever heard of who loves sinners. False gods—the gods of human manufacturing —despise sinners, but the Father of Jesus loves all, no matter what they do. But of course this is almost too incredible for us to accept. Nevertheless, the central affirmation of the Reformation stands: through no merit of ours, but by His mercy, we have been restored to a right relationship with God through the life, death, and resurrection of His beloved Son. This is the Good News, the gospel of grace.

With his characteristic *joie de vivre*, Robert Capon puts it this way: "The Reformation was a time when men went blind, staggering drunk because they had discovered, in the dusty basement of late medievalism, a whole cellarful of fifteen-hundred-year-old, two hundred proof grace—of bottle after bottle of pure distillate of Scripture, one sip of which would convince anyone that God saves us single-handedly. The word of the Gospel—after all those centuries of trying to lift yourself into heaven by worrying about the perfection of your bootstraps—suddenly turned out to be a flat announcement that the saved were home before they started.... Grace has to be drunk straight: no water, no ice, and certainly no ginger ale; neither goodness, nor badness, nor the flowers that bloom in the spring of super spirituality could be allowed to enter into the case."[4]

Matthew 9:9–13 captures a lovely glimpse of the gospel of grace: "As he moved on, Jesus saw a man named Matthew at his post where taxes were collected. He said to him, 'Follow me.' Matthew got up and followed him. Now it happened that, while Jesus was at table in Matthew's house, many tax collectors and those known as sinners came to join Jesus and his disciples at dinner. The Pharisees saw this and complained to his disciples, 'What reason can the Teacher have for eating with tax collectors and those who disregard the law?' Overhearing their remark, he said, 'People who are in good health do not need a doctor; sick people do. Go and learn the meaning of the words, "It is mercy I desire and not sacrifice." I have come not to call the self-righteous but sinners.'"

Here is revelation bright as the evening star: Jesus comes for sinners, for those as outcast as tax collectors and for those caught up in squalid choices and failed dreams. He comes for corporate executives, street people, superstars, farmers, hookers, addicts, IRS agents, AIDS victims, and even used car salesmen. Jesus not only talks with these people but dines with them—fully aware that His table fellowship with sinners will raise the eyebrows of religious bureaucrats who hold up the robes and insignia of their authority to justify their condemnation of the truth and their rejection of the gospel of grace.

This passage should be read, reread, and memorized. Every Christian generation tries to dim the blinding brightness of its meaning because the gospel seems too good to be true. We think salvation belongs to the proper and pious, to those who stand at a safe distance from the back alleys of existence, clucking their judgments at those who have been soiled by life. In the name of Grace, what has been the verdict of the Christian community on the stained life of the late Rock Hudson? To the disclosure (the $4.5 million settlement to his lover Marc Christian notwithstanding) that he called a priest to his deathbed, confessed his sins, and cried out to God for forgiveness?

Jesus, who forgave the sins of the paralytic (thereby claiming divine power), proclaims that He has invited sinners and not the self-righteous to His table. The Greek verb used here, *kalein*, has the sense of inviting an honored guest to dinner.

In effect, Jesus says the Kingdom of His Father is not a subdivision for the self-righteous nor for those who feel they possess the state secret of their salvation. The Kingdom is not an exclusive, well-trimmed suburb with snobbish rules about who can live there. No, it is for a larger, homelier, less self-conscious cast of people who understand they are sinners because they have experienced the yaw and pitch of moral struggle.

These are the sinner-guests invited by Jesus to closeness with Him around the banquet table. It remains a startling story to those who never understand that the men and women who are truly filled with light are those who have gazed deeply into the darkness of their imperfect existence. Perhaps it was after meditating on this passage that Morton Kelsey wrote: "The church is not a museum for saints but a hospital for sinners."

The Good News means we can stop lying to ourselves. The sweet sound of amazing grace saves us from the necessity of self-deception. It keeps us from denying that though Christ was victorious, the battle with lust, greed, and pride still rages within us. As a sinner who has been redeemed, I can acknowledge that I am often unloving, irritable, angry, and resentful with those closest to me. When I go to church I can leave my white hat at home and admit I have failed. God not only loves me as I am, but also knows me as I am. Because of this I don't need to apply spiritual cosmetics to make myself presentable to Him. I can accept ownership of my poverty and powerlessness and neediness.

As C. S. Lewis says in *The Four Loves*, "Grace substitutes a full, childlike and delighted acceptance of our need, a joy in total dependence. The good man is sorry for the sins which have increased his need. He is not entirely sorry for the fresh need they have produced."

As the gospel of grace lays hold of us, something is radically right. We are living in truth and reality. We become as honest as the ninety-two-year-old priest who was venerated by everybody in town for his holiness. He was also a member of the Rotary Club. Every time the club met, he would be there, always on time and always seated in his favorite spot in a corner of the room.

One day the priest disappeared. It was as if he had vanished into thin air. The townsfolk searched all over and could find no trace of him. But the following month, when the Rotary Club met, he was there as usual sitting in his corner.

"Father," everyone cried, "where have you been?"

"I just served a thirty-day sentence in prison."

"In prison," they cried. "Father, you couldn't hurt a fly. What happened?"

"It's a long story," said the priest, "but briefly, this is what happened. I bought myself a train ticket to go into the city. I was standing on the platform waiting for the train to arrive when this stunningly beautiful girl appears on the arm of a policeman. She looked at me, turned to the cop and said, 'He did it. I'm certain he's the one who did it.' Well, to tell you the truth, I was so flattered I pleaded guilty."[5]

There's a touch of vanity in the holiest men and women. They see no reason to deny it. And they know that reality bites back if it isn't respected.

When I get honest, I admit I am a bundle of paradoxes. I believe and I doubt, I hope and get discouraged, I love and I hate, I feel bad about feeling good, I feel guilty about not feeling guilty. I am trusting and suspicious. I am honest and I still play games. Aristotle said I am a rational animal; I say I am an angel with an incredible capacity for beer.

To live by grace means to acknowledge my whole life story, the light side and the dark. In admitting my shadow side I learn who I am and what God's grace means. As Thomas Merton put it, "A saint is not someone who is good but who experiences the goodness of God."

The gospel of grace nullifies our adulation of televangelists, charismatic superstars, and local church heroes. It obliterates the two-class citizenship theory operative in many American churches. For grace proclaims the awesome truth that all is gift. All that is good is ours not by right but by the sheer bounty of a gracious God. While there is much we may have earned—our degree and our salary, our home and gar- den, a Miller Lite and a good night's sleep—all this is possible only because we have been given so much: life itself, eyes to see and hands to touch, a mind to shape ideas, and a heart to beat with love. We have been given God in our souls and Christ in our flesh. We have the power to believe where others deny, to hope where others despair, to love where others hurt. This and so much more is sheer gift; it is not reward for our faithfulness, our generous disposition, or our heroic life of prayer. Even our fidelity is a gift. "If we but turn to God," said St. Augustine, "that itself is a gift of God." My deepest awareness of myself is that I am deeply loved by Jesus Christ and I have done nothing to earn it or deserve it.

In my ministry as a vagabond evangelist, I have extolled certain saints and contemporary Christians, speaking of at what cost they have struggled to surpass lesser men and women. O God, what madness I have preached in sermons! The Good News of the gospel of grace cries out: we are all, equally, privileged but unentitled beggars at the door of God's mercy!

Besides, as Henri Nouwen notes, the greater part of God's work in the world may go unnoticed. There are a number of people who have become famous or widely known for their ministries, but much of God's saving activity in our history could remain completely unknown. That is a mystery difficult to grasp in an age that attaches so much importance to publicity. We tend to think that the more people know and talk about something, the more important it must be.

In Luke 18, a rich young man comes to Jesus asking what he must *do* to inherit eternal life. He wants to be in the spotlight. It is no coincidence that Luke juxtaposes the passage of Jesus and the children immediately preceding the verses on the young aristocrat. Children contrast with the rich man simply because there is no question of their having yet been able to merit anything. Jesus' point is: there is nothing that any of us can do to inherit the Kingdom. We must simply receive it like little children. And little children haven't done anything. The New Testament world was not sentimental about children and had no illusion about any pretended innate goodness in them. Jesus is not suggesting that heaven is a huge playground for Cajun infants. Children are our model because they have no claim on heaven. If they are close to God, it is because they are incompetent, not because they are innocent. If they receive anything, it can only be as a gift.

Paul writes in Ephesians: "It is by grace you have been saved through faith; not by anything of your own, but by a gift from God; not by anything you have done so that nobody can claim the credit" (2:8–9).

If a random sample of one thousand American Christians were taken today, the majority would define faith as belief in the existence of God. In earlier times it did not take faith to believe that God existed—almost everybody took that for granted. Rather, faith had to do with one's relationship to God—whether one trusted in God. The difference between faith as "belief in something that may or may not exist" and faith as "trusting in God" is enormous. The first is a matter of the head, the second a matter of the heart. The first can leave us unchanged, the second intrinsically brings change.[6]

Such is the faith described by Paul Tillich in his famous work *The Shaking of the Foundations*: "Grace strikes us when we are in great pain and restlessness. It strikes us when we walk through the dark valley of a meaningless and empty life.... It strikes us when, year after year, the longed-for perfection does not appear, when the old compulsions reign within us as they have for decades, when despair destroys all joy and courage. Sometimes at that moment a wave of light breaks into our darkness, and it is as though a voice were saying: 'You are accepted. You are accepted, accepted by that which is greater than you, and the name of which you do not know. Do not ask for the name now; perhaps you will find it later. Do not try to do anything now; perhaps later you will do much. Do not seek for anything, do not perform anything, do not intend anything. Simply accept the fact that you are accepted.' If that happens to us, we experience grace."[7]

And Grace calls out: you are not just a disillusioned old man who may die soon, a middle-aged woman stuck in a job and desperately wanting to get out, a young person feeling the fire in the belly begin to grow cold. You may be insecure, inadequate, mistaken, or potbellied. Death, panic, depression, and disillusionment may be near you. But you are not just that. You are accepted. Never confuse your perception of yourself with the mystery that you really are accepted.

Paul writes: "The Lord said, 'My grace is enough for you: my power is at its best in weakness.' So I shall be very happy to make my weaknesses my special boast so that the power of Christ may stay over me" (2 CORINTHIANS 12:9). Whatever our failings may be, we need not lower our eyes in the presence of Jesus. Unlike Quasimodo, the hunchback of Notre Dame, we need not hide all that is ugly and repulsive in us. Jesus comes not for the super-spiritual but for the wobbly and the weak-kneed who know they don't have it all together, and who are not too proud to accept the handout of amazin' grace. As we glance up, we are astonished to find the eyes of Jesus open with wonder, deep with understanding, and gentle with compassion.

Something is radically wrong when the local church rejects a person accepted by Jesus: when a harsh, judgmental and unforgiving sentence is passed on homosexuals; when a divorcée is denied communion; when the child of a prostitute is refused baptism; when an unlaicized priest is forbidden the sacraments. Jesus comes to the ungodly, even on Sunday morning. His coming ends ungodliness and makes us worthy. Otherwise, we are establishing at the heart of Christianity an utterly ungodly and unworthy preoccupation with works.

Jesus sat down at table with anyone who wanted to be present, including those who were banished from decent homes. In the sharing of a meal they received consideration instead of the expected condemnation. A merciful acquittal instead of a hasty verdict of guilty. Amazing grace instead of universal disgrace. Here is a very practical demonstration of the law of grace—a new chance in life.

Any church that will not accept that it consists of sinful men and women, and exists for them, implicitly rejects the gospel of grace. As Hans Küng says, "It deserves neither God's mercy nor men's trust. The church must constantly be aware that its faith is weak, its knowledge dim, its profession of faith halting, that there is not a single sin or failing which it has not in one way or another been guilty of. *And though it is true that the church must always dissociate itself from sin, it can never have any excuse for keeping any sinners at a distance.* If the church remains self-righteously aloof from failures, irreligious and immoral people, it cannot enter justified into God's kingdom. But if it is constantly aware of its guilt and sin, it can live in joyous awareness of forgiveness. The promise has been given to it that anyone who humbles himself will be exalted."[8]

The story goes that a public sinner was excommunicated and forbidden entry to the church.

He took his woes to God, "They won't let me in, Lord, because I am a sinner."

"What are you complaining about?" said God. "They won't let Me in either."

Often hobbling through our church doors on Sunday morning comes grace on crutches—sinners still unable to throw away their false supports and stand upright in the freedom of the children of God. Yet, their mere presence in the church on Sunday morning is a flickering candle representing a desire to maintain contact with God. To douse the flame is to plunge them into a world of spiritual darkness.

There is a myth flourishing in the church today that has caused incalculable harm—once converted, fully converted. In other words, once I accept Jesus Christ as my Lord and Savior, an irreversible, sinless future beckons. Discipleship will be an untarnished success story; life will be an unbroken upward spiral toward holiness. Tell that to poor Peter who, after three times professing his love for Jesus on the beach and after receiving the fullness of the Spirit at Pentecost, was still jealous of Paul's apostolic success.

Often I have been asked, "Brennan, how is it possible that you became an alcoholic after you got saved?" It is possible because I got battered and bruised by loneliness and failure, because I got discouraged, uncertain, guilt-ridden, and took my eyes off Jesus. Because the Christ-encounter did not transfigure me into an angel. Because justification by grace through faith means I have been set in right relationship with God, not made the equivalent of a patient etherized on a table.

We want ever-sharp spirituality (push-pull, click-click—one saint that quick) and attempt to cultivate a particular virtue at a given point in time. Prudence in January, humility in February, fortitude in March, temperance in April. Score cards are provided for toting up gains and losses. The losses should diminish if you expect to meet charity in May. Sometimes May never comes. For many Christians, life is a long January.

According to an ancient Christian legend, a saint once knelt down and prayed, "Dear God, I have only one desire in life. Give me the grace of never offending You again."

When God heard this, He started laughing out loud. "That's what they all ask for. But if I granted everyone this grace, tell Me, whom would I forgive?"

Because salvation is by grace through faith, I believe that among the countless number of people standing in front of the throne and in front of the Lamb, dressed in white robes and holding palms in their hands (REVELATION 7:9), I shall see the prostitute from the Kit-Kat Ranch in Carson City, Nevada, who tearfully told me she could find no other employment to support her two-year-old son. I shall see the woman who had an abortion and is haunted by guilt and remorse but did the best she could faced with grueling alternatives; the businessman besieged with debt who sold his integrity in a series of desperate transactions; the insecure clergyman addicted to being liked, who never challenged his people from the pulpit and longed for unconditional love; the sexually-abused teen molested by his father and now selling his body on the street, who, as he falls asleep each night after his last 'trick,' whispers the name of the unknown God he learned about in Sunday school; the deathbed convert who for decades had his cake and ate it, broke every law of God and man, wallowed in lust and raped the earth.

"But how?" we ask. Then the voice says, "They have washed their robes and made them white in the blood of the Lamb."

There they are. There *we* are—the multitude who so wanted to be faithful, who at times got defeated, soiled by life, and bested by trials, wearing the bloodied garments of life's tribulations, but through it all clung to the faith.

My friends, if this is not good news to you, you have never understood the gospel of grace. ❖

CHAPTER NOTES

1. Anthony De Mello, *Taking Flight: A Book of Story Mediations* (New York: Doubleday, 1988), 105.

2. Fyodor Dostoevsky, *Crime and Punishment*, trans. Constance Garnett (New York: Random House Inc., 1950), 322.

3. Jaroslav Pelikan, *Jesus Through the Centuries, His Place in History of Culture* (New Haven, Conn.: Yale University Press, 1985), 158. This is a work of vast and carefully concealed scholarship which traces the images of Jesus from New Testament times down to the twentieth century. Pelikan suggests that the way a particular age depicted Jesus is an essential key to understanding that age. The later chapters of the book show that "as respect for the organized church has declined, reverence for Jesus has grown."

4. Robert Farrar Capon, *Between Noon and Three* (San Francisco: Harper & Row, 1982), 114–15, quoted in Donald W. McCullough, *Waking from the American Dream* (Downers Grove, Ill.: InterVarsity Press, 1988).

5. De Mello, 113–14.

6. Marcus S. Borg, *Jesus, A New Vision, Spirit, Culture and the Life of Discipleship* (New York: Harper & Row, 1987), 35.

7. Paul Tillich, *The Shaking of the Foundations* (New York: Scribner's, 1948), 161–62.

8. Hans Küng, *On Being a Christian* (New York: Doubleday, 1976), 507–08. Küng is one of those rare thinkers incapable of superficial thought. I find it difficult to state the value and importance of this book in my life without hyperbole.

What is my Purpose?

by Rick Warren

Chapter:
It All Starts With God

Book:
The Purpose Driven Life

Look for your coupons for this and other featured titles in the back of this book.

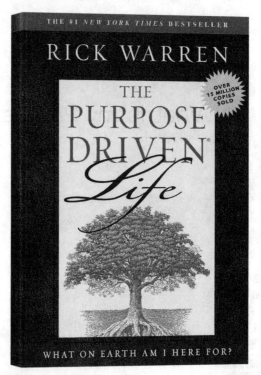

Author's Bio

Rick Warren is the founding pastor of Saddleback Church in Lake Forest California, one of America's largest and best-known churches. His previous book, *The Purpose Driven® Church* has sold over a million copies in 20 languages. Winner of the Gold Medallion, it was selected as one of the 100 Christian Books That Changes the 20th Century.

What Is My Purpose?

by Rick Warren

> For everything, absolutely everything, above and below,
> visible and invisible,… everything got started in him and
> finds its purpose in him.
> —COLOSSIANS 1:16 (MSG)

> Unless you assume a God, the question of life's purpose
> is meaningless.
> —Bertrand Russell, atheist

The purpose of your life is far greater than your own personal fulfillment, your peace of mind, or even your happiness. It's far greater than your family, your career, or even your wildest dreams and ambitions. If you want to know why you were placed on this planet, you must begin with God. You were born by his purpose and for his purpose.

The search for the purpose of life has puzzled people for thousands of years. That's because we typically begin at the wrong starting point—ourselves. We ask self-centered questions like What do I want to be? What should I do with my life? What are my goals, my ambitions, my dreams for my future? But focusing on ourselves will never reveal our life's purpose. The Bible says, "It is God who directs the lives of his creatures; everyone's life is in his power."[1]

Contrary to what many popular books, movies, and seminars tell you, you won't discover your life's meaning by looking within yourself. You've probably tried that already. You didn't create yourself, so there is no way you can tell yourself what you were created for! If I handed you an invention you had never seen before, you wouldn't know its purpose, and the invention itself wouldn't be able to tell you either. Only the creator or the owner's manual could reveal its purpose.

I once got lost in the mountains. When I stopped to ask for directions to the campsite, I was told, "You can't get there from here. You must start from the other side of the mountain!" In the same way, you cannot arrive at your life's purpose by starting with a focus on yourself. You must begin with God, your Creator. You exist only because God wills that you exist. You were made *by* God and *for* God—and until you understand that, life will never make sense. It is only in God that we discover our origin, our identity, our meaning, our purpose, our significance, and our destiny. Every other path leads to a dead end.

◆

Focusing on ourselves will never reveal our life's purpose.

◆

Many people try to use God for their own self-actualization, but that is a reversal of nature and is doomed to failure. You were made for God, not vice versa, and life is about letting God use you for *his* purposes, not your using him for your own purpose. The Bible says, "Obsession with self in these matters is a dead end; attention to God leads us out into the open, into a spacious, free life."[2]

I have read many books that suggest ways to discover the purpose of my life. All of them could be classified as "self-help" books because they approach the subject from a self-centered viewpoint. Self-help books, even Christian ones, usually offer the same predictable steps to finding your life's purpose: Consider your dreams. Clarify your values. Set some goals. Figure out what you are good at. Aim high. Go for it! Be disciplined. Believe you can achieve your goals. Involve others. Never give up.

Of course, these recommendations often lead to great success. You can usually succeed in reaching a goal if you put your mind to it. But being successful and fulfilling your life's purpose are *not at all* the same issue! You could reach all your personal goals, becoming a raving success by the world's standard, and *still* miss the purposes for which God created you. You need more than self-help advice. The Bible says, "Self-help is no help at all. Self-sacrifice is the way, my way, to finding yourself, your true self."[3]

This is not a self-help book. It is not about finding the right career, achieving your dreams, or planning your life. It is not about how to cram more activities into an overloaded schedule. Actually, it will teach you how to do *less* in life—by focusing on what matters most. It is about becoming what *God* created you to be.

How, then, do you discover the purpose you were created for? You have only two options. Your first option is *speculation*. This is what most people choose. They conjecture, they guess, they theorize. When people say, "I've always thought life is ...," they mean, "This is the best guess I can come up with."

For thousands of years, brilliant philosophers have discussed and speculated about the meaning of life. Philosophy is an important subject and has its uses, but when it comes to determining the purpose of life, even the wisest philosophers are just guessing.

Dr. Hugh Moorhead, a philosophy professor at Northeastern Illinois University, once wrote to 250 of the best-known philosophers, scientists, writers, and intellectuals in the world, asking them, "What is the meaning of life?" He then published their responses in a book. Some offered their best guesses, some admitted that they just made up a purpose for life, and others were honest enough to say they were clueless. In fact, a number of famous intellectuals asked Professor Moorhead to write back and tell them if he discovered the purpose of life![4]

◆

You were made by God and for God—and until you understand that, life will never make sense.

◆

Fortunately, there is an alternative to speculation about the meaning and purpose of life. It's *revelation*. We can turn to what God has revealed about life in his Word. The easiest way to discover the purpose of an invention is to ask the creator of it. The same is true for discovering your life's purpose: Ask God.

God has not left us in the dark to wonder and guess. He has clearly revealed his five purposes for our lives through the Bible. It is our Owner's Manual, explaining why we are alive, how life works, what to avoid, and what to expect in the future. It explains what no self-help or philosophy book could know. The Bible says, "God's wisdom ... goes deep into the interior of his purposes.... It's not the latest message, but more like the oldest—what God determined as the way to bring out his best in us."[5]

God is not just the starting point of your life; he is the source of it. To discover your purpose in life you must turn to God's Word, not the world's wisdom. You must build your life on eternal truths, not pop psychology, success-motivation, or inspirational stories. The Bible says, "It's in Christ that we find out who we are and what we are living for. Long before we first heard of Christ and got our hopes up, he had his eye on us, had designs on us for glorious living, part of the overall purpose he is working out in everything and everyone."[6] This verse gives us three insights into your purpose.

1. You discover your identity and purpose through a relationship with Jesus Christ. If you don't have such a relationship, I will later explain how to begin one.

2. God was thinking of you long before you ever thought about him. His purpose for your life predates your conception. He planned it before you existed, *without your input!* You may choose your career, your spouse, your hobbies, and many other parts of your life, but you don't get to choose your purpose.

3. The purpose of your life fits into a much larger, cosmic purpose that God has designed for eternity. That's what this book is about.

Andrei Bitov, a Russian novelist, grew up under an atheistic Communist regime. But God got his attention one dreary day. He recalls, "In my twenty-seventh year, while riding the metro in Leningrad (now St. Petersburg) I was overcome with a despair so great that life seemed to stop at once, preempting the future entirely, let alone any meaning. Suddenly, all by itself, a phrase appeared: *Without God life makes no sense.* Repeating it in astonishment, I rode the phrase up like a moving staircase, got out of the metro and walked into God's light."[7]

You may have felt in the dark about *your* purpose in life. Congratulations, you're about to walk into the light. ❖

THINKING ABOUT MY PURPOSE

◆   Point to Ponder: It's not about me.

◆   Verse to Remember: "Everything got started in him and finds its purpose in him." *(COLOSSIANS 1:16B MSG)*

◆   Question to Consider: In spite of all the advertising around me, how can I remind myself that life is really about living for God, not myself?

CHAPTER NOTES

1.   Job 12:10 (TEV).

2.   Romans 8:6 (Msg).

3.   Matthew 16:25 (msg).

4.   Hugh S. Moorhead, comp., *The Meaning of Life According to Our Century's Greatest Writers and Thinkers* (Chicago: Chicago Review Press, 1988).

5.   I Corinthians 2:7 (msg).

6.   Ephesians 1:11 (msg).

7.   David Friend, ed., *The Meaning of Life* (Boston: Little, Brown, 1991), 194.

Aren't There Tough
Questions About God?
by Norman Geisler

Chapter:
Tough Questions About God

Book:
Who Made God?

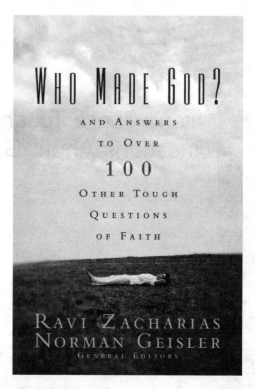

Author's Bio

Norman Geisler is an award-winning
author and coauthor of over fifty books
and hundreds of articles. He holds a
Pd.D. in Philosophy from Loyola University
and has taught at the university and
graduate level. Many of Dr. Geisler's
works are used as textbooks in Christian
colleges and seminaries, including books
as *A General Introduction to the Bible*,
When Skeptics Ask, *When Critics Ask*,
Christian Apologetics, and *Baker
Encyclopedia of Christian Apologetics*.

Aren't There Tough Questions About God?

by Norman Geisler

My daughter Ruth, a pastor's wife, told her oldest son, Samuel, who was then about four years old, "Go ask your grandfather." A moment later I was confronted with this tough question: "Grandpa, where is the mind in the brain?" This question is easy enough to answer for a college or seminary philosophy student who knows what a category mistake is, but how do you explain it to a four-year-old?

As parents and church leaders who have ministered to small children know, the toughest questions typically come from the youngest members of the congregation. Often these are about God—such as, "Daddy, who made God?" More than a few parents have heard this question before, but only a few can answer it.

We must be prepared to give an answer (1 PETER 3:15) to every sincere question we are asked (COLOSSIANS 4:6). Here are some of the toughest ones I've been asked over the past fifty years of ministry. I will try my best to answer them so that even young boys and girls can understand.

WHO MADE GOD?

Who made God? No one did. He was not made. He has always existed. Only things that had a beginning—like the world—need a maker. God had no beginning, so God did not need to be made.

For those who are a little older, a little more can be said. Traditionally, most atheists who deny the existence of God believe that the universe was not made; it was just "there" forever. They appeal to the first law of thermodynamics for support: "Energy can neither be created nor destroyed," they insist. Several things must be observed in response.

First, this way of stating the first law is not scientific; rather, it is a philosophical assertion. Science is based on observation, and there is no observational evidence that can support the dogmatic "can" and "cannot" implicit in this statement. It should read, "[As far as we have observed,] the amount of actual energy in the universe remains constant." That is, no one had observed any actual new energy either coming into existence or going out of existence. Once the first law is understood properly, it says nothing about the universe being eternal or having no beginning. As far as the first law is concerned, energy may or may not have been created. It simply asserts that if energy was created, then as far as we can tell, the actual amount of energy that was created has remained constant since then.

Further, let us suppose for the sake of argument that energy— the whole universe of energy we call the cosmos—was not created, as many atheists have traditionally believed. If this is so, it is meaningless to ask who made the universe. If energy is eternal and uncreated, of course no one created it. It has always existed. However, if it is meaningless to ask, "Who made the universe?" since it has always existed, then it is equally meaningless to ask "Who made God?" since he has always existed.

If the universe is not eternal, it needs a cause. On the other hand, if it has no beginning, it does not need a cause of its beginning. Likewise, if a God exists who has no beginning, it is absurd to ask, "Who made God?" It is a category mistake to ask, "Who made the Unmade?" or "Who created the Uncreated?" One may as well ask, "Where is the bachelor's wife?"

WHY COULDN'T THE WORLD ALWAYS HAVE EXISTED?

Christians naturally believe there must be a God because the world had a beginning. And everything that had a beginning had a beginner. But the tough question to answer is how we know the world had a beginning. Maybe the world always existed.

Famous agnostic Bertrand Russell presented this dilemma: Either the world had a beginning, or it did not. If it did not, it did not need a cause (God). If it did, we can ask, "Who caused God?" But if God has a cause, he is not God. In either case, we do not arrive at a first uncaused cause (God).

The answer to this tough question is that it, too, asks a meaningless question: Who made God? To put it another way, it wrongly assumes that "*everything* must have a cause" when what is claimed is that "*everything that had a beginning* had a cause." This is quite a different matter. Of course, everything that had a beginning had a beginner. Nothing cannot make something. As Julie Andrews once sang, "Nothing came from nothing. Nothing ever could." So God does not need a cause because he had no beginning.

This being the case, we need only to show that the universe had a beginning, to show that there must have been a cause of it (i.e., God). Two strong arguments will be offered as evidence that the universe had a beginning. One is from science—the second law of thermodynamics. The second is from philosophy, namely, the impossibility of an infinite number of moments.

According to the second law of thermodynamics, the universe is running out of usable energy.[1] But if the universe is running down, it cannot be eternal. Otherwise, it would have run down completely by now. While you can never run out of an unlimited amount of energy, it does not take forever to run out of a limited amount of energy. Hence, the universe must have had a beginning. To illustrate, every car has a limited amount of energy (gas). That is why we have to refuel from time to time—more often than we like. If we had an unlimited (i.e., infinitely) large gas tank, we would never have to stop for gas again. The fact that we have to refill shows that it was filled up to begin with. Or, to use another example, an old clock that gradually unwinds and has to be rewound would not unwind unless it had been wound up to begin with. In short, the universe had a beginning. And whatever had a beginning must have had a beginner. Therefore, the universe must have had a beginner (God).

Some have speculated that the universe is self-winding or self-rebounding. But this position is exactly that—pure speculation without any real evidence. In fact, it is contrary to the second law of thermodynamics. For even if the universe were rebounding, like a bouncing ball in reverse, it would gradually peter out. There is simply no observational evidence that the universe is self-winding.

Even agnostic astronomers like Robert Jastrow have pointed out: "Once hydrogen has been burned within that star and converted to heavier elements, it can never be restored to its original state." Thus, "minute by minute and year by year, as hydrogen is used up in stars, the supply of this element grows smaller."[2]

If the overall amount of actual energy stays the same but the universe is running out of usable energy, it has never had an infinite amount—for an infinite amount of energy can never run down. This would mean that the universe could not have existed forever in the past. It must have had a beginning. Or, to put it another way, according to the second law, since the universe is getting more and more disordered, it cannot be eternal. Otherwise, it would be totally disordered by now, which it is not. So it must have had a beginning—one that was highly ordered.

A second argument that the universe had a beginning—and hence a beginner—comes from philosophy. It argues that there could not have been an infinite number of moments before today; otherwise today never would have come (which it has). This is because, by definition, an infinite can never be traversed—it has no end (or beginning). But since the moments before today have been traversed—that is, we have arrived at today—it follows that there must only have been a finite (limited) number of moments before today. That is, time had a beginning. But if the space-time universe had a beginning, it must have been caused to come into existence. This cause of everything else that exists is called God. God exists.

Even the great skeptic David Hume held both premises of this argument for God. What is more, Hume himself never denied that things have a cause for their existence. He wrote, "I never asserted so absurd a proposition as that anything might arise without a cause."[3] He also said that it was absurd to believe there were an infinite number of moments: "The temporal world has a beginning. An infinite number of real parts of time, passing in succession and exhausted one after another, appears so evident a contradiction that no man, one should think, whose judgment is not corrupted, instead of being improved, by the sciences, would ever be able to admit it."[4] Now if both of these premises are true, it follows that there must have been a creator of the space-time universe we call the cosmos—that is, God exists.

HOW CAN GOD MAKE SOMETHING OUT OF NOTHING?

If God and nothing else existed prior to the creation of the world, the universe came into existence from nothing. But isn't it absurd to say that something can come from nothing? It is absurd to say that nothing caused something, because nothing does not exist and has no power to do anything. But it is not absurd to say that someone (i.e., God) brought the universe into existence from nonexistence. Nothing cannot make something, but someone (i.e., God) can make something out of nothing.

In fact, if the universe had a beginning (as demonstrated earlier), then there was once no universe and then there was— after God created it. This is what is meant by creation "out of nothing" (Latin, *ex nihilo*). It does not mean that God took a "handful of nothing" and made something out of it, as though "nothing" were something out of which he made the world. There was God and simply nothing else. Then God brought something else into existence that had not existed to that point.

Or to put it another way, creation "out of nothing" simply means that God did not create out of something else that which already existed alongside himself, as in certain forms of dualism in which there are two eternal substances of entities. This is really creation *ex materia*, that is, out of some preexisting matter outside of God. The Greek philosopher Plato held this view.

Neither did God create the world out of himself (i.e., *ex Deo*). That is, God did not take part of himself and make the world out of it. In fact, the orthodox Christian God has no parts. He is a simple whole that is absolutely one. Thus there is no way God could have taken part of himself and made the world. God is infinite and the world is finite. And no amount of finite parts can make an infinite, since no matter how many parts or pieces one has, there could always be one more. But there cannot be more than an infinite. Hence, no amount of parts would ever equal an infinite. So God

could not have created the world out of part of himself
(i.e., *ex materia*).

The world came *from* God but is not *of* God. He was its cause
but not its substance. It came into existence **by** him, but it is not
made *of* him. However, if the world was not created out of God
(*ex Deo*) or out of something else (*ex materia*) existing alongside God,
it must have been created out of nothing (*ex nihilo*). There is no
other alternative. God made something that before he made it did
not exist, either in him or in anything else.

The only place the world "existed" before God made it was as
an idea in God's mind. Just as a painter has an idea of his painting
in his mind before he paints it, so God had an idea of the world
before he made it. In this sense, the world preexisted in God's mind
as an idea before he brought it into existence.

WHAT WAS GOD DOING BEFORE
HE MADE THE WORLD?

Another tough question often asked about God is this: What
was God doing with all his time before he created? The famous
fifth-century A.D. Christian teacher Augustine had two answers to
this question, one humorous and one serious. The first answer was
that God was spending his time preparing hell for people who ask
questions like this! The serious answer was that God didn't have
any time on his hands, since there was no time before time was
created. Time began with creation. Before creation, time did not
exist. So there was no time for God to have on his hands. The world
did not begin by a creation *in* time but by a creation *of* time. But,
you may think, *if there was no time before time began, what was there?*
The answer is, eternity. God is eternal, and the only thing prior to
time was eternity.

Further, the question implies that an infinitely perfect
being like God could get bored. Boredom, however, is a sign of
imperfection and dissatisfaction, and God is perfectly satisfied.
Thus, there is no way God could be bored, even if he had long time
periods on his hands. An infinitely creative mind can always find

something interesting to do. Only finite minds that run out of interesting things to do get bored.

Finally, the Christian God has three persons who are in perfect fellowship. There is no way such a being could get bored or lonely. There is not only always someone to "talk to," but someone of perfect understanding, love, and companionship. Boredom is impossible in such a being.

HOW CAN THERE BE THREE PERSONS IN ONE GOD?

How can God be three and yet one? Isn't this a contradiction? It would seem that God could be one and not three, or three and not one. But he cannot be both three and one at the same time. It would be a violation of the most fundamental law of thought, namely, the law of noncontradiction.

First of all, the Christian belief in a Trinity of three persons in one God is not a contradiction. A contradiction occurs only when something is both A and non-A at the same time and in the same sense. God is both three and one at the same time but not *in the same sense*. He is three persons but one in essence. He is three persons but only one in nature.

It would be a contradiction to say that God had three natures in one nature or three persons in one person. But it is not a contradiction to claim that God has three persons in one nature. God is like a triangle. At the same time it has three corners and yet it is only one triangle. Each corner is not the same as the whole triangle. Or, God is like one to the third power (1^3). $1 \times 1 \times 1 = 1$. God is not $1 + 1 + 1 = 3$, which is tritheism or polytheism. God is one God, manifested eternally and simultaneously in three distinct persons.

God is love (1 JOHN 4:16). But to have love, there must be a lover (Father), a loved one (Son), and a spirit of love (Holy Spirit). So, love itself is a tri-unity.

Another illustration of the Trinity is that God is like my mind, ideas, and words. There is a unity between them, yet they are distinct from each other.

Of course, the Trinity is a mystery. It goes beyond reason without going against reason. We can apprehend it, but we cannot completely comprehend it. As someone wisely said, "If we try to understand God completely, we may lose our mind, but if we do not believe in the Trinity sincerely, we will lose our soul!"

HOW CAN A GOOD GOD SEND PEOPLE TO HELL?

This question assumes that God sends people to hell against their will. But this is not the case. God desires everyone to be saved (SEE 2 PETER 3:9). Those who are not saved do not will to be saved. Jesus said, "O Jerusalem, Jerusalem, you who kill the prophets and stone those sent to you, how often I have longed to gather your children together, as a hen gathers her chicks under her wings, but you were not willing" (MATTHEW 23:37).

As C. S. Lewis put it, "The door of hell is locked on the inside." All who go there choose to do so. Lewis added: "There are only two kinds of people in the end: those who say to God, 'Thy will be done,' and those to whom God says, in the end, 'Thy will be done.' All that are in hell, choose it." Lewis believed "without that self-choice there could be no hell. No soul that seriously and constantly desires joy will ever miss it. Those who seek find. To those who knock it is opened."[5]

Furthermore, heaven would be hell for those who are not fitted for it. For heaven is a place of constant praise and worship of God (REVELATION 4–5). But for unbelievers who do not enjoy one hour of worship a week on earth, it would be hell to force them to do this forever in heaven! Hear Lewis again: "I would pay any price to be able to say truthfully 'All will be saved.' But my reason retorts, 'Without their will, or with it?' If I say 'Without their will,' I at once perceive a contradiction; how can the supreme voluntary act of self-surrender be involuntary? If I say 'With their will,' my reason replies 'How if they *will not* give in?'"[6]

God is just and he must punish sin (HABAKKUK 1:13; REVELATION 20:11–15). But he is also love (1 JOHN 4:16), and his love cannot force others to love him. Love cannot work coercively but only persuasively. Forced love is a contradiction in terms. Hence, God's love demands that there be a hell where persons who do not wish to love him can experience the great divorce when God says to them, "Thy will be done!"

HOW CAN GOD BE BOTH LOVING AND JUST?

It would seem that love and justice are incompatible attributes. If God is just, he must punish sin. But if he is loving, he would forgive sin. How then can he be both?

The attributes (characteristics) of God are not contradictory. He is both absolutely just and yet unconditionally loving. Each attribute complements the other. God is "justly holy" and "holy just." That is, his justice is administered in love, and his love is distributed justly.

The perfect example of how God's love and justice kiss is in the cross. In his love, God sent his Son to pay the penalty for our sins so that his justice could be satisfied and his love released. For "the wages of sin is death" (SEE ROMANS 6:23). And sin against the eternal God demands eternal death (SEE REVELATION 20:14–15). So when Christ died for our sins (SEE ROMANS 5:8), the Just suffered for the unjust (SEE I PETER 3:18) that he might bring us to God. "God made him who had no sin to be sin for us, so that in him we might become the righteousness of God" (2 CORINTHIANS 5:21).

God's justice demands that sin be punished, but his love compels him to save sinners. So by Christ's death for us his justice is satisfied and his love released. Thus, there is no contradiction between absolute justice and unconditional love. To illustrate, God is like the judge who, after passing out the punishment to the guilty defendant, laid aside his robe, stood alongside the convicted, and paid the fine for him. Jesus did the same for us on Calvary. Surely justice and mercy kissed at the cross.

CONCLUSION

Even little children like my grandson can ask tough questions, but there are good answers for all these "God questions." And the Bible exhorts us to find them and give them. Paul wrote, "Let your conversation be always full of grace, seasoned with salt, so that you may know how to answer everyone" (COLOSSIANS 4:6).

By the way, my grandson just graduated from college and is preparing to attend seminary to study apologetics (defending the faith). Soon he will be prepared to answer the same kinds of questions he asked. One can only wonder what he would be doing if no one had answered his.

QUESTIONS FOR REFLECTION AND DISCUSSION

1. Read 1 Peter 3:15 and Colossians 4:6. Given that these verses are addressed to all believers, what can we do to put them into practice?

2. When, if ever, should questions asked by unbelievers not be answered? Consider Proverbs 26:4 and Matthew 7:6 in your response.

3. Why is it so important to answer questions about God? How does belief in God relate to our belief that the Bible is the Word of God and that Jesus Christ is the Son of God?

CHAPTER NOTES

1. Of course, the actual amount of energy remains constant; only the usable amount is decreasing.

2. Robert Jastrow, *God and the Astonomers* (New York: W.W. Norton, 1978), 15–16.

3. David Hume, *The Letters of David Hume*, vol. 1, ed. J.Y.T. Greig (Oxford: Clarendon, 1932), 187.

4. David Hume, *Enquiry Concerning the Human Understanding*, ed. Chas. W. Hendel (New York: Liberal Arts, 1955), 165–66.

5. C.S. Lewis, *The Abolition of Man* (New York: Macmillan, 1947), 69.

6. C.S. Lewis, *The Problem of Pain* (New York: HarperCollins, 2001, reprint; first published, 1944), 120.

Why Does God Allow Bad Things to Happen?
by Bruce Marchiano

Chapter:
Why, Oh Lord?

Book:
Jesus Wept

Look for your coupons for this and other featured titles in the back of this book.

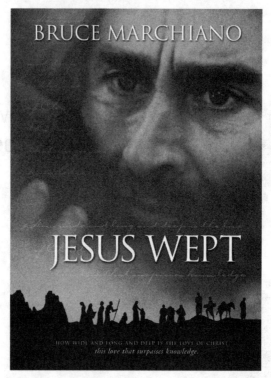

Author's Bio

Bruce Marchiano is an actor, speaker, and writer and is well-known for his poignant portrayal of Christ in the movie *The Gospel According to Matthew*. He is the author of the best-selling book *In the Footsteps of Jesus* and *Yesterday, Today and Forever*. Bruce lives out his commitment to Christ, reaching out to the destitute of Africa and the world.

Why Does God Allow Bad Things to Happen?
by Bruce Marchiano

"If it hurts Him so much, why does He allow terrible things to happen?"

It's the age-old question: If God is who He says He is, then why all the pain in life, why all the horror? Why in heaven and earth doesn't He do something? Why doesn't He intervene?

How long, O Lord?

Will you hide yourself forever?

It's a question that was asked the whole world over on the morning of September 11. It's a question that's been asked a million times by millions of people caught in the grip of millions of private and personal "September 11s."

It's a question that was asked two thousand years ago, on that first-century September 11, as Jesus faced Lazarus's grave.

Swirling all around Him as He stood there weeping was a froth of arrogant whispers: "Could not he who opened the eyes of the blind man have kept this man from dying?" (JOHN 11:37).

Oh, the aloneness of Jesus! They wouldn't even allow Him to grieve.

He had given everything that they might have life and life abundantly (SEE JOHN 10:10). In the coming days, He would give even more that they might have life and life eternally. But such treasures, it seems, are paltry to men and women. On this Lazarus day—a day like every day—these treasures were met with abundant complaints and grumblings. They were met with gossip and opinions eternally.

"Why this?"

"How come that?"

"You're not who You say You are. I can tell by what's happening to me!"

Man judging God: It is the most widespread of crimes, the very oldest of professions. Man assuming that his wisdom and understanding is superior to that which hurled the sun into the afternoon sky: What a horror! What a slap in His face!

Jesus.

In the pages of Scripture, the answer to every question, every accusation, lies free for the seeking, obvious and true:

For all have sinned and fall short of the glory of God. (ROMANS 3:23)

The wages of sin is death. (ROMANS 6:23)

For the creation was subjected to frustration ... [and] bondage to decay. (ROMANS 8:20–21)

In the way of righteousness is life, and in its pathway there is no death. (PROVERBS 12:28 NKJV)

Then there is the most answering scripture of all—words from the lips of Jesus Himself as He spilled His heart on the pavement of Jerusalem's temple courts for everyone to see: "How often I have longed to gather your children together, as a hen gathers her chicks under her wings, but you were not willing. Look,"—open your eyes and see!—"your house is left to you desolate" (MATTHEW 23:37–38).

It's true: The "desolations" that you and I suffer in this life are not the product of an aloof and uncaring God. How uncaring can He be—to step out from heavenly glory to be born in a barn, to work with His hands, to sleep in the fields, to suffer the mockery of common men, to be hung like a rag on a tree?

For God so loved the world.

Are such choices born out of apathy? No, they're born out of care—care beyond what any of us could imagine care to be. They're born out of passion and hope and desire. They're born out of longing—His longing. His longing for you. His longing for me.

In the book of Revelation the apostle John records a heavenly vision that captures this passionate longing, this unimaginable care. It is a startling image, a shocking revelation that very well could be the most revealing in all of Revelation: Standing in the center of the throne of heaven at the right hand of the Father is a lamb, "looking as if it had been slain" (REVELATION 5:6).

Jesus.

It is God's devotion in a single image. It is His response to mankind's rebellion and sin; the passionate urgency with which He reaches and woos; the unyielding commitment He extends—even as man continues to scoff and laugh in His torn and battered face.

You are worthy ... because you were slain, and with your blood you purchased men for God.

No, the problem is not Jesus. The hole in Creation through which evil oozes, gurgles, and putrefies everything in its wicked and vicious path is not a hole torn by an angry and distant God. It's a hole ripped open by us: "But you were not willing." In the grip of our sin nature, it's a hole torn by you and me.

Inch by inch
> generation by generation
>> sin by sin

and rebellion by rebellion—wider and wider the hole is torn by a billion yous and a billion mes across the expanse of time and humanity. Like a silent crawl of consuming lava, like an avalanche roar, it grows and it grows, as does the danger it presents. Ravenous and insatiable, it swallows and destroys everything in its random and reckless path.

To you I call, O Lord my Rock; . . .

Hear my cry for mercy.

And may we make no mistake; may there be no illusion. Sin takes no prisoners. Horror plays no favorites. It doesn't pick and choose who will be its next victim. It doesn't decide who deserves all and who deserves none. It just flows and flows. It reeks and reeks. It feeds with gluttonous frenzy on anything close and everything near—you, me, the good people next door—vomiting disease, desolation, and tragedy all the more.

Cancer strikes; drunkenness flows. Dad has heart disease; Mom doesn't hear like she used to. Two cars collide; a family writhes in divorce. A gunshot splits a big-city night; a child is stolen on a small-town day. An airplane hits a building; Jesus weeps before His friend's grave.

Come quickly to me, O God.

You are my help and my deliverer.

All of it is the fallout, the by-product, the putrid refuse of sin. It infiltrates, cripples, and rots the very Creation of which you and

I are a part. It can never be said too often or strongly enough: Not a pin-drop of it did He ever want to be!

And yes, He could easily intervene. In the past He has intervened; and as His Word guarantees, He'll intervene in the future even more. The day will surely come when all the laughter that's done in the dark will be paraded openly in the light. All bets will be called in. Right will prevail.

He will turn back upon them their own iniquity. . . . The Lord our God will wipe them out.

Truth be told, He intervenes in the here and now too. But his intervention seldom looks like we want it to look; and in our world of

    shouts and screams

        bells and whistles

            racing from this to that

it comes in a whisper that cries to be heard. But He intervenes nonetheless—24/7, He intervenes.

There isn't one of us in the midst of our choices who doesn't hear His still, small, intervening voice in the private place of our conscience. "No," He whispers. "That's not the way you should go. That way will surely lead to your harm. That path will devastate your family."

There isn't one of us in the midst of our choices who doesn't walk by His still, small, intervening voice sitting, leather-bound, on our coffee tables and bookshelves. "Sin leads to death; don't take the risk. I have plans for your future; walk in My ways. Remember mercy, holiness, self-control. Come to Me and I will give you rest for your soul."

A man sits on the couch, beer in hand, and clicks on the TV. A preacher is there. "Friend," the preacher pleads, "Jesus died for your sins and offers you the free gift of eternal life." The man hears the words—words as intervening as words can be. He swigs his beer. He makes a choice. He flips the channel to football ...

A woman follows her friends into a dark, loud place. The music pounds, the laughter echoes. Smells of perfume and sweat, whiskey and leather collide. A man she doesn't know touches her as if she did. The Lord whispers, "This guy doesn't care. He'll only hurt you." The woman hears the plea; for a moment, perhaps, she even listens. She makes a choice. She touches the man in return.

A husband and father packs a suitcase. His pastor said no, his friends and family said no; and through every one of them, the Lord begged him, "No!" But the car is running, and a young woman waits. He pulls the ring from his finger. He makes a choice. He closes the bag and heads for the door ...

People making day-to-day choices in their day-to-day freedom to make their own choices. And oh, what a terrible price is paid for that privilege—

what tragedy

what pain and loss

what brokenness.

It is a price born by the chooser and, willfully or otherwise, imposed on everyone in the chooser's path. It's imposed on every life and heart, every child and grownup, every stranger and stranger's family who just happens to be in the vicinity when the horrific choice is made.

Now choose life, so that you
and your children may live.

I picture a man in a cheap motel room. An angry man. A man far from the country of his birth. Day after day, night after night, for many days and many nights, he has been sitting in the company of cigarettes and coffee, take-out pizza, and inexpensive beer. He has a plan. A well-thought-out plan. A plan that will cost lives—many lives, he hopes.

A cell phone, a rented car, maps, cash: It's all ready. It is September 10, 2001. And unbeknownst to the nation that has opened its arms to him, come sunrise he will park his rented car in an airport parking lot and execute his plan.

How many times did this angry man sit at coffee-shop counters, and through the smiles and gentle conversation of people he'd been taught to hate, hear the living God cry, "No! It's all lies. These people are good, and everything you've learned is lies!" How many times in how many of those faces did he picture men and women lying beneath the rubble of his freedom to make choices—even as the living God continued to plead from deep within, "What you're planning to do is wrong!"

How many times did he pass a little boy or girl, their mother holding their small hands, and think of all the little boys, all the little girls, who would suffer the fallout of his decision—perhaps even his own little boy, his own little girl? How many times did his own basic sensibilities revolt against what he'd set his mind to pursue? How many times did the living God explode through that window of sensitivity and plead and plead, "No, no, no!"

And it's so far outside our capacity to accept, I know—but how many times and in how many ways did the living God try to reach in to save his eternal soul?

It is not the will of your Father who
is in heaven that one ... should perish.

I picture this same angry man weeks earlier, driving through town on a Sunday morning. Perhaps he stops at a red light, and his attention is suddenly arrested by music and singing cascading through open windows from a church on the corner. It is unlike the rote, religious chanting he is accustomed to. It is warm and exciting, joyous and alive.

With every note and chorus, the living God pleads at the door of the angry man's heart. With tears unceasing—tears for the angry man and tears for the lives he plans to destroy—the living God begs and begs, "Come! I'll give you rest for your soul."

But the angry man's answer is no. He makes a choice. The light turns green, and he slides his foot from the brake to the gas pedal. He drives on, maybe in fear, maybe in confusion. Maybe the anger and lies are just

so entrenched

so enthroned

so rampant

—so "Legion"—that he just drives on.

Or maybe the angry man hesitates. Maybe something deep inside him cries out for freedom from all the lies—for any excuse to escape and run from them. Maybe the vise grip strangling his heart has hurt so much for so long that his heart longs to breathe, longs to know truth and joy.

And maybe on the wings of that music coming from the church, a whisper of God's cry to him slips between the cracks of his yearning. For a moment he thinks about turning his wheel and driving his rented car into that church parking lot. And in that moment, all the angels in heaven get their dancing shoes ready in anticipation of another life saved—of thousands of lives saved.

But then maybe there is another man in the car behind him who isn't so angry but forever in a hurry—a self-important hurry. Maybe he grows impatient with the angry man in front of him; and in his same freedom to make choices, he blasts his horn, shattering the softness that was beginning to take hold in the angry man's heart.

Maybe, God forbid, the impatient man is about to turn into the church parking lot himself. O Lord, let it not be so! Maybe in his hurry to get to God, he makes a liar out of God in the mind of the angry man.

And maybe the angry man becomes even angrier. Maybe that impatient blast kicks and twists the life-giving words that God has been speaking and, in the skilled hands of hell's manipulation, actually affirms the lies. Maybe it leaves the angry man even more convinced that his cause is just, that his evil perversion of right is right indeed.

But have no fear—the living God is not a God who gives up on anyone, especially with so much at stake. So He continues to reach and reach, pursuing ever more, inviting and intervening, never tiring, never ceasing, pleading and pleading: "Jesus, Jesus. Come to Jesus!"

Where can I go from your Spirit?
Where can I flee from your presence?

Maybe the angry man stabs at the radio as he drives his rented car, and there is that music again—the exalted worship of a Christian broadcast. Leaping through the car speakers with outstretched arms, the living God trumpets His glory in invitation: "I've set before you the path of life. Choose Jesus!"

Later the man clicks on the TV in his cheap motel room and hits upon a preacher's passion. Again the Spirit swarms his heart: "Jesus, Jesus! 'I am' Jesus!"

Each day before September 11, he drives past cross after cross on hilltop and steeple; and like the blood of Jesus that flowed two thousand years before on Golgotha, the testimony spills and splashes against the walls of his willingness. Its impassioned shout reverberates in his soul and spirit: "Eternal life! Come to Jesus!"

How many men and women did the living God send along the angry man's path—in a post-office line, on a bus ride to Florida, at a donut-shop counter? How many of His children did the living God nudge and prompt, beg and lead, "Go talk to that guy about My Son. Go talk to him about Jesus!"

He is the living God, and His beckoning is constant, desperate, through every means imaginable—desperate, astoundingly so, for even the angry man's life. Desperate—oh, how desperately desperate—for the lives of the many the man hopes to destroy.

Seek me and live.

Untiring, unyielding, passion unceasing, the very voice that spoke heaven and earth into existence cries out to the very last seconds: "Steer away! Choose Jesus! Steer a—"

But the answer is no. Like the cold steel of a Roman spear, an airplane thrusts itself through the living God's heart. Like the cruel mass of a Roman crossbeam, tons of concrete crumble upon His back. Like His blood that flowed till there was no more, the voluminous cries of the dying and wounded, the broken and shattered, the wives and husbands, parents and children pour forth into the dust and soot-filled morning air.

And so He weeps. "My babies, My babies! Look what they did to My babies!"

He weeps
and He weeps
and He weeps.
Jesus.

This is the verdict"—He phrases the words with human lips on a distant Jerusalem night, two thousand years ago—"light has come into the world. . . ." His voice breaks; His gaze turns away. Divine foresight swells from within His eyes and spills down His very human cheekbones, staining the weave of His most blessed beard.

"But men loved darkness instead" (JOHN 3:19).

Jesus. ❖

How Do I Become a Christian?

by Tim Way

Author's Bio

Tim Way is senior book buyer for Family Christian Stores. He has more than 20 years experience in Christian retailing. Tim serves as an elder at Daybreak Community Church in Hudsonville, Michigan, where he assists in the development and teaching of spiritual growth classes. He's been married for more than 30 years and has three children and two grand children.

How Do I Become a Christian?
by Tim Way

Grand Haven, Michigan is a popular tourist town nestled on the banks of Lake Michigan on the far southwestern side of the state. Aside from the lake itself, the most notable landmark in the town is its massive pier, which juts 1,300 feet out into the cold waters of Lake Michigan. On the tip of this formidable concrete and rock structure stands a bright red lighthouse that serves as a regional landmark, a popular scene on local post cards and tourist brochures. In the summer this huge pier is lined with fishermen, sunbathers, and tourists just out for a stroll.

Lake Michigan is more like an inland sea; one of the largest fresh water lakes in the world. It is almost 50 miles from the end of the Grand Haven pier straight west across the lake to the city of Milwaukee. Yet the drive from Grand Haven to Milwaukee is a grueling five hours heading south down the shoreline of the Michigan Peninsula, around the bottom of the huge lake, through downtown Chicago, then north up the busy Illinois/Wisconsin shoreline. Even taking the "shortcut," a ferry across the lake, takes about three hours - four hours if you include the trip to the ferry dock. Bottom line; there is just no easy way to get from Grand Haven, Michigan, to Milwaukee, Wisconsin. The lake is an overwhelming obstacle.

On a particular warm summer day, a young man is standing on the beach in front of the pier. He is in the process of shedding sweat pants and shirt, stripping down to a snug pair of swim trunks. He then begins a warm-up process that he has gone through at least three thousand times. This is the day his dream will come true. This is the day he will make history. For the past ten years, this young man has worked five hours a day practicing and training. He has honed his skills as a broad jumper until there is none in the world equal to him. In practice, he has already broken the world record, and surpassed his own best jumps many times.

Now he is ready. Kicking off his running shoes, he leans forward and takes a deep breath and begins his sprint down the pier. The water is a quarter of a mile away, plenty of space to get up to top speed. With each step he runs faster. He barely notices the searing heat of the concrete beneath his feet. His eyes are fixed on the end of the pier still a thousand feet ahead. In under a minute he has covered almost the entire length of the long pier, flashing by people in a virtual blur. Finally, with a mighty push of his muscular legs, he launches himself out over the water, his feet still pumping in midair as he struggles with all of his might to gain another moment of airtime and space between the end of the pier and the lake. Finally, gravity takes over and he plunges with a graceful splash into the cold water.

The crowd on the pier is stunned. First of all, no one ever really intentionally jumps into the water at the end of this pier. The rocks are too hard to clear, and it would be a dangerous stunt for the average human. But this is no average human. This is a highly trained athlete, and he has easily cleared the rocks, landing in the deep water out from the breakwater. At first there is silence, but when the young man bobs to the surface the crowd breaks into a loud cheer. It is obvious to all that have seen this event that this young man has jumped further than any human being has ever jumped before.

As the young man surfaces, he looks around. A look of utter dejection and disappointment becomes evident on his face. As he slowly swims back to the end of the pier and is helped to the top by the waiting crowd of fishermen and tourists, the tears begin to flow.

"What's wrong?" an old man who is giving him a hand up the rocks asks him. With a sigh the young man turns around and with tears coursing down his face says, "I missed my goal." "What was your goal?" the man asks. "That was an absolutely spectacular jump. I've watched track and field events for years and have never seen anything like that!"

"But it wasn't good enough," the young man replies. "I was trying to jump across to Milwaukee."

The man laughs out loud. "Jump to Milwaukee!" he exclaims, bending over and slapping his leg. "My ambitious friend, that's impossible!"

Sounds a bit ridiculous, doesn't it? Anyone who has ever stood on the shores of Lake Michigan and looked out across this enormous body of water knows that, without a very reliable boat, no one will ever cross over this lake to the other side.

Yet this is exactly what millions of people try to do every day. In fact, what they are trying to do is even more impossible than jumping a 50 mile body of water. They are attempting to get across from where they stand to the other side of an impossible gulf between themselves and God through their own efforts.

We try to make this entire "religion thing" far too difficult. It all comes down to this: If you were to stand before God tonight and he was to say to you, "Why should I let you into my heaven?" how would you respond? That is the one key question that we will all have to answer one day.

It all boils down to "Whom do you trust?" Do you trust in what you have accomplished, or do you trust what God has already done for you?

That is the first key difference between true Christianity and every other world religion. Every world religion provides a list of things that you do to earn your way into God's presence—prayers, works of charity and good deeds, moral laws to obey, pilgrimages to take. True Christianity says that it is impossible to work your way to God. No amount of good works, no sheer number of prayers, no long pilgrimages, and no large amounts of money given to charity will ever be enough to earn a place in God's Heavenly Kingdom. These acts are all like trying to jump across Lake Michigan. They all fall far short of the goal.

This is a very intentional principle. God does not want anyone to be able to boast about being in His Kingdom by their own merit. All of the credit for our salvation belongs to God from beginning to end. When we work for something, we get paid what we are owed. This is a wage. When we are given something that we have not earned, it is a gift. God said this about His salvation: "For the wages of sin is death, but the gift of God is eternal life in Christ Jesus our Lord." (ROMANS 6:23)

God loves it when we do good deeds and try to live good lives. This pleases Him. However, when we are counting on these things to get us into His Heaven, He says, "It isn't enough."

Another thing that people do is to attempt to choose their own path to God. "A little of this and a little of that ought to get me there." Or, "This sounds good. I'll try it." In fact, in today's world of tolerance and acceptance, it is considered intolerant to suggest that there is only one way to heaven. That being the case, Jesus was definitely intolerant. He said this: "I am the way, and the truth and the life. No one comes to the Father except through me." (JOHN 14:6) That statement is the great dividing line. No matter how you try to reinterpret it, in the end it pretty much eliminates every other way to God. Jesus plainly said that the way to God is through Him or not at all.

And this brings us to the second key difference between Christianity and every other religion. Study every world religion and you will find that it has as its founder a man who said, "Listen to me and I will show you the way to God." Jesus Christ is unique. He didn't say, "I will show you the way." Jesus said, "I AM the way." How is He able to make that claim? Because Jesus is God in the flesh. The Bible says this about Jesus: "In the Beginning was the Word (another name for Jesus), and the Word was with God, and the Word was God." (JOHN 1:1 [WORDS IN PARENTHESIS ADDED]) Jesus is far more than just a good teacher. He is God.

So, if you can't work your way to God, and if you can't pick another path to Him, what can you do?

Again, the answer is found in the verse above from Romans. "For the wages of sin is death, but the gift of God is eternal life." When someone presents you with a gift, to receive that gift you simply reach out and take it. That is exactly what God wants you to do with His gift of salvation; simply reach out and take it.

Is it really that easy? Yes, it's really that easy.

Here is a key verse from the Bible: "For it is by grace you have been saved, through faith – and this not from yourselves, it is the gift of God – not by works, so that no one can boast." (EPHESIANS 2:8) God wants to bring you into His Kingdom because He loves you and wants a relationship with you. It is His gracious love that calls you and saves you. This grace is put into action through simply having faith in what He has already done for you. God does the work. You only have to trust and believe (have faith) that this work of God will save you. And what is the work that God has done? He has sent His Son, Jesus Christ, to die for you on the cross for the forgiveness of your sins, and then to be raised from the dead three days later so that you can have eternal life.

Think of grace as a car. You can trust that the car will get you from point "A" to point "B," but unless you put the key in the ignition and turn it, nothing is going to happen. Having faith in God's work completed for you in Jesus Christ is the key. When you turn the key of faith, amazing things happen.

What is faith? Well, it is a little like standing on the top of a tower with a bungee cord tied around your ankle, and then taking that amazing step off into thin air. You are trusting that this rubber-band-like cord will actually stop your fall before you hit the bottom. That is faith. Having faith in God's work is the same thing. It is stepping off into thin air and saying "God, I trust you completely, now and for eternity. I have no other safety net."

Here's another fact about faith: You don't "work up" faith in God on your own. God places it there for you. Look again at the verse mentioned above. "For it is by grace you have been saved, through faith – and this is not from yourselves, it is the gift of God…" Even the faith comes from God. It is His salvation from beginning to end. The very desire you have to know God is His calling you to Himself. It is God from start to finish.

God has promised in His Word, the Bible, that if you will trust in Him, he will save you and give you eternal life. In the last book of the Bible, John's Revelation, Jesus said this: "Here I am! I stand at the door and knock. If anyone hears my voice and opens the door, I will come in and eat with him, and he with me." (REVELATION 3:20) There is a famous painting by Warner Sallman that depicts Jesus standing outside the door of a home with His hand poised to knock on the door. He is leaning forward expectantly as if listening to see if anyone on the inside will open the door for Him. If you examine this painting carefully, you will note that there is no doorknob on the outside of the door. It can only be opened from the inside. That is the way it is with us. God is a gentleman, and He does not come in where He is uninvited. But He does gently knock on our heart's door and willingly comes in if we will but open the door to Him. In another place in the Bible it says this: "If we confess our sins, he is faithful and just and will forgive us our sins and purify us from all unrighteousness." (1 JOHN 1:9). Forgiveness is ours for the asking.

It is no accident that you have this book in your hands. Hopefully it will answer most of your questions. In the end it all comes down to this: "God so loved the world (that includes you!) that he gave his one and only Son (that's Jesus), that whoever believes in him shall not perish but have eternal life." (JOHN 3:16 WORDS IN PARENTHESES ADDED) In other words, the bungee cord of faith is Jesus Christ. He is the way that God has provided for your salvation. All you have to do is to agree with Him that you are a sinner and can't earn it on your own, and say, "I put my trust in you."

Are you ready to do that? If so, here is a simple prayer to God that you can repeat right now:

"Father, I am a sinner. I have broken Your laws. I come to You with nothing to offer of my own, but totally trust in the death and resurrection of Your Son, Jesus Christ, for my salvation. Starting this day I give my life over to You. I confess that I am a sinner. Forgive me of my sins. Come to live in my heart. Thank You. In Jesus name, amen."

If you have just prayed that simple prayer and meant every word of it, you are now a child of God!

Is it that simple? Yes, it's just that simple.

If you've prayed this prayer and have decided to follow Jesus Christ, we'd like to know. You can e-mail us at Family Christian Stores at info@fcsdirect.familychristian.com. If you would like recommendations on books or a Bible that will help you get started on your Christian walk, let us know. We will be glad to help.

May God who gives all things abundantly and freely, richly bless you as you walk with Him. ❖

What If God Won't Accept Me?

by Cindi McMenamin

Chapter:
Knowing He Accepts Me

Book:
Letting God Meet Your Emotional Needs

Look for your coupons for this and other featured titles in the back of this book.

Author's Bio

Cindy McMenamin, an award-winning writer and national speaker, is the author of when Women Walk Along. She is a contributing author to several devotional books and Christian magazines. She is the director of women's ministries at Valley Bible church in San Marcos, California, and has been actively involved in ministering to women for nearly 20 years.

What if God Won't Accept Me?
by Cindi McMenamin

I grew up believing I had to earn my father's love. When I received good grades, held coveted positions, or earned honors or awards, my dad was proud. And when he felt proud, I felt loved. I don't remember my dad expressing affection toward me verbally, except when he would say, "I'm proud of you, Ceenee." Because I interpreted that as, "I love you, Cindi," I became an overachiever. My life was focused on making Dad proud and feeling acceptable in his sight.

I vividly remember the day I felt Dad's love withdrawn. I was a sophomore in high school and brought home my first "B" on my report card—in geometry. My father hit the roof! He immediately drove down to the school and blamed my teacher for not teaching me adequately and for having the nerve to give his daughter anything less than an "A." In his sadly twisted way, Dad was trying to express that he loved me by insisting that I only be given the best grades. But at the same time, I felt I had blown it in his eyes, and I was no longer accepted by him.

Three years later, I brought home my first speeding ticket. Dad was furious and accused me of being irresponsible. It became a crucial point in our relationship. I feared his anger and what he might do to me. Shortly afterward I moved out of my parents' house and into an apartment with my sister. I feared ever disappointing *anyone* again. And it took me a long time to feel accepted again by my father.

Because of the work of the Holy Spirit, my father is a different person today. He recognizes my humanity and admits he has made many mistakes. I am now confident that he loves me for who I am, not what I've done and will continue to do. But my perception of unconditional love—whether from my husband or my heavenly Father or anyone else—had already been shaped.

DEALING WITH OUR FEARS

It's difficult for me to understand that my Heavenly Father loves me for who I am, not what I've done and will do. And to this day, when I disappoint the Lord with a heart that isn't right or sin that should've been avoided, I still fight those thoughts in the back of my mind—that I am no longer accepted by Him and that He doesn't love me anymore.

My insecurities about being accepted continued into my marriage relationship. In the first few years of my marriage I was terribly fearful that if my husband discovered who I *really* was, he wouldn't want me anymore. When we married, he was under the impression that I had a gentle, quiet spirit and that I was soft-spoken, well refined, and emotionally all-together. He soon found out I was a talker and that I could get quite loud, especially around members of my family. He discovered I had a bad habit of interrupting people and I was much more emotionally fragile than he'd ever imagined. About the same time he discovered the *real* me, I was finding out that he wasn't the stellar communicator I thought he was. While I had grown up in a family in which everyone talked at once and freely expressed how they felt, he grew up in a silent home, where he was taught to stuff his feelings deep inside and never talk about them. After years of lashing out at him for not opening up and talking to me, he finally admitted the ugly truth: He never talks to me because he can't get a word in edgewise! He would *start* talking, he said, if I could *stop* talking. How humiliating! And, because of my fears of not being accepted, how very threatening!

The most difficult task for both of us in our marriage has been accepting each other's flaws. I didn't want to accept that my husband may never be the communicator I thought he was when we married. But by accepting that as a part of the complete package that is him, it teaches me to love him a little more unconditionally. And by his accepting the fact that I may never have the quiet and gentle composure he believed me to have when we married, he shows me how very deeply he must love me.

Our longing for acceptance is often just as strong as our fear of rejection. So we tend to hide the parts about us that we fear will not be accepted in order to feel loved and avoid rejection. Sometimes it's our bad habits, deeply ingrained in us since childhood, that we hide from others, as Hugh and I tried to do. But sometimes it's stuff much deeper than that ... deep, dark secrets of our past that we hope no one will find out.

WHAT ABOUT OUR PAST?

Everyone goes into a relationship with baggage. Some baggage is a little easier to sort through than others. Shortly after I was married, I made the mistake of going through one of my husband's bags that would have been better left alone. But, by discovering some painful things in his past, I learned something more about acceptance.

My husband had a night job, which meant he would return home late. One evening as I was waiting for him to come home, I found his old high school yearbook and began flipping through the pages. I knew my husband had had a girlfriend in high school before he became a Christian. And he had leveled with me about his mistakes, in general, before he began walking with the Lord. But I was curious about the details. Although I was convicted in my heart not to delve into this matter, because it was a relationship prior to his knowing the Lord, I also felt I had a right to know more.

I didn't even know the girl's name, but it didn't take me long to figure out which signature in his yearbook was hers. I read what she wrote and felt sick to my stomach. I would have been better off not reading about the details and things she implied on that page.

That night, when my husband got home and inquired about my mood, I mentioned briefly that I had found his yearbook and read through it. He wasn't offended at my invasion of his privacy, as I expected him to be. He, instead, was hurt ... at having to be reminded of his past and see me hurt by it as well. After a long time, he broke the silence.

"I did a lot of dumb things before I gave my life to the Lord," he admitted to me, with tears in his eyes. "And I'm not proud of them. I don't want to think about the way I used to live. That's not me anymore. I'm a different person now in God's eyes."

I realized then that acceptance means love without condition, without certain expectations of the past or the future. It is a decision to love no matter what happened yesterday and no matter what happens tomorrow. By bringing up my husband's past, I had hurt him deeply. God forgave my husband's sin and threw away his past when he became saved. Who was I to bring this up again when God had wiped his slate clean? That night, I decided I would spend the rest of my life trying to show my husband how very much I love him for *who* he is, not for what he's done or what he will do. And by trying to do that through the years, I've learned how precious it is not only to be fully accepted myself, but to fully accept another person regardless of their past, present, or future.

WHAT ARE YOU HIDING?

Whether it's something about our personality or something buried in our past, many women enter relationships hoping the other person will never know the deep, dark secrets they hide. Past relationships or reputations, abortions or addictions … the list abounds of things we would rather not expose about ourselves for fear of not being accepted.

Some of us never go beyond a certain point in relationships, fearing that if we become too close to a person, we will eventually be hurt because they might not accept us for who we really are. No matter how you look at it, knowing we are accepted is crucial to feeling secure and loved in any relationship.

I have a friend who was afraid to admit to her adult son that she had had an abortion many years before he was born. After much prayer, counsel, and consideration, she admitted it to him one evening. But rather than hearing words of condemnation, as she had feared, she heard the sweet sound of grace: "Mom, God has forgiven you, and so have I." After hearing her son express forgiveness and acceptance toward her, this friend of mine was able to finally forgive herself and better grasp the fact that she was forgiven by God as well. Unconditional love means we are accepted and forgiven no matter what we've done.

JESUS KNEW THE ART OF ACCEPTANCE

Jesus feels the same way about us. When Jesus was passing through a town called Samaria, He stopped near a well to have a conversation with a woman—a woman with a worldly reputation. He struck up the conversation by asking her to draw some water for Him. Not only was this woman of a nationality that Jesus' people, the Jews, found offensive, but she was a sinner, one that you'd think God would find offensive. Jesus crossed a cultural barrier by speaking to this woman on a deserted road. But regardless of this woman's nationality, sex, and troubled past, Jesus talked with her and asked her for some water.

The woman hesitated. *If he knew the kind of woman I was, he wouldn't be talking to me*, she must have thought.

Jesus knew what she was thinking. "Where's your husband?" He asked.

"I don't have one," she replied, perhaps a bit flustered.

She *didn't* have a husband—at least not at the moment. She'd been through quite a few husbands, however. And she was now living with a man who wasn't her husband. Why hadn't he married her? Because of her reputation? Because she was afraid to tell the latest man her true story? All we know is that she wasn't completely honest with Jesus when He asked if she was married. Most likely, she didn't want to talk about it.

Yet Jesus knew. And despite this woman's past, He offered her living water.[1]

He offers us the same. In addition to the life-giving forgiveness of our past, He offers us the water of relief and refreshment in a life in which we no longer have to keep things hidden. We can be up-front with Him and it will not affect His love for us one bit.

FINDING OUR ACCEPTANCE

There is only one way we become acceptable to God and that is when we have accepted His Son, Jesus Christ, and are depending on Him for our salvation. Jesus, God's obedient Son, is holy and perfect in God's eyes. And when we are trusting in Jesus, we become holy and perfect as well, because He represents us and His righteousness becomes ours.[2] Once we have repented of our sin and trusted in Jesus for salvation, there is nothing we can do to be "unaccepted" in God's eyes.

Now, that's a wonderful concept. That means that if I mess up, I'm still okay with Him. If I make a wrong choice and push the line with Him, I may have consequences to bear because of my actions, but I am still loved. That means I can be completely honest with Him without any fear that He might cast me away.

When was the last time you told the Lord, your Heavenly Husband, how you were really feeling? Have you ever tried sharing with Him the things you refuse to tell anyone else? If not, draw it out for Him. By doing this, you will lift a burden that you've been carrying far too long.

In Matthew 11:28-30, Jesus told us to come to Him with our burdens and He'll lighten our load. That means we can tell Him what's on our mind. We can unload the things we're afraid to tell anyone else and we can experience the relief of no longer having to carry that burden alone. We can draw out for Him what is buried deep in our hearts and He will give us the water of relief and refreshment in return.

ASSESSING YOUR FEARS

Some of the women I've counseled have been afraid to admit to their husbands their previous sexual relationships. One woman I know has buried the guilt of past abortions deep in her heart and mind, unwilling to talk about it to her husband, family, or friends, for fear of being judged and condemned by them. Other women I've counseled have hidden a past of sexual molestation by family members, feeling they will be looked at differently if their past is revealed.

Take a moment to think about some things in your past that you feel embarrassed or ashamed about—things about yourself that you wouldn't necessarily want others to know. Do you have *anyone* in your life that you can reveal these things to without fearing rejection?

Now, let's look at how the Lord views the things that linger in our past.

He considers them in the past and no longer relevant

The Bible says anyone who has a relationship with Christ is just like a new person. The past is forgotten and everything is new again *(2 CORINTHIANS 5:17)*. That means any sin or mistake we make prior to knowing God is erased from our history. We get a clean slate when we come to Him.

He doesn't let our past mistakes affect how we look in His eyes

Isaiah 1:18 says, "'Come now, and let us reason together,' says the Lord, 'Though your sins are as scarlet, they will be as white as snow; though they are red like crimson, they will be like wool.'" Again, He loves us for who we are, not what we do and don't do.

He chooses to forget our mistakes and He never keeps an account

In Isaiah 43:25 God says, "I, even I, am the one who wipes out your transgressions for My own sake; and I will not remember your sins." A big part of being accepted is being assured of the fact that our past won't be brought up time after time. The Lord assures us that things we've repented of are behind us and will never have to haunt us again.[3] In Psalm 103:12, David eloquently describes this freedom from our mistakes: "As far as the east is from the west, so far has He removed our transgressions from us."

When we come to Christ and He cleans our slate, we get a new start. He still knows who we are and where we came from. But He doesn't hold that against us. Sometimes I think He considers it a delightful challenge to see how much He can transform us into His likeness and how far He can take us in our new life with Him

(SEE 1 CORINTHIANS 1:26-31).

God knows us intimately and still loves us. Psalm 139, which tells of the Lord's intimate knowledge of us, reminds us that He formed us in the womb and saw our unformed bodies and already ordained for us the number of days we would live before we had even been born.[4] That tells us that He not only knows our past, but He planned us out, meaning He had a hand in how we came about and what we were before we came to know Him. With that in mind, of course He accepts us so willingly. We're His creation, His special project that has come back to Him after a run on our own. And we didn't even have to prove ourselves to Him so He would take us back.

Romans 5:8 says, "God demonstrates His own love toward us, in that *while we were yet sinners*, Christ died for us" (emphasis added). We didn't even have to clean up our act before He decided He would save us. Because there was nothing we could do to earn His love, there's nothing we can do to lose it. Face it, my friend: You are accepted in the beloved.

ACCEPTED, BUT NOT EXCUSED

It's important for us to know that although we are accepted by God, we are not excused for the things that He clearly disapproves of. God grieves at our sin. But He loves us as individuals.

I am grieved when my husband doesn't communicate. But I accept that it's difficult for him and therefore I try to be patient in working with him in this area of vulnerability. I was grieved at discovering things about my husband's past, but I didn't let it affect how I love him today. And, although I accept him regardless of his past, there are certain things I would not accept today if he were to revert back to the person he used to be.

When we are forgiven by God and accepted into His family, we are not given a license to continue sinning.[5] When we know something is wrong and we do it anyway, it is never acceptable to God. It is forgivable, when we are truly sorry for it. But His grace and forgiveness never give us a go-ahead to continue in sinful behavior. Sometimes coming to God with something that we are ashamed of or struggling with involves confrontation—His Spirit convicting us to get the help we need and to make the necessary changes in our lives.

When Jesus talked to the Samaritan woman, He accepted her, but He did not excuse her lifestyle. Later, when Jesus came upon a woman accused of adultery, He refused to condemn her. But He didn't excuse her actions. In fact, He told her "From now on sin no more."[6] Again, our continued forgiveness is contingent upon our willingness to make the desired changes.

If you are struggling with a pattern of life that is destructive (dishonesty, compulsive behavior, substance abuse, addictions, habitual sin, and so on) God's desire for you is to get the help you need. Confess this problem to the Lord and then talk to a pastor or Christian counselor who can direct you, if possible, to a biblically based recovery program, support group, or accountability relationship. Depend on the Lord and the accountability group He leads you to in order to make a turnaround. Sometimes our acceptance depends greatly on our sincerity and desire to change. God knows our hearts. He knows when we truly desire forgiveness and change, and when we are just continuing to take advantage of grace.

When we truly desire acceptance in God's eyes, we can pray, as David did:

> Search me, O God, and know my heart; Try me and know my anxious thoughts; And see if there be any hurtful way in me, And lead me in the everlasting way.[7]

ACCEPTING THE TRUTH

No matter what is in our past, no matter what we may be struggling with in our present, God loves and accepts us like no other. When we realize how generously God has accepted us, it not only deepens our trust and intimacy with Him, but it enables us to more generously accept others, bringing harmony to our earthly relationships. Remember, since you didn't earn this acceptance from God (it was given to you freely), you can't lose it, either. His acceptance of you was there before the beginning of time and it will be there on into eternity. Living in the light of this acceptance can make you a confident, capable person of God as you realize that you are His creation, His pride and joy, His much-loved bride. So take heart, my friend, and stand tall. You and I are accepted by our Beloved. ❖

Chapter Notes:

1. John 4:5–26.

2. Romans 5:18-19.

3. See also Hebrews 8:12 and Hebrews 10:17.

4. Psalm 139:13, 15–16.

5. Romans 6:1-2 says, "Are we to continue in sin that grace might increase? May it never be!" See also verses 14–15.

6. John 8:1-11.

7. Psalm 139:23–24.

What is the Christian Life?
by Mark D. Roberts

Chapter:
What is the Christian Life?

Book:
After I Believe

Look for your coupons for this and other
featured titles in the back of this book.

After

"I Believe"

EXPERIENCING AUTHENTIC

CHRISTIAN LIVING

MARK D. ROBERTS

Author's Bio

Mark D. Roberts is senior pastor of Irvine
Presbyterian Church in Southern California
and teaches courses in New Testament at
Fuller Theological Seminary. Previously, he
served on the pastoral staff of Hollywood
Presbyterian Church with Lloyd Ogilvie.
He has earned A.B., M.A. and Ph.D. from
Harvard. The author of *Ezra, Nehemiah,
Esther* in the Communicator's
Commentary Series, Mark lives with
his wife, Linda, and two children in
Irvine, California.

What is the Christian Life?

by Mark D. Roberts

"I, Mike, take you, Allison ... As a gift from God ... To be my wedded wife ..." With such revered phrases, I lead earnest grooms to commit their lives to their radiant brides. Then I help the brides return the favor.

Often I'm caught up in the supreme sentiment of a wedding. But, I must confess, there are times when, observing a youthful couple as they gaze adoringly into each other's eyes, I want to shout, "Do you really know what you're getting into?"

Let me reassure you. I don't actually holler during wedding ceremonies. Besides, I don't really need to ask that question because I know the answer already. Do the bride and groom really know what they're getting into? Of course not. Nobody actually knows what marriage is all about before experiencing the unexpected joys and unforeseen sorrows of married life.

Yet those whom I marry have previously satisfied me with their rudimentary knowledge of marriage. In premarital counseling, I always ask couples, "What is marriage?" Answers vary, but they usually reflect several basic perspectives:

- Marriage is a friendship that lasts for a lifetime.
- Marriage is a business partnership.
- Marriage is a means to leave my own family and make a fresh start.
- Marriage is a gift from God.

Each of these answers captures a part of what marriage is all about. But each is also less than adequate, in my opinion.

If a couple begins marriage with an inadequate sense of marriage, they threaten the health and longevity of their relationship. For example, marriage is indeed like a business partnership in many ways. But if a spouse sees marriage *primarily* as a business arrangement, problems ensue when the cost-benefit ratio of the relationship falls below an acceptable range. What if a wife believes she is contributing more to the marriage than her husband and is receiving less benefit than her investment merits? If she views marriage simply as a business venture, she has a convincing reason to terminate the marriage partnership.

If, in contrast, two people see marriage as a divinely sealed, lifelong covenant between a man and a woman, they will form a solid foundation for a lasting, fruitful marriage. If they hold on to this vision during the inescapable frustrations of married life, they will have a much better chance of growing through conflict to enjoy the abundant blessings of wedded life. Having a correct understanding of marriage does not guarantee a successful marriage, but it certainly gets newlyweds headed in the right direction.

As with marriage, so it is with the Christian life. How we understand Christian living will impact the health and longevity of our relationship with God. The closer we come to seeing the Christian life accurately, the more likely we will be to thrive as Christians. Yet many of us have only the foggiest notion of Christian living.

When we first became Christians, most of us had almost no conception of the Christian life. By God's Spirit at work in us, we recognized how much we had messed up our lives by rejecting God's will for us. We perceived that a vast chasm separated us from God, and we realized that we could not bridge that gap by ourselves. We needed serious help, God's help, to clean up our lives and to get right with him. Then we heard the good news of what God had done for us in Jesus, who took upon himself our separation from God so that we could know God intimately, just as Jesus himself does (2 CORINTHIANS 5:21). All we had to do was acknowledge that our sin had corrupted our relationship with God and put our trust in Jesus to save us (ROMANS 3:21-26). As we trusted in him, in his death on the cross for us, we were reborn. We received new life from God above, the best sort of life there is, what the Bible calls "eternal life" (JOHN 3:1-16). From that moment on, we had the chance to live in a completely different way, relying on God's goodness, following God's directives, and enjoying God's presence.

Just as newborn infants have little idea of what life will be like, so it is for most of us who, through faith in Jesus, are reborn as spiritual babies. A few people trust their lives to Christ after an extensive process of examining Christianity. Most of us, however, begin our Christian journey with little idea of where the road leads or what our form of travel will be. God does not require the spiritual equivalent of premarital counseling before someone enters into a permanent covenant with Jesus Christ. Thus, as we begin to live in this relationship, we may well wonder, "What is the Christian life?"

BASIC IDEAS ABOUT THE CHRISTIAN LIFE

Like marriage, the Christian life is too complex to be captured fully in one simple statement. Biblical metaphors for the Christian life abound, including: walking (GALATIANS 5:16; EPHESIANS 4:1, 5:2), athletic competition (1 CORINTHIANS 9:24-27; PHILIPPIANS 3:12-14; HEBREWS 12:1), citizenship (PHILIPPIANS 3:20), stewardship (1 PETER 4:10), servanthood (2 CORINTHIANS 5:18; EPHESIANS 4:12), and apprenticeship (MATTHEW 28:19; LUKE 14:25-33).

Most Christians, even those who are new to the faith, have some rudimentary idea of the life they have begun. As a pastor, I have listened to scores of people describe their conceptions of Christianity. These notions usually reflect one of four basic ideas of the Christian life. Each of these captures one vital aspect of that life. But each also overlooks integral parts.

Idea #1: The Christian Life Is Reserved for Heaven

The assurance of heaven is one of the most precious possessions of any Christian. A couple of years ago, I sat near the bedside of Helen, a dear woman in my congregation whose body had just about given up after eighty plus years of life. Helen knew that her death was near, and she knew it with joyful confidence. "I'm ready to go," she admitted. "It's time. I want to see Jesus." What could be more reassuring than to know that when we die, we will not so much end life as begin a new, enhanced, everlasting life?

We stand on biblical bedrock when we embrace the hope of heaven: "For God has reserved a priceless inheritance for his children. It is kept in heaven for you, pure and undefiled, beyond the reach of change and decay" (1 PETER 1:4). But blissful existence after death does not fully capture the Christian life. The apostle Paul proclaims that, once we have been saved by grace through faith, we join Christ in heaven right now, in a spiritual sense (EPHESIANS 2:6). Jesus speaks of eternal life, that which we associate with afterlife, as a present and a future reality for those who believe in him (JOHN 5:24). Therefore, the Christian life is not only "pie in the sky when you die," to repeat a hackneyed phrase. Rather, the Heavenly Cook lets us stick our fingers into the batter of heaven while it's being prepared. The Christian life happens not just in the future but right now.

Idea #2: The Christian Life is Feeling Joy and Peace in the Lord

Sometimes new believers discover the present reality of the Christian life right away. Many converts, though certainly not all, tingle with joy in the seconds following their first step of faith. Others find their emotional burdens lifted as they taste "God's peace, which is far more wonderful than the human mind can understand" (PHILIPPIANS 4:7). This initial blush of emotion might linger for days, refreshed through corporate worship and private devotions. The dynamism of joy, so invigorating, healing, and empowering, can lead us to believe that feeling this joy is the essence of the Christian life.

Indeed, Jesus promises overflowing joy to those who live in him (JOHN 15:11). But we must beware of the tendency to reduce Christianity to feelings alone. The culture in which we live, with its loss of respect for truth, has enthroned feelings as the measure of all things. This emotional orientation to life has infected the Western world, including the church. In some quarters of the church, Jesus has become primarily the one who makes us feel better, not the one who saves us from our sin.

Christian living involves every aspect of our being, including our emotions. We are to love God with all that we are (MARK 12:30).

We must not reject the emotional dimension of Christian experience, but we shouldn't condense Christian living to emotions alone.

Idea #3: The Christian Life Is Believing the Right Things about God

According to the New Testament, joy and peace come as we believe in Jesus (ROMANS 15:13; 1 PETER 1:8). So, if these emotions do not constitute the core of the Christian life, but are gratifying adjuncts to it, is the Christian life primarily a matter of believing?

The Bible unabashedly proclaims the existence and magnitude of truth. Speaking through the Old Testament prophet Isaiah, God says, "I publicly proclaim bold promises. I do not whisper obscurities in some dark corner so no one can understand what I mean. And I did not tell the people of Israel to ask me for something I did not plan to give. I, the LORD, speak only what is true and right" (ISAIAH 45:19).

To such a truth-speaking God, the psalmist cries out, "Teach me your ways, O Lord, that I may live according to your truth!" (PSALM 86:11). The New Testament echoes this commitment to truth. Jesus says, "You are truly my disciples if you keep obeying my teachings. And you will know the truth, and the truth will set you free" (JOHN 8:31-32; SEE ALSO JOHN 14:6; 2 THESSALONIANS 2:13; AND 1 TIMOTHY 4:3).

We begin the Christian life by believing the "word of truth," the good news of what God has done in Jesus (EPHESIANS. 1:13 NRSV). We grow as Christians by "speaking the truth in love" (EPHESIANS. 4:15 MDR).[1] Abandoning the basic truth of God endangers both the correctness of our theology and the genuineness of our relationship with God (2 JOHN 1:9).

Christians care about right belief, what theologians call "orthodoxy." Consequently, we find ourselves increasingly alienated from a culture that denies the value or even the possibility of knowing truth. We do not affirm the popular, relativistic slogan, "It doesn't matter what you believe, as long as you believe it." For us it makes all the difference in the world what a person believes. Christians do not have faith in faith but faith in a God who has revealed himself in history, in human experience, in the Bible, and most of all in Jesus.

Yet right belief, as important as it is, does not sum up the whole Christian life. Christian faith is not just "believing that" but "believing in." Not only do we *believe that* Jesus died on the cross, but we also *believe in* him to forgive us. We trust him completely for our salvation. Christian faith is an act of mind and will.

Moreover, true faith must be expressed in action. Jesus said, "Anyone who listens to my teaching and obeys me is wise, like a person who builds a house on solid rock" (MATTHEW 7:24). So, genuine Christian faith involves *believing* key truths about God, *trusting* Christ personally for salvation, and *putting our belief and trust into action* each day.

Idea #4: The Christian Life Is Doing What God Commands

Throughout the Bible, God cares about what we do. His very first words to human beings tell us to do something: "Be fruitful, and multiply" (GENESIS 1:28 KJV). Throughout the Old Testament, God continues to give directions to the Israelites, even though he anticipates their inevitable disobedience. The Law and the prophets repeatedly call God's people to live rightly and to avoid sin. This emphasis continues in the New Testament, every book of which contains imperatives, with hundreds coming from the mouth of Jesus himself. The Bible contains a total of 5,953 verbs in the imperative mood. Obviously, God cares about what we do and assumes the right to tell us what to do.

Because the Bible frequently gives directions for living, believers in Jesus have been tempted to turn the Christian life into a to-do list of good works. It makes relating to God so much more predictable if we can enumerate and then check off everything we're required to do. This form of the Christian life can be mastered through astute time management.

Unfortunately for those of us who are drawn to this approach to Christian living, it contradicts the essence of God's work in our lives. We are saved by grace through faith, and we continue to live by grace, not by our best efforts (EPHESIANS 2:8-10; PHILIPPIANS 2:12-13). If we turn the Christian life into a list of works, we run the risk of nullifying God's grace (GALATIANS 2:20-21). If a to-do list becomes the essence of our Christian experience, we have lost our center in Christ.

THE CHRISTIAN LIFE AS INTIMATE FELLOWSHIP

The four common ideas outlined above capture crucial components of the Christian life but must not be equated with that life. Each is essential, but none is fully adequate by itself. We must keep looking for a concept broad enough to incorporate the diversity represented by the four common ideas, yet pointed enough to keep Jesus Christ at the center.

We find this concept in the opening chapter of the first letter of John in the New Testament. He begins by talking a lot about life, mentioning, "the Word of life," "life from God" and "eternal life" (1 JOHN 1:1-2). What is this multiform life? Or, better yet, *who* is this life? None other than Jesus Christ. In this identification of Jesus as life we hear echoes of the Gospel of John. There, as the Word of God, Jesus created physical life (JOHN 1:1-4, 10). As the Son of God, he is the source of "eternal life" (JOHN 3:16). As the Good Shepherd, he offers "life in all its fullness" (JOHN 10:10). Jesus is "the way, the truth, and the life," through whom we receive life that conquers death (JOHN 14:6; 11:25-26).

John's equation of Jesus with life is, of course, a figure of speech. It suggests an inseparable connection between him and the divine life, a life John identifies in his letter by the word "fellowship." He is writing about Jesus as eternal life "so that you may have fellowship with us. And our fellowship is with the Father and with his Son, Jesus Christ" (1 JOHN 1:3). If we know Jesus as the Word of life, we will enter into fellowship, the essence of the Christian life.

We often associate fellowship with informal friendliness. Many churches have a "fellowship hall," a place for casual conversation, often complemented with donuts and coffee (the American church's unofficial sacrament). But this casual sense of "fellowship" falls short of the meaning of the Greek word *koinonia*. This term, translated as "fellowship" in 1 John, means far more than spending time with friendly people. Among Greek speakers in the Roman Empire, *koinonia* was used for a business partnership. Early Christians used the word for their celebrations of the Lord's Supper, which we call "communion." Marriage could be called "the fellowship of life," and sexual intimacy between spouses could be called *koinonia*.[2] Clearly, *koinonia* implies a depth of relationship we don't usually associate with fellowship halls.

It's hard to find an English word that unites the various connotations of *koinonia*. "Fellowship," "partnership," and "sharing" highlight limited facets of the word's meaning. "Communion" gets much closer, but its religious tone limits the full sense of *koinonia*. The best translation I can conceive for *koinonia* uses two English words: "intimate fellowship." God's kind of life involves neither a casual relationship with him over donuts and coffee nor an exclusively religious moment when we "receive communion" in church, but deep fellowship with him at all times and in all places.

What a wonder! The Creator of heaven and earth seeks an intimate relationship with you and me. In our preoccupation with our own search for God, we easily forget that he has been searching for us too. That's the story of the Bible: God's search for humankind, God's effort to reestablish the fellowship between himself and his human creatures that was broken because of sin. Jesus Christ came to save us from sin and death so that we might have a close, lasting relationship with God. As the source of eternal life from God, Jesus welcomes us into *koinonia* with God—but not with God alone.

INTIMATE FELLOWSHIP WITH GOD AND GOD'S PEOPLE

The Christian life is intimate fellowship with God *and God's people*. John writes his letter so that his readers "may have fellowship with us" as well as "with the Father and with his Son" *(1 John 1:2-3)*. The human dimension of *koinonia* is essential to full Christian fellowship. John reiterates this point in 1 John 1:6-7, where "fellowship with God" is interchangeable with "fellowship with each other." You can't have one without the other because they are inescapably entwined.

The equation of fellowship with God and fellowship with God's people might seem surprising. Isn't the Christian life really about a relationship with God? Isn't the human dimension secondary in significance? If we had to choose between relationship with God and relationship with people, we'd rightly join up with God. But, by making this distinction, we miss the indivisibility of divine and human fellowship that's taught in the Bible. We echo the bias of our culture rather than the revealed word of God.

Many popular versions of the Christian life separate that which the Bible holds together so consistently. American individualism has infected our conceptions of Christianity. All that really matters, we are told, is our personal relationship with God. But in biblical perspective, that personal relationship always has corporate implications. We tend to equate personal with private, but the Bible links personal and corporate. A genuine personal relationship with God draws us into genuine personal relationships with people.

Consider the vast sweep of biblical revelation. When God creates a solitary man, God says that it is not good for him to be alone. Therefore, God forms a partner for the man (GENESIS 2). God promises to bless Abraham, not all by his lonesome, but by making him the father of a nation and by blessing all the families of the earth through him (GENESIS 12). God sets his people free from Egypt not so each Israelite will please God individually but so the congregation of the Israelites will be a "holy nation" together (EXODUS 19:6).

Turning to the New Testament, Jesus prayed for those who would one day believe in him, that we might be "perfected into one," even as he was one with his heavenly Father (JOHN 17:22-23). Our Savior died on the cross for our personal salvation and to create one new humanity between formerly divided peoples (EPHESIANS 2). God's ultimate plan is to "bring everything together" in Christ (EPHESIANS 1:10). In New Testament visions of the afterlife, you will not end up sitting on your own private cloud playing a harp. Rather, you will join a vast heavenly choir, worshipping God in a way that is intensely personal and inescapably corporate (REVELATION 7:9-10). That's not all we will do in heaven, but whatever else we do, it won't involve an eternity of playing spiritual solitaire. C. S. Lewis writes that isolation from other people is an essential characteristic of hell, not heaven.[3]

One of the highlights of my life occurred when I was three and a half years old. The spring afternoon was warm as my parents drove across town to finish a process that had taken many long months. When we finally arrived at our destination, I clutched a special teddy bear in one hand while nervously grabbing my mother's fingers in the other. After walking down a long corridor, we stopped at a room. It was sparsely furnished, with a plain wooden crib in the corner. In that crib was a three-month-old baby, my parents' newly adopted son, Gary. My heart raced as I peered at him for the very first time. Dangling the teddy bear before his giant blue eyes, I swelled with pride when Gary smiled at me. This was not just my parents' son. He was my brother.

This remained true throughout our lives, whether we liked it or not. I was still Gary's brother four years after his adoption when I ditched him in the hills above our home and he was lost for hours. Gary was still my brother when he clobbered me on the head with the sharp claw of a hammer just to see what would happen to my head. We were joyfully brothers when we stood together in each other's wedding ceremonies and shared the wonder of holding each other's babies only moments after they were born.

Through the best of times and the worst of times, fellowship with our heavenly Father includes fellowship with his other children. Eternal life is personal life and shared life. It is intimate fellowship with God and, necessarily, with God's people.

INTIMATE FELLOWSHIP AND FORGIVENESS

Once we experience genuine *koinonia*, we begin to live in a completely different way. Before we had fellowship with God, we lived in spiritual darkness, blinded by our sin (*1 John 1:6*). But when we entered into *koinonia* with God, we began to live in the light of divine truth (*1 John 1:7*). It's impossible, John explains, to have fellowship with God and to continue in a lifestyle of pervasive sin. This does not mean, however, that Christians are sinless, that we always live up to God's standards. When we do fall short, and at times we all do, we don't grit our teeth and strain for greater perfection. Rather, we come before God with an honest admission of our failures: "If we confess our sins to him, he is faithful and just to forgive us and to cleanse us from every wrong" (1 JOHN 1:9).

I am thankful that John mentions sin and forgiveness in his discussion of the Christian life. Even though my theology warns against it, my heart keeps trying to turn the Christian life into a matter of perfect performance. A part of me thinks I will finally live as a Christian if I only try hard enough, if I only do all the right things. Of course, I fall short of this unrealistic goal, both by failing to do many right things and by doing many wrong ones instead. Yet my shortcomings do not separate me from fellowship with God because the blood of Jesus his Son cleanses me from all sin (1 JOHN 1:7). The Christian life is not a matter of perfection, but process, not performance for God, but relationship with a God who offers forgiveness and cleansing through Christ.

INTIMATE FELLOWSHIP INCLUDES THE FOUR COMMON IDEAS ABOUT THE CHRISTIAN LIFE

The concept of intimate fellowship encompasses the four ideas of the Christian life that we examined above. According to *Idea #1*, the Christian life is being in heaven after death. This notion correctly identifies a central hope of our faith, but it puts too much emphasis on postmortem existence, overlooking the present reality of Christian living. When we think of the Christian life as intimate fellowship with God and God's people, we need to understand that this fellowship *begins* the moment we believe in Jesus and *extends* forever. Our *koinonia* continues beyond death, though we don't have to wait until we die to experience it.

Intimate fellowship also clarifies the biblical sense of heaven. Though Scripture speaks of heaven as a place, it is, most importantly, the experience of God's presence. To be "in heaven" is to be "with God," in the company of God's people (1 THESSALONIANS 4:17; PHILIPPIANS 1:23). For this reason, heaven is a present reality for Christians because we already live with God through Christ (EPHESIANS 2:6) and already have joined the heavenly assembly (HEBREWS 12:22-23).

Idea #2 pictures the Christian life as feeling joy and peace in the Lord. Although this notion overemphasizes certain emotions, these feelings often proceed from fellowship with Christ and participation in the Christian community. Jesus makes this clear when he says that abiding in him—another way of talking about *koinonia*—will lead to overflowing joy (JOHN 15:11). Moreover, when in times of worry we share in fellowship with God through prayer, often receiving the supportive prayers of our Christian family, we "will experience God's peace, which is far more wonderful than the human mind can understand" (PHILIPPIANS 4:7).

Proponents of Idea #3 highlight the content of faith. For them, the Christian life is believing the right things about God. From John's perspective, right belief leads to genuine *koinonia* but is not equivalent to it. We must correctly understand who Christ is as the "Word of life" so that we might live in fellowship. *Koinonia* is not some squishy, subjective relationship with a god of our own formulation. It is a substantive, spiritual relationship with the one God who has revealed himself in Jesus Christ, and with all of those who confess a common faith in Christ.

According to Idea #4, Christian living is doing what God commands. As we have seen, true fellowship with God influences our whole life. Our way of walking—our daily behavior—will reflect our relationship with God. We will do what God commands as a result of our intimacy with him, but without separating our good works from their divine source. Because the Christian life is not equivalent to obedience, individual acts of disobedience do not kill that life. Our relationship with God depends on his grace and not on our acts of obedience. Therefore, occasional sin is more like a bad flu than a terminal illness. *Koinonia* with God heals our sickness and vaccinates us from the virus of sin. Moreover, God places us in fellowship with other Christians so that we might help one another avoid sin and live in a way that pleases God.

INTIMATE FELLOWSHIP AND COMPLETE JOY

Failure to engage in fellowship with other Christians won't cause you to lose your salvation or to be hit by a divine lightning bolt. It will, however, keep you from experiencing the fullness of the Christian life, including the joy of the Lord. John writes his first letter not only to promote *koinonia* but also so that "that *our* joy will be complete" (*I JOHN 1:4, ITALICS ADDED*). Although John already has deep fellowship with God, his full joy depends to a great extent on his fellowship with other Christians. Likewise, only if we share together in our relationship with the Lord will our joy be complete.

I learned this lesson last summer when my family and I spent a week in the High Sierra of California. One afternoon I set off by myself for a sightseeing hike to Sherwin Lakes. Without my young children tagging along, nothing interrupted my brisk pace or my alpine meditations. Sheer granite peaks, pungent cedar forests, shimmering alpine lakes—I was just about in heaven. Could I be more joyful than this?

The next day I loaded my backpack with all the provisions for an overnight stay at Sherwin Lakes. This time I didn't go alone. My six-year-old son, Nathan, accompanied me for his first backpacking trip. With him as my partner, I didn't hike as quickly as I had the day before. I didn't see as many sights as I had seen when walking alone or have the leisure to appreciate them without distraction. But my joy was even more supreme than it had been because it was now shared. I could show Nathan the cliffs that had stirred my soul earlier, and he could marvel at them with me: "Dad, they're just hunormous!" Nathan helped me get pleasure from natural trifles I had overlooked just the day before: pine cones, water bugs, and sticks just right for throwing. Every aspect of that trip thrilled my son, whether we were gathering wood for the campfire or bundling up in our sleeping bags. My joy was magnified through fellowship with someone I love.

That's the way it is in the Christian life. I've seen it again and again; *koinonia* with God *and* God's people leads to complete joy. ❖

PRACTICAL QUESTIONS AND ANSWERS

1. *"How can I begin to experience intimate fellowship with God and God's people?"*

    Christian koinonia comes as a result of trusting Jesus Christ as Savior and Lord. If you have taken this step of faith, you have already begun to experience intimate fellowship. If you have not put your trust in Jesus, I'd urge you to do so.

2. *"I've always thought the Christian life was really a matter of my personal relationship with God, so I haven't ever become a part of a church. How can I find a good church?"*

    There's no simple answer to this question. First, let me urge you to pray about it. If you faithfully seek the Lord's guidance, he will lead you to a church that is right for you. Second, talk with Christians who live near you. Ask about their churches and consider their recommendations. Most people find a church through friends and family members. Third, check the local Yellow Pages or church web sites. You can find out a lot of information this way.

    When you're considering a church, look for evidence that it honors Jesus Christ as Lord and Savior. When you visit the church, see if the worship facilitates intimate fellowship with God, if the preaching is biblically based, and if the people are friendly. Look for programs that might help you grow in full koinonia. If you have children, be sure to check out ministries for children and youth.

    Before you decide to join a church, I encourage you to meet with the pastor. (In a large church, you might meet with one of the associates, not the senior pastor.) Bring a list of the questions that matter most to you. Remember: No church is perfect.

CHAPTER NOTES

1. When well-known English translations of the bible are not accurate enough for the purposes of this book, I will supply my own translation, noted by my initials MDR.

2. Henry Liddell and Robert Scott, revised by Henry Jones, A *Greek-English Lexicon* (Oxford: Clarendon Press, 1968), 970.

3. C.S. Lewis, *The Great Divorce* (New York: Touchstone, 1996), 13–26.

How Do I Pray?
by Stormie Omartian and Jack Hayford

Chapter:
The Power of One

Book:
Power of Praying Together

Look for your coupons for this and other
featured titles in the back of this book.

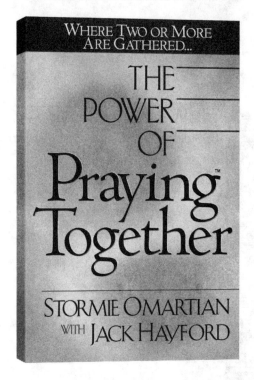

Author's Bio

Stormie Omartian is the bestselling author
of the The Power of a Praying books (more
than 5 million copies sold), *Stormie*, and
Just Enough Light for the Step I'm On.
Stormie and her husband, Michael, have
been married for 30 years and have three
grown children. Jack Hayford is the
Chancellor of The King's College and
Seminary in Los Angeles. A pastor, author,
and songwriter, Jack has been married to
his wife, Anna, for 49 years. They have
four children and eleven grandchildren.

Excerpted from *The Power of Praying Together* ©2003
by Stormie Omartian with Jack Hayford. Used by
permission of Harvest House Publishers. All
rights reserved.

How Do I Pray?
by Stormie Omartian and Jack Hayford

One Sunday morning Pastor Jack stood before the congregation and said he wanted to share an area of failing he had in his life. I knew right away it was not going to be an earth-shattering revelation. He was not getting a divorce, and I was sure he had not robbed a bank, murdered anyone, or committed adultery. So I couldn't imagine what he was going to say.

He had always been very candid about his own frailties and humanity, which was one of the things that endeared him to so many. He would share from his heart and experience for the purpose of helping us to grow.

What he told us was that he had been awakened by the alarm and had gotten up to pray when the Lord spoke to his heart saying, "You have forgotten the discipline of daily devotional habit."

But that's what I am up doing, he thought.

"I didn't feel that God was mad at me," he told us. "It was more like the Lord had something to teach me. And I understood what God was dealing with me about. I had learned so much about intercession and worship in the immediately preceding years that I was spending less *intimate* time with Jesus. It was a call to go back to the childlike basics of presenting myself to the Lord."

It wasn't that Pastor Jack had stopped being a person of prayer. He prayed all the time. He always responded to what he called "Holy Spirit-prompted intercession." Whenever the Holy Spirit signaled a prompting to pray, Pastor Jack stopped whatever he was doing at the time and prayed about that. He consulted with the Lord regularly and sought Him for wisdom about everything. He was a praise and worship person consistently, and he prayed daily in prayer groups with other people. No one could have accused Pastor Jack of not being a praying person. After all, he was in the middle of praying when God spoke to him about this. But he had lost the essential discipline of a daily devotional prayer time.

From his teens through college and the early years of his public ministry, Pastor Jack had learned to be with the Lord every morning.

"I don't know when it changed," he explained. "I couldn't tell you an exact time. I didn't one day say that I'm not going to get up and pray anymore. It just got sporadic and irregular, and finally I'd lost the discipline. But something has come clear to my understanding, and I am persuaded that it will never be lost again."

Most of us can relate to what he described. We've all struggled with maintaining a consistent and regular prayer time alone with God at some point in our lives. However, at the time he spoke about it to our congregation, I was faithfully doing it. I would get up early every day and go before the Lord to pray with Him alone. It was no struggle for me then because I had been in such bad shape when I received the Lord. I had come out of a life of drugs, alcohol, the occult, depression, fear, anxiety, and unforgiveness, and I knew I couldn't get through a day without being with God first. Hearing Pastor Jack talk about his struggle amazed me because I realized if it could happen to him, it could happen to anyone—including me.

And then one day, a long time later, it did.

A few years ago my devotional prayer life began to slip. I had been extremely sick off and on for about five months. Each time I had an attack of nausea, vomiting, and severe stomach pain, my husband took me to the emergency room, but no one could find anything wrong with me.

I tried different hospitals, doctors, and specialists, but there were still no answers. Finally in the middle of one very miserable night, I felt something explode in my body so violently that I knew I would die if I didn't get help immediately. My husband rushed me to the hospital again because it was obvious I didn't have time to wait for an ambulance.

In the emergency room I endured a number of excruciating tests, but still no one could find out what was wrong with me. Finally the specialist called in a surgeon who was courageous enough to say, "We don't know what's causing your pain and sickness, but I believe your appendix has ruptured. I'm going to take you into surgery and if I'm wrong, I'll find out what the problem is."

As it turned out, he was right. After I awakened from the anesthetic he told me, "In another hour I would not have been able to save you."

I was in such bad shape that the surgeon had to make a huge vertical incision from the sternum to the pubic bone. And worst of all, he had to leave the incision open rather than sew it up. That's because it had to be opened every day and cleaned out, and tubes had to be left in to keep it draining by means of a special wound vacuum machine. The wound was never sewed up, and it took five months for it to close itself from the inside out.

During those months of illness before the surgery, I had gotten out of the habit of praying first thing in the morning. Because I never felt well, I had to sleep, eat, and work whenever I was able to. The sicker I became, the harder it was to stay on any kind of normal schedule and the more difficult it was to pray consistently. I continued praying for my husband and children and a few close friends and family members, and of course for my healing, but that was about it.

After my appendix ruptured, however, I had difficulty praying anything beyond the "Help me, Jesus! Heal me, Lord!" kind of desperation prayers. The recovery was so gruesome and agonizing that it was hard to concentrate, and many times I wondered if I would ever be able to do anything normal again. But I felt the sustaining prayers of other people lifting me up and keeping me from getting discouraged and losing heart in the midst of it all. I was grateful for them because they carried me through that time.

Two months into my recovery period, however, I suddenly started having the same kind of abdominal pain and nausea I'd had in the months prior to my appendix rupturing. I couldn't believe that after all I had been through, I still had not gotten rid of the problem. Here I was, not even half healed from the first surgery and still not walking well because of a huge gaping hole in my body, and I had to go back into surgery again. This time the doctor had to remove my gallbladder, which he now believed was the problem from the beginning.

My recovery from the second surgery was extremely slow, as if my body were saying, "This was one too many!"

My prayer time and Bible reading had been continually slipping, but after this second surgery, both fell off dramatically. I'd had so much anesthetic and been on so many drugs that it was hard to concentrate. I read the Bible a little every day, but I felt as though I were reading through a thick fog. Plus, I was in so much pain that I couldn't sit up for very long at a time. I felt frail because I couldn't do anything by myself, not even the basics. The extent of my prayer life centered entirely around healing and surviving the day.

Of course, I had to cancel all speaking engagements and book deadlines that year, and I felt guilty about letting so many people down. But Pastor Jack said, "If a soldier is wounded in battle, during his recovery time no one expects him to be out doing daily drills he is in no condition to do. We can become casualties in the spiritual battle sometimes, and though we are still in the army, the agenda is to get well."

I was grateful to still be in God's army.

In spite of the prayers of other people sustaining me through that time, I still felt empty in my spirit. I realized how much I had fallen out of the discipline of being alone with the Lord in prayer every day. And it went beyond having sickness as an excuse. I was completely out of the habit. As a result, I had a hard time hearing God's voice speaking to my soul. I knew that I, like Pastor Jack, had to start learning this discipline all over again.

When I was well enough, I went back and reviewed all that Pastor Jack had taught us that day on devotional prayer. I gained a renewed sense of perspective, and I was reminded of some things I had forgotten along the way. Things I want to share with you in this chapter. The prayers of others are vital and can help us survive, but to really sense the fullness of God's presence in our lives, we have to be alone with Him every day.

The more time we spend alone with God, the more powerful our prayers will be when we pray with others. It's not that praying with other people is less effective than praying alone. There is great power when we pray in numbers, and convincing you of that is the very reason for writing this book. But praying with other people *without* spending time alone with God will compromise the effectiveness and power of your prayers. In other words, you will be a more effective prayer partner if you have not neglected your time alone with the Lord.

When I used to play the violin, I found that I was a greater asset to the orchestra I played with if I practiced on my own. The more I played alone, the better I was with the group. It's the same way with prayer.

WHAT IS PRAYER, EXACTLY?

Prayer is communicating with God. Each time we pray, we come in contact with God in a profound and life-changing way.

When we face hopeless situations in our relationships, businesses, work, finances, health, emotions, or children, praying to the God of hope can change the situation. When we struggle with such things as unrealized dreams, an unfulfilling life, lack of mental clarity, or emotional pain, we have access to the God who can touch every area of our lives to transform them and bring about wholeness. He wants to reach down and touch *us*, but first we have to reach up and touch *Him* in prayer. When we pray, we're saying, "I know You are real, Lord, and I want to spend time with You."

Prayer is praising and worshiping God for who He is. This takes our focus off of ourselves and places it on Him. It positions Him first in our hearts and allows Him full access to our lives. Pastor Jack taught us that there are two sides to prayer. There is the *fellowship side* and the *partnership side*.

"The fellowship side of prayer is when we come just to be with God in the intimacy of relationship," he explained. "The partnership side is when we exercise the responsibilities of partnering with Him to see the reintroduction of His rule into our circumstances. Worship, praise, adoration, and exaltation are an important part of fellowship with God, but it is also a means of partnering with Him to drive back the darkness."

When we pray we're saying, "Lord, You are wonderful, almighty, all-powerful, the God and Creator of all things. I exalt You above everything, and I worship You for who You are."

Prayer is telling God we love and adore Him. It's coming humbly before God and speaking to Him the way we would to someone we dearly love. Prayer is telling God how grateful we are that He loved us before we were even aware He existed. When we pray, we're saying, "I love You, Lord, and I thank You for loving me."

Prayer is telling God we need Him. When we *don't* pray, it implies that we think we can handle everything on our own. But the truth is we can't handle *anything* on our own. We need God for everything. We need Him to save us, forgive us, heal us, deliver us, fill us, restore us, redeem us, free us, guide us, protect us, lift us above our limitations, and move us into the plans and purposes He has for us. We can't get there without Him. When we pray we're saying, "I can't live without You, Lord. If You don't intervene in my life, nothing good is going to happen."

Prayer is making our requests known to God. It's sharing with Him all that is on our hearts, knowing that He cares about each one of those things. God promises to give us all we need, but we still have to ask. Just as He instructs us to ask for our daily bread, we are to come before Him and ask for whatever else we need too.

Prayer is not a last resort, something we turn to when all else fails, a stab at something in the dark, or an exercise in positive thinking to try and make ourselves feel better. Prayer changes things. But we have to talk to God about the things that need to be changed. Prayer is acknowledging that, even though what we are praying for may seem impossible to us, with God all things are possible (MATTHEW 19:26). When we pray, we're saying, "Lord, I have these needs, and I know You care about them and will hear my requests."

Prayer is serving God His way. It's not just about us getting *our* needs met, although that's an important part of prayer. God's plan is to rule earth through His delegated authority. That's us— we who believe in Him. God wants us to bring His kingdom to bear upon the issues of the earth. God has things for each of us to do, and they start with prayer.

Pastor Jack said, "If we think that a future in heaven is the sum of Christ's gift to us, we will live out a spiritually immature existence, pointed toward heaven, but pointless on earth."

Pastor Jack was never one to be vague about the truth.

"People need to understand why God doesn't just do everything on His own initiative," he said. "It goes back to God giving the responsibility for governing earth's affairs to humankind (GENESIS 1:26,28). He ordained that everything on earth would be determined by human choice. 'The heaven, even the heavens, are the LORD's; but the earth He has given to the children of men' (PSALM 115:16). But it only works when man keeps in relationship with God. The will of God and the works and power of God do not simply flow without an invitation into earth's scene. The Lord has transmitted to His people the responsibility of inviting the presence of the kingdom. It's not because God *can't* do something without us, but because He *won't* do it without us."

Some people believe that God is going to do whatever He is going to do no matter what, so there is no reason to pray. But the truth is there are things God will not do on earth except in answer to prayer.

"There are people who don't like this idea because they don't want the responsibility that it carries with it," said Pastor Jack. "They just want God to do what He's going to do. But God wants to grow up His sons and daughters, and He waits to move where they invite Him to move. That's what He *wants* to do! His decree is clear about this. But we need to be equally clear: This emphasis does not minimize the sovereignty of God. The power is all His! But views of God's sovereignty can overlook His will to involve His children in advancing His redemptive purposes. The Sovereign God Almighty has decreed that what takes place on earth shall be realized through the willing activities of people who submit to His will and invoke His presence and power."

This explains why the earth is in the mess it's in. God has delegated everything to man, and we have reaped what we've sown. God has determined, and chosen to abide by, this sovereign decree: He works on earth in answer to our prayers, and we have neglected to pray.

The good news is that it's never too late to sow the seeds of prayer and gain a different harvest than the seeds of sin and death we have produced in our world. We can invite God's power to enter specific situations right now. When we pray, we're saying "Lord, I want to be Your instrument through which You do what You want to do on this planet. Help me to pray according to Your will, so that *Your* will is done on earth."

This is what it means to pray "Your kingdom come, Your will be done."

WHAT MAKES PRAYING SO HARD SOMETIMES?

There are a surprising number of people who believe in God but do not pray very much. They say they find praying difficult. I took a short survey of the people who mentioned feeling that way, and here are some of the reasons they gave. See if you recognize yourself in any of these.

"I find praying difficult because there are many different kinds of prayer, and I'm not sure how to pray." It's true. There are many kinds of prayers. There is *praise* and *worship*, which is glorifying God. There is *confession*, where we open our hearts to God and ask Him to reveal all that is in them so He can cleanse them. There is *petition*, where we tell Him of our needs and the concerns of our heart. There is *intercession*, where we pray for others. How do we know which one to do and when to do it? What if we do the wrong thing? When we have more questions than answers about prayer, praying becomes too complex in our minds and we tend to avoid it. But God is not asking us to take a theology course before we come to Him. He simply wants us to share honestly from our heart. The right way to pray comes out of a heart that loves God and desires to communicate with Him.

"I find praying difficult because I don't do it very well." People are often hesitant to pray because they expect too much of themselves. They have heard the eloquence and power of the prayers of certain others, and they feel they must live up to that. They think they need to sound like the greatest preacher on earth.

But God looks on our heart not our proficiency as a public speaker. Besides, nobody starts out as a powerful intercessor. We all begin with simple prayers that come from the heart. And there is nothing wrong with praying a prayer that someone else wrote, or saying a memorized prayer if it's a prayer your heart resonates to and you believe God could answer it. Just because someone else wrote the prayer doesn't mean God will not hear it coming from you. Start with that and grow from there.

"I find praying difficult because down deep I doubt whether prayer really works." Many people doubt that God is actually listening when they pray. And if He is listening, they think, *Why would God listen to me? He is the God of the universe, and I'm just a tiny speck in comparison.* Or they may think prayer works, but just not *their* prayers. They don't understand how God has set it up. They think, *Why bother to ask?* But He has set Himself to act in response to our asking.

"I find praying difficult because I feel I am not good enough to deserve an answer." Many people feel God is not pleased with them because they have fallen short of what they should be or do. Because of their failures, or what they have *not* done, they think they are not worthy of His time. The truth is none of us is worthy. None of us have done all that we should. We have all fallen short. Only Jesus makes us worthy. Only the grace of God and the enabling power of the Holy Spirit helps us to live His way. God is loving and compassionate. He is not waiting to strike us with lightning because we didn't do everything right. He is waiting for us to come to Him and confess our sins so He can *make* everything right.

"I find praying difficult because I see God as being distant." People who don't really know God well think of Him as being a long way off, and they believe their prayers have to travel too far to reach Him. They envision their prayers evaporating in the air immediately after they pray them. If you feel your prayers are not powerful enough to make it up to God's ears, you are not alone. You would be surprised at how many people feel that way. But when we receive Jesus, He becomes the mediator between us and God.

He has also given us the Holy Spirit, who is now living *in* us, thereby giving us a direct line to the Lord. Our prayers don't have to travel far at all.

"I find praying difficult because I am not sure I am praying in line with God's will." People often fear that if they were to ask for the wrong thing, it could mean trouble. They fear they might be punished for an inaccurately conceived prayer. Or that their prayer might be answered and produce a bad thing because they ask unwisely.

"The primary thing to understand about God's will is this—He *wills* that we should pray!" explained Pastor Jack. "We aren't called to analyze everything perfectly or pray excellently, but to bring our heart cry and limited perceptions to Him who is perfect and excellent and rest these matters with Him. We don't have to fear that inept praying may somehow sneak up on God's blind side and cause Him to inadvertently answer a prayer that doesn't serve the purposes of His will. An imperfect prayer won't cause a cosmic accident by slipping into heaven and sliding through the machinery of God's providence without His knowing. God will never find Himself awkwardly glancing toward earth and wondering, 'How did I ever let that prayer get answered?' "

No matter how experienced we are in prayer, we will never be perfect in our praying. We won't always have full understanding of the way God wants us to pray in every situation. But we don't have to know His perfect will *before* we pray. We can find it *as* we pray.

"Ask boldly. Ask largely. Ask in faith," Pastor Jack instructed us. "Ask as His child and then praise Him in the confidence He will work His will. But ask!"

The bottom line is that it's God's *will* for us to pray. We don't have to worry about whether it is His will to *answer* the way we prayed. God isn't going to be forced into answering something that is not His will. And we don't have to worry about asking for too much, because God doesn't have a limited supply of resources. He will not run out of anything. The solution to praying according to God's will is to always say, "Lord, may Your will be done in this matter."

"I find praying difficult because it requires too much of my time to be effective." Often people believe that in order to be an effective praying person, they have to spend hours a day in prayer the way great prayer warriors of history have done. While it's true that the more time you spend in prayer, the more you can pray about and the more answers to prayer you will see, it doesn't mean that a quick prayer will be less likely to get answered. God hears every word we pray, especially when it is from a pure and loving heart. "The effective, fervent prayer of a righteous man avails much" (JAMES 5:16). Every prayer counts, no matter how little time it took to pray it.

WHAT MAKES PRAYER WORK?

Prayer works because of what Jesus did. God created the earth, and then He created man to rule over it. Man lost his rule of the earth because of disobedience to God's laws. Satan gained control, and his goal is to destroy God's purpose for every person. God sent His Son, Jesus, to die for our sins and break the power of the enemy. In other words, Jesus took the penalty for man's disobedience, which is death, so those who believe in Him can live fruitfully on earth and spend eternity with God.

When Jesus rose from the dead, He commissioned everyone who believes in Him to *destroy* the rulership of the enemy and restore rulership to man. This is done through prayer.

When we pray we are applying Jesus' victory through the cross, taking the rule away from Satan and establishing the rule of God. In that way we stop the devil's work and establish the Lord's will. We take things that are wrong and make them right.

God doesn't want us just waiting around for Jesus to come back or for us to die and go to heaven. There are things He has for us to do in the meantime. He wants us to expose the enemy's lies and proclaim God's truth. He wants us to bring down the enemy's strongholds and set the captives free. He wants us to bring health where there is sickness, love where there is fear, forgiveness where there is condemnation, revelation where there is spiritual blindness, and wholeness where there is a shattered life. God's

Word reveals that this can be accomplished when we pray.

Prayer works because we live God's way. In order to get our prayers answered, we need to walk in obedience to God's laws. "Whatever we ask we receive from Him, because we keep His commandments and do those things that are pleasing in His sight" (1 JOHN 3:22). For starters, we need to love God with all our heart, soul, mind, and strength, and love others as ourselves (MARK 12:30-31). You may be thinking that this is enough to disqualify you right there. But God is merciful in this too, because we can pray about these issues as well. He will even help us to obey if we ask Him.

Remember, answers to prayer are not earned by our obedience. But our privilege to pray boldly is rooted in our relationship with Father God. And He has called us to walk as obedient children.

Prayer works because we don't hesitate to ask. God wants us to be bold in our asking. Being bold isn't stomping into the throne room of God and demanding what we think we deserve, but it is recognizing that God wants to do above and beyond what we think possible (EPHESIANS 3:20). This knowledge makes us courageous to ask God to do great things in us, through us, and around us.

Jesus said, "Which of you shall have a friend, and go to him at midnight and say to him, 'Friend, lend me three loaves; for a friend of mine has come to me on his journey, and I have nothing to set before him'; and he will answer from within and say, 'Do not trouble me; the door is now shut, and my children are with me in bed; I cannot rise and give to you'? I say to you, though he will not rise and give to him because he is his friend, yet because of his persistence he will rise and give him as many as he needs" (LUKE 11:5-8). This suggests that we not only ask persistently, but boldly as well.

I once had someone tell me they prayed only about the big stuff because they didn't want to waste any of their prayers on small things, as if God only allows us a certain number of prayer requests per lifetime so we had better make our prayers count. God says we are to ask continually—to pray without ceasing. Not like a chant or saying the same thing over and over, but praying *all* the time about *everything*, knowing that God has no limits and is never too busy or preoccupied. He is always ready to hear from us. He wants us to ask because He wants to answer.

Prayer works because God has set it up that way. The way God works His purposes in this world is through people who believe in Jesus. God says that if we pray, He will move on our behalf. And He will not only move, He will do what is impossible for us.

"There has long been a debate between human responsibility and divine sovereignty," explained Pastor Jack. "To some, an emphasis on the responsibility of man suggests that eternal issues are sacrificed on the altar of man's obvious imperfection. To others, an emphasis on divine sovereignty suggests a deterministic universe in which God's will irresistibly makes everything happen. Too much of human responsibility produces an erratic world; too much of divine sovereignty, a fatalistic one."

Maybe we can't settle this issue to everyone's satisfaction, but we can at least agree that God has assigned us free will and He wants us to take charge of our part of this world in prayer. It begins in the prayer closet alone with Him.

WHAT CAN I DO TO MAINTAIN A DAILY PRAYER HABIT?

Because our culture idolizes the intellect, we don't often give value to prayer. We give greater value to reading and knowing the Bible intellectually. We would rather study the Bible because we can verify that we have covered a certain amount of ground. We can see what we have accomplished. But when we pray, we can't always see results right away. It's not a matter of disqualifying the importance of the intellect or our Bible study, it's a matter of our giving more time and value to prayer than we do.

I have been guilty of doing that myself, and that's why I have found it is better for me to pray first, *before* I read the Bible. When I start my devotional time by reading the Bible, I find it's hard to stop reading and allow enough time for prayer. But if I *pray* first, I will still read the Bible at some time during the day.

The day Pastor Jack spoke to us regarding his daily devotional habit, he taught us a practical way to structure our prayer time so that it would be more effective.

"Don't try to decide *how much* time you will devote to prayer or you will feel defeated if you can't live up to it," he instructed us. "It will become a task rather than a point of entry into devotional relationship with the living God. If you say you want to spend 30 minutes and you only pray for 15, you will feel like you failed. And feelings of failure are defeating in your efforts to have consistent prayer. If you don't set a time goal, it will never become a bondage to you—it will be a rejoicing to you instead."

Of course, we do need to determine what time each day we can be with God alone or the opportunity will slip through our fingers. I have found that it is best to pray in the morning when I first get up. If I don't do it then, it becomes much harder later, and I find myself struggling to have something more than a pray-and-run time. But it might be better for you at midmorning, lunchtime, sometime in the afternoon, or in the evening after dinner. I've tried having my main prayer time before I go to bed, but I am usually so tired by then that I spend a lot less time and I am not as clear thinking. Also, doing it then doesn't provide the advantage of having the day covered from the beginning. Regardless of when you do it, the point is to *allow* time for daily prayer so it becomes a good habit.

Ask God to *help* you carve out the time you need to spend with Him. He will show you things you can eliminate from your schedule, or at least shorten to the point of giving you an extra 20 to 30 minutes. I have found that if I can get on my knees and pray *before* I do much else, then my day is not off and running without me while I am trying to catch up. Just as you would never leave the house in the morning without brushing your teeth, it should also be that you wouldn't think of starting your day without being alone with God—even if it is only for a few minutes. If you only get a short time with God in the morning and then try to fit in a more extensive time later, you have at least started the day on the right track.

It is good to have some paper and a pencil handy when coming before God so that you can write down what He speaks to your heart in your prayer time. He may remind you of something you would otherwise have forgotten. He might bring to mind something you need to do that you would not have thought of. These kinds of things make your life easier and less confusing or haphazard.

Your personal prayer time with God is the foundation for all other kinds of effective prayer. It's not that you *can't* pray with other people until you have prayed alone with God. If that were the case, most of us would not even be saved. Nor would we have experienced the healing, deliverance, or restoration we have due to the prayers of others for us. And we've all had times where the troubles in our lives were so great that we were sustained only by the prayers of others. But eventually, in order to move on in the things of God, we have to establish our own personal prayer time with the Lord.

WHAT DO I DO NOW THAT I'M ON MY KNEES?

I have found that it is much harder to stay focused in prayer when you have only a vague idea of what you are doing. If you have a plan of some sort when you pray, it helps you to get down to prayer more quickly and experience a more fruitful prayer time. Below are some steps I learned from Pastor Jack, plus what I learned through experience, that have really helped me to pray with clear purpose. They will help you get started, and you can go on from there as the Holy Spirit leads. You may even end up spending the whole time on just *one* of these steps, and that is fine. The point is to get you before the Lord, where all prayer begins.

Step 1: Acknowledge God as your heavenly Father.

Say, *"Lord, I come before You today and thank You that You are my heavenly Father."* This establishes your relationship with God in the clearest of terms, because this is who God ultimately is to you.

Step 2: Praise God for who He is and what He has done.

Say, *"Lord, I praise You for who You are and all that You have done."*

Then praise Him for everything else that comes to your mind. Recognize how much you have to praise God for every single moment of your life.

Do you ever have days where everything seems to go wrong? Does it ever feel that your whole life is off track, or some of the things you are doing are not right on target? Does it ever seem as though you are invisible, as if no one sees or hears you when you say something? Do you feel as if you are insignificant or irrelevant? Or do you have the opposite experience where you think that everything you do attracts unwanted attention and you feel as though you stick out like a sore thumb? The way to combat all of these things is through praise and worship of God. That's right. I know it sounds as though those things don't relate, but they do. When you start your day with praise and worship and then tell God all that you are thankful for, you get the focus off of yourself and onto the Lord. Then the presence of God is welcomed into your life in a transforming way.

"Where worship takes place by people who know what they're doing and who they are approaching, you have more than merely the glib exercise of what could seem fanatical to the watcher," said Pastor Jack. "You find something that is a knowledgeable, perceptive, conscious participation with the Almighty Creator in making room for His rule and presence to invade what otherwise would be the chaotic scene of the world where we live—whether it's our home, our business, our block, our town, or our nation. Worship is the fountainhead of power."

This is something you should never forget. If you feel powerless, praise God for who He is. It's not that you will suddenly feel as though you are powerful, but you will immediately be aware that you have access to a source of power that is second to none. "If anyone is a worshiper of God and does His will, He hears him" (JOHN 9:31). Those words alone should convince you.

Step 3: Choose one of God's names, attributes, or characteristics and thank Him for being that to you.

Say, "Lord, I thank You that You are Almighty God. You are stronger

and more powerful than anything I face or any enemy that opposes me."
Then choose another attribute of God you are especially thankful
for that day. What has He been to you lately? What do you need
Him to be to you today? For example, has He been your Deliverer,
Counselor, Peace, Rewarder, Wisdom, Shield, Refiner, Overcomer,
God who forgives, God who loves, or God who gives peace? Then
praise Him for having been that to you. Do you need Him to be
your Healer, Comforter, Redeemer, Forgiver, Strength, Resting Place,
Provider, Light, or Refuge from the storm? Then thank Him for
being that to you now.

"Require of yourself to go back into the *preceding* day and pick
out one situation in which a specific characteristic of God was
shown to you and make that a point of praise," instructed Pastor
Jack. "Keep it current so you aren't always living on the basis of
historic things He's done, as wonderful as they may be."

This is great advice because we often recall the greatest things
God has done in our lives, which are good to remember, but forget
the most recent ones, for which we also need to be grateful. We
should acknowledge the Lord's hand in our lives every day, in
every way we see it, because this strengthens our faith and gives
us a heart full of thanksgiving and praise. There are many blessings
we take for granted in our lives, and we need to praise God for
them all.

Step 4: Present your day to the Lord.

Say, "Lord, I present my day to You and ask You to bless it in every
way." I have found that when the first thing I do is ask the Lord to
be in charge of my day and to put it in order, things go a lot
smoother and there are far fewer unpleasant surprises.

Have you ever had big plans for your day and definite ideas
about how it should go, and then it started getting crazy until
nothing turned out the way you expected? Some of that is just part
of life, but a lot of it can be alleviated by a personal and intimate
time with God in the morning, setting your day before Him and
putting it in His hands.

Everyone has challenges and difficulties in their lives. We all have times of worry, anxiety, loneliness, sadness, depression, despair, or pain. We all have things we're concerned about every day. But no matter what you face in your day, if you lay it all before the Lord and surrender it to Him, He will be in charge of it. Be specific about each detail, concern, event, or activity. Don't think that the details of your day are too insignificant to bring before God. If He cares about the hairs on your head enough to number them, then surely He cares about the things that fill your day.

Say, "Lord, I surrender my day to you." And then list before Him the things your day contains, or at least what you plan for it to contain. There are always things we don't expect, and sometimes we can't get everything done we would like to, but when you set your day before the Lord, you will see yourself make greater headway.

The Bible says, "In all your ways acknowledge Him, and He shall direct your paths. Do not be wise in your own eyes; fear the LORD and depart from evil" (PROVERBS 3:6-7). Whenever we think we can handle our day by ourselves, we are being wise in our own eyes. And that is what going without prayer says to God. Even when we are about to do something we have done many times before, we still should ask God to help us. Just because we did it a certain way before and all went well doesn't mean we should assume everything will go smoothly now so we don't need to pray.

Tell the Lord specific ways you want Him to guide you. Say, "Lord, I lift before You the meeting I have this morning, the trip I'm going to take, the plans I must develop, the thing I need to purchase, the decisions I have to make, the talk I need to have, the bill I have to pay, the letter I must write," or whatever else is ahead of you that day. Then ask Him to order your day for you and be in charge of it. Ask Him to give you peace about it so that no matter what comes into it, whether expected or by surprise, you'll know that God is Lord over it all.

As you pray about your day, God will bring things to mind that you need to know or remember. He may make you aware of something you should do that you would not have otherwise thought about. He might open up opportunities for you that would not have happened otherwise. I found that presenting my day before the Lord in the morning keeps it from getting out of control later on. It seems to cut down on the unexpected, or at least make me better able to handle the unexpected when it happens. I could especially tell that this was true on the days I *didn't* present my day to the Lord and saw how out of control and tyrannized by the unexpected it became.

When you order your day before the Lord and put Him in charge of it, He will help you walk through it with great success.

Step 5: Present your body to the Lord.

Say, " *Lord, I present my body to You this day as a 'living sacrifice' and ask You to help me be a good steward of this temple of Your spirit."* When you present your body as a "living sacrifice, holy, acceptable to God" (Romans 12:1), it means you are submitting your entire being totally to Him.

It means acknowledging your dependence upon Him physically as well as spiritually and emotionally.

"If your body is presented to the Lord at the beginning of the day, you will find the spirit of the world less able to entice your body into any expression of disobedience," Pastor Jack explained. "Whether it's one end of the spectrum, such as temptation to sexual disobedience, or across the spectrum of potential verbal, visual, or attitudinal disobedience, or to the other end, such as the temptation to nutritional disobedience, presenting your body to God changes everything."

I have found that this is especially helpful when trying to take proper care of my health. It's almost as if the moment I present my body to the Lord, He shows me what I need to do or stop doing. He doesn't show me in a condemning way, but rather in a way that encourages and strengthens me. I sense greater motivation and resolve in myself, and I feel better able to make good choices throughout the day. Choices I might not otherwise have made.

Step 6: Confess your sins before God and ask Him to help you live His way.

Say, "Lord, search me and know my heart. Try me and know my anxieties. See if there is any wicked way in me, and lead me in the way everlasting (PSALM 139:23-24). Help me to live in obedience to your ways."

We all feel terrible when we know we have disobeyed God or have not chosen His best for our lives. But Satan wants us to feel so condemned about it that we are too ashamed to come before God. He wants us to struggle with guilt to the point that we can't even pray. Yet the Lord has given us a way out of condemnation. It's called confession.

"People don't often know the difference between condemnation and conviction," said Pastor Jack. "The difference is that conviction will always drive you *to* the Lord while condemnation will drive you *from* Him. So if you feel condemned, know it is the adversary and turn to the Lord."

Nothing works in our lives when we don't live God's way, not the least of which is that our prayers are not answered. The Bible says, "Your iniquities have separated you from your God; and your sins have hidden His face from you, so that He will not hear" (ISAIAH 59:2). Don't let unconfessed sin separate you from God. We all fail at times, so don't let any failure on your part hinder your prayers in any way. If you take care of this issue by yourself with God in the morning, you won't have to be dealing with it when you are trying to rest at night.

Ask God every day to keep you undeceived. And when He reveals any sin, confess it immediately so that you can be cleansed of it.

If you can't think of any sin in your life, ask God to show you whatever you need to see in that regard. All of us get things in our hearts, souls, minds, and emotions that shouldn't be there and are not God's best for our lives. Often we have sin in our hearts and lives and don't even realize it until we start paying the conse- quences for it. We need to keep ourselves current with those things. The Bible says, "If we say that we have no sin, we deceive ourselves, and the truth is not in us. If we confess our sins, He is faithful and just to forgive us our sins and to cleanse us from all unrighteousness" *(1 John 1:8-9)*. It can't get any easier than that.

Step 7. Ask God to help you speak only words that bring life.

Say, *"Lord, may the words of my mouth and the meditation of my heart always be acceptable in Your sight (Psalm 19:14). May they bring life and truth to everyone who hears them."* We are all capable of saying the wrong things or speaking words that can be hurtful to others, even if we don't mean any harm by them. What comes out of our mouths can cause trouble for our lives, but it doesn't have to happen.

The Bible says that "the preparations of the heart belong to man, but the answer of the tongue is from the LORD" *(Proverbs 16:1)*. It also says that "out of the abundance of the heart the mouth speaks" *(Matthew 12:34)*. Prepare your heart by filling it with God's Word. And ask Him to put a monitor on your mouth so that every word proceeding from your lips is loving, truthful, kind, comforting, edifying, wise, encouraging, and God-glorifying. He will do that.

Step 8. Ask God for what you need.

Say, *"Lord, I ask You to meet all of my needs today. Specifically I ask for the following things."* Then tell the Lord whatever it is you need.

"God gives the birds what they need, and you're going to get what you need too," Pastor Jack explained. "But He still says you need to ask. In other words, the fact that God makes promises doesn't mean that they fall out of the sky. Just because God promised something doesn't mean He is obligated to do it automatically. There is a contingency that if you don't pray, you don't get it. Salvation is free, but nobody gets it who doesn't ask for it. God says not to worry about what you need, but you must obey His instructions and ask."

Step 9. Pray for God's will in your life.

Say, *"Lord, may Your will be done in my life this day and every day."* When someone asked Pastor Jack, "How can I know the will of

God?" he told them to ask for it every day. The more we ask God to keep us in His perfect will, the less chance we will end up outside of it.

The Lord may not show you the exact details of His will for you the moment you pray, but as you look back over a week, month, or year of your life, you will see how God led you, even when you weren't too sure you were on the right path at the time. And He did it because you submitted your life to His will every day.

Step 10. Pray for other people.

Say, *"Lord, I pray for the following people."* Then list all who come to your mind. Start with the people closest to you, like immediate family members and close friends. Mention each one by name and bring them under the covering of God's blessings. Then pray for your church family and the people you will likely see in your day wherever you go. Ask God to show you whom you should be praying for during the day. He may suggest someone you don't even know to adopt in prayer. Pastor Jack told us, "The logical extension of your devotional time with the Lord is intercessory prayer." We will naturally turn to prayer for others when we've been alone with God.

WHAT IF I NEED MORE POWER?

The greatest source of power is the name of Jesus. He told His disciples that they had not asked anything in His name before, but now they should ask *everything* in His name and they would receive from God. When we walk close to God and pray in Jesus' name, we too will see great power unleashed through us and amazing answers to our prayers (JOHN 16:24-26). This places all focus on Jesus' person and what He accomplished on the cross.

"Praying in Jesus' name affirms your dependence upon who He is and what He has achieved through the cross," explained Pastor Jack. "Through the cross He broke the power of darkness so His purpose could be done. Prayer in His name is doing the same thing on behalf of other situations."

Another way to have more power and breakthrough in your prayers—especially for the tougher issues—is through fasting. Fasting and prayer brings your body into submission by informing it that it is not in charge.

"What happens when a person lets his body boss him around, whether it's sensually, sexually, or in any other dimension, is that he begins to be ruled by something other than the power by which he was created to be ruled, and that's the power of God," explained Pastor Jack. "Fasting is a way of saying, 'I'm a spirit being before I'm a physical being. I'm physical, so I need to eat, but I'm spiritual too, so I'll sometimes assert the supremacy of my spiritual allegiance beyond and before my allegiance to my body and its cry.' Fasting is an instrument that cripples the power of spiritual and evil forces in the realm of the darkness so they cannot sustain their grip on human life, minds, and circumstances."

When I fasted with Mary Anne for those three days and then was prayed for to be set free from depression, I witnessed the power of God in a way I had never imagined. I don't believe it happened randomly or by accident. I don't believe God was just having a good day and feeling benevolent toward me at that moment. God is always having a good day because everything about Him is good. He is always feeling benevolent because He is the God of love. But some things just don't happen unless we fast and pray. When we understand that powerful things occur in the spirit realm every time we fast and pray, it will no longer seem like merely starvation.

If you are facing what seem like insurmountable obstacles and you need more power in your prayers, don't just try to *survive* the battle when you can win the war through fasting and prayer.

WHAT SHOULD I DO IF MY PRAYERS ARE NOT ANSWERED?

There are many different reasons why our prayers are not answered. It may be that they just haven't been answered *yet*, because the timing isn't right for the answer to come. Or perhaps we have prayed something that is not God's will. Or our prayers *have* been answered, but we can't see it because they weren't answered the way we thought they would be.

Sometimes our prayers are not answered because we ask from a wrong heart. Perhaps our heart harbors unforgiveness towards someone. "If I regard iniquity in my heart, the Lord will not hear" (PSALM 66:18). Perhaps our heart is selfish or our motivation is off. "You ask and do not receive, because you ask amiss, that you may spend it on your pleasures" (JAMES 4:3).

Jesus promised that if we will spend time with Him, learn of Him, get to know Him, be honest with Him, and acknowledge our sin against Him, then we can ask of Him whatever we want and He will answer. "If you abide in Me, and My words abide in you, you will ask what you desire, and it shall be done for you" (JOHN 15:7). The key is wanting what *He* wants. When we do that, we end up *doing* His will and we find our prayers answered.

When I first came to know the Lord, I prayed about everything and was disappointed when all my prayers weren't answered. As I matured in the things of God, I realized that He and I are on the same side and my praying is actually working in partnership with Him to see His will done on earth. Then I became more consistent in prayer and not so disappointed if my prayers weren't answered immediately or exactly the way I prayed them. I trusted Him to answer in the time and way He chose. I concentrated on the praying instead of on the answers. It was freeing.

Once you have prayed, release your concerns. This doesn't mean you can't pray about the same thing again, but once you've finished a prayer, allow the issue to be surrendered into His hands so you can rest and be at peace. Don't worry about whether He heard you or if you did it right. Trust Him to take care of it. Learn to *partner* with God. "For the eyes of the LORD run to and fro throughout the whole earth, to show Himself strong on behalf of those whose heart is loyal to Him" (2 CHRONICLES 16:9). If you partner with God alone, you'll see more power in your prayers when you partner with others. ❖

PRAYER POWER

Heavenly Father, I thank You this day for who You are and all that You have done. I enter Your gates with thanksgiving and Your courts with praise *(PSALM 100:4)*. I worship Your holy name. This is the day that You have made, and I will rejoice and be glad in it *(PSALM 118:24)*. Thank You that You are my Savior, Healer, Redeemer, Deliverer, Provider, Counselor, and coming King. I specifically thank You that You are *(name what you are most thankful for about the Lord that reflects His character)*.

I present my day to You and ask You to bless it in every way. I surrender all the details of it into Your hands. In everything I face today, I ask You to be with me. I trust You with all my heart, and I will not lean on my own understanding. I acknowledge You in all my ways and ask You to direct my paths *(PROVERBS 3:5-6)*. Order my day and be in charge of it. Help me to do all I need to do. Give me peace in the midst of the unexpected.

Lord, I present my body to You as a living sacrifice, holy and acceptable *(ROMANS 12:1)*. Teach me how to treat it with care and be a good steward of it. Help me not to mistreat it in any way or use it improperly. Enable me to make good decisions with regard to maintaining healthful habits. Thank You that You are my healer. Specifically I pray for *(name any area where you need the Lord to help you or heal you)*.

Teach me from Your Word so that I will know Your ways and walk in them. Help me to live in obedience to Your commands. I don't want anything to hinder my prayers. Show me any sin in my life so that I can confess it to You and be cleansed. Keep me undeceived in my heart and mind. Where I have sinned against You, I ask You to forgive and restore me. Specifically, I confess before You *(name any area where you have fallen short of God's ways for your life)*. I repent of this and thank You that You are a God who forgives. Thank You that my sin doesn't have to separate me from You because by repenting of it and confessing it to You, I can be set free.

Show me anyone against whom I have unforgiveness, and I will confess that unforgiveness to You as sin. Specifically, I pray about my relationship with *(name anyone you need to forgive)*. Create in me a clean heart and renew a right spirit within me *(PSALM 51:10)*. Set me free so that my heart can be clean when I come before You. I don't want anything to keep me from fulfilling Your ultimate purpose for my life.

Lord, You have said that we will have to give account of every idle word in the day of judgment *(MATTHEW 12:36)*. Help me to keep my tongue from evil and my lips from speaking deceit *(1 PETER 3:10)*. Help me to speak only words that are true, noble, just, pure, lovely, of good report, virtuous, excellent, or praiseworthy *(PHILIPPIANS 4:8)*. Help me to always be able to give the reason for the hope that is within me *(1 PETER 3:15)*. Help me to speak the truth in love *(EPHESIANS 4:15)*. Fill me with Your love so that it flows from me in the words I speak.

I pray that You would bless my family and friends. Specifically, I lift up to You *(name family members and friends)*. I also lift up to you my church family and people I see in my work and throughout my day *(name specific people who come to mind)*. Show me anyone else You want me to pray for today.

Lord, I ask that You would meet all my needs this day. Thank You that You have provided for my needs in the past and will continue to provide for me in the future, as You have promised in Your Word. Help me to live in Your will. Thank You that Your will is not beyond knowing and that You reveal Yourself to me when I ask You to. Help me to abide in You so that I can understand Your ways and Your heart. In Jesus' name I pray.

How Do I Overcome Temptation?
by Steve McVey

Chapter:
Victory is a Gift

Book:
Grace Walk

Look for your coupons for this and other
featured titles in the back of this book.

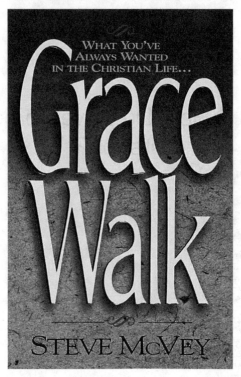

WHAT YOU'VE
ALWAYS WANTED
IN THE CHRISTIAN LIFE...

Grace
Walk

STEVE MCVEY

Author's Bio

Steve McVey is the President of Grace
Walk Ministries, a discipleship-training
ministry in Atlanta, Georgia, as well as
a sought-after leader of Grace Walk
conferences. Steve and his wife, Melanie,
have four children and reside in Atlanta.

How do I Overcome Temptation?
by Steve McVey

"I tried everything I could think of to experience victory, but all to no avail. I didn't know that it was by my dying, not doing, that victory was possible. Like all Christians, I had a sincere desire to glorify God. That desire is inherent to the new nature of every believer. At the core of our being, our spirit yearns to express the righteousness of Christ. A Christian whose lifestyle contradicts the holy nature of Christ will inevitably experience anxiety. A sinning Christian is behaving in a way that is unnatural. The spirit is the core of one's being, and at the spirit level the believer was made righteous. So for a Christian to sin is to act against his own nature. Anytime a person behaves unnaturally, he won't feel right about his behavior. There may be a temporary and shallow pleasure in sin, but beneath it all will be a restlessness within the Christian whose lifestyle is sinful. People who do not have the nature of Christ aren't bothered when they sin. They are doing what comes naturally.

Does this mean that Christians will enjoy sinless perfection? Of course not. Our old nature was put to death with Jesus at the cross, but there is another obstacle to a victorious lifestyle which we must understand. While the old man is dead, the flesh is still an enemy to be reckoned with every day. *The flesh* is defined as "the techniques we use to try to meet our needs, independent of Jesus Christ." The expression of flesh life might be obviously wicked, as evidenced in the life of a person who commits adultery to gratify a sexual or emotional desire. Or the flesh might appear respectable, as in a person who eloquently teaches the Bible in order to gain a sense of significance and affirmation from his ministry. *To walk after the flesh simply means to live a lifestyle which does not rely on Christ as its source.*

All of us have developed flesh patterns. We have learned specific techniques that minimize the risk of painful circumstances in our lives and maximize the opportunity for self-gratification.

Until we understand the reality of Christ as our life, our lifestyle will be characterized by these fleshly behavior patterns. One unavoidable result of a flesh-oriented lifestyle is that the spiritual life is always up and down, characterized by inconsistency.

THE FLESH AND SERVICE

Without a proper understanding of how the flesh operates in our life, our whole perspective on walking in victory will be distorted. For many years my evaluation of my own spiritual life was that I was either "close to God" or "away from the Lord." When I felt defeated I would conclude that I was out of fellowship and needed to get back close to the Lord again. Before I understood that Christ was my life, I was doomed to constant defeat. When I considered myself close to God, I would pour my energy into doing all the things for God that I could do. When I felt I was away from the Lord, I was miserable. Self-condemnation would increase until I finally rededicated myself to Him and started busily doing things for Him again.

I was a manic-depressive Christian! Have you experienced this distorted kind of Christianity? I felt close to God when doing the things I believed that He expected, and far from the Lord when I neglected those responsibilities. However the truth is that God is never closer to us or further from us at any point. If Christ is always in us and we are in Him, how can we ever get closer than that? We may *feel* far from God, but Jesus Christ is always within us, having promised never to leave us.

The victorious Christian life is nothing less than the life of Christ being expressed through the child of God. *Any* behavior which is not dependent on Him living His life through us comes from the flesh. That suggests that it is even possible to be busy doing things *for* God while our actions still stem from the energy of the flesh. *The exchanged life means we depend on His resources, not our own. Flesh life means depending on what I can do.* We may be well respected for our zeal and service to Christ and yet be relying on the flesh. God has no desire to help us to live the Christian life or

do the work of Christian ministry. He wants to do it Himself—
through us. Major Ian Thomas has said:

> There is nothing quite so nauseating or pathetic as the
> flesh trying to be holy! The flesh has a perverted bent for
> righteousness—but such righteousness as it may achieve
> is always self-righteousness; and self-righteousness is
> always self-conscious righteousness; and self-conscious
> righteousness is always full of self-praise. This produces
> the extrovert, who must always be noticed, recognized,
> consulted, and applauded. On the other hand, when the
> flesh in pursuit of self-righteousness fails, instead of
> being filled with self-praise, it is filled with self-pity, and
> this produces the introvert. A professional "case" for
> professional counselors![1]

Trying to do something *for* God is a flesh trip! It is possible
to be sincere in trying to do something for Him, yet be sincerely
wrong. Religious flesh is often a hard pattern for a person to
recognize because it is usually applauded by other Christians.
Religious service may cause you to be pleased with yourself. Or it
may leave you feeling spiritually and emotionally drained. If you
find yourself in either place, God may be trying to show you the
problem. Many Christians today are exhausted because they
understand the Christian life to be primarily a life of service for
God. But that isn't true. The Christian life is primarily a life of
intimacy *with* God.

> There may have been created within you a genuine
> desire to serve God, out of a sincere sense of gratitude
> to Christ for dying for you; you may be impelled out of
> a sense of duty as a Christian, to seek conformity to
> some pattern of behavior that has been imposed upon
> you as the norm for Christian living; you may be deeply
> moved by the need of others around you, and holy
> ambitions may have been stirred within your heart, to
> count for God; if, however, all that has happened is that
> your sins have been forgiven, because you have
> accepted Christ as the Savior who died for you, leaving
> you *since* your conversion only with those resources
> which you had *before* your conversion, then you will
> have no alternative but to "Christianize" the flesh and

> try to teach it to "behave" in such a way that it will
> be godly.
>
> That is a sheer impossibility! The nature of the flesh
> never changes. No matter how you may coerce it or
> conform it, it is rotten through and through, even with
> a Bible under its arm, a check for missions in its hand,
> and an evangelical look on its face![2]

Any person whose Christian life is centered on service is doomed to a life of frustration. I speak from personal experience. It was a painful realization when God showed me that I was more in love with the ministry than with the One who called me to the ministry. Sooner or later, a person whose life revolves around service will experience burn out. And what a wonderful realization when that day comes—the realization that human energy and efforts *can* burn out, but that the life of Christ will never burn out! Christian service which doesn't overflow from our walk with Christ is nothing but flesh. God cannot receive glory from flesh, regardless of how dedicated it might be.

THE FLESH AND SINS

A Christian who lives according to the flesh will often find his spiritual experience to be high voltage some of the time and a drained battery at other times. Such a person is always on the lookout for anything that will give another "spiritual charge." I have read books, been to conferences and seminars, attended revival meetings, listened to tapes, and done a hundred other things in an effort to "get my battery charged" for Jesus. It was discouraging that life always drained my battery faster than I could keep it recharged. Have you experienced that problem? When my "spiritual battery" was weak, I found myself vulnerable to sinful flesh patterns. When I sinned I would sooner or later feel guilty and ask the Lord to help me to live for Him. I resolved to do whatever it took to keep myself charged.

However a Christian doesn't experience victory over sins by keeping himself charged up for Jesus. Christ Himself is our power over sin. As we allow Him to express His life through us, we will experience continuous victory over temptation. It is important to make this distinction: Christ does not *give* us the victory; instead, He *is* our victory! Consider these promises from God concerning the source of victorious Christian living:

- *"But thanks be to God, who gives us the victory through our Lord Jesus Christ"* (1 CORINTHIANS 15:57). The Bible clearly says here that victory is a *gift* that comes through Jesus Christ. So if we have the Lord Jesus Christ, victory is ours.

- *"Now thanks be to God who always leads us in triumph in Christ, and through us diffuses the fragrance of His knowledge in every place"* (2 CORINTHIANS 2:14). How often does God lead us in triumph? Always! What is the source of the triumph we may experience daily? Christ!

- *"Yet in all these things we are more than conquerors through Him who loved us"* (ROMANS 8:37). Life will get tough at times (VERSES 35-36), but we aren't just conquerors—we are *more* than conquerors *through* Him!

Do you get the picture? We don't experience victory by fighting, instead we enjoy it by faith! As we abide in Christ and allow Him to live His life through us, we live in victory. *"And this is the victory that has overcome the world—our faith"* (1 JOHN 5:4). Why would Christians want to get their spiritual batteries charged, when we have an omnipotent "power plant" within us that can continuously be activated by faith in Him?

FOCUSING ON HIM, NOT ON SIN!

A guaranteed way to be defeated by the flesh is to focus on the sins that we want to avoid. That's like going on a diet and then reading the menu at Pizza Hut every day just so we'll know the foods we want to avoid! We don't experience victory over the flesh by being preoccupied with it. We are to be obsessed with Jesus, not sin. "For those who live according to the flesh set their minds on the things of the flesh, but those who live according to the Spirit, the things of the Spirit. For to be carnally minded is death, but to be spiritually minded is life and peace" (ROMANS 8:5-6).

Philip had been involved in adultery several times over the past few years. He had come from a home where his own parents had what has been called "an open marriage." They both often brought other partners into the home. What would happen during those times was no secret. Neither of his parents expressed their love for him. The only affection he had seen them give to anyone was toward those with whom they had affairs. Philip's own low self-esteem, coupled together with the absence of a proper role model for marriage, influenced his adulterous lifestyle. He had received Christ and wanted to be faithful to his wife, but he was afraid. For many years he had been programmed for erotic behavior. "I am scared that I'm going to fall back into that life again," he expressed one day. "I don't want to, but everywhere I turn, the temptation is in front of me." In an effort to keep from failing, Philip had given away his television because of all the sexual stimuli on the screen. He was apprehensive about going to any movies, for fear that what he saw might put him in the wrong frame of mind. "I can't even look at some of the billboards as I drive to work each morning," he complained. He felt that he was walking through a minefield where he might accidently step into a temptation and suddenly see his Christianity be blown apart.

Philip's outlook is not uncommon, but he was giving more credit to the enemy than he deserves. Satan can't *make* a Christian sin. But an attitude like Philip's will lead to sin if it isn't adjusted to God's truth. The Bible says that God is able "to keep you from stumbling" (JUDE 24). His problem wasn't that he was spiritually weak; the omnipotent power of Almighty God is in him. His problem was that he focused on the temptation to sin and not on Christ. He confessed greater confidence in Satan's ability to cause him to fall than in the ability of the Holy Spirit to keep him from falling.

God's purpose is that the focus of our whole life be on Him. Our minds are to be set continuously on the Spirit of Christ. When our minds are fixed on Jesus, we will experience a quality of life characterized by the peace of God. But preoccupation with sin stimulates internal conflict that will ultimately enslave us to the very sins we are trying to avoid.

"Walk in the Spirit, and you shall not fulfill the lust of the flesh" (GALATIANS 5:16). The key to overcoming the flesh is walking in the Spirit. There has been much discussion among Christians about the Spirit-filled walk. The heart of walking in the Spirit is allowing the Spirit of Christ to do the walking through us. That is God's prescribed order. We often reverse the order and try to overcome the sinful desires of the flesh, so that we might be able to walk in the Spirit. However, we can't clean up our act to become spiritual. It isn't possible to do things backwards from what God says and also experience success!

It is the life of Christ within us that gives us the victory. Just as His death and resurrection delivered us from the penalty of sin, so His life frees us from sin's power as we faithfully abide in Him. "For if when we were enemies we were reconciled to God through the death of His Son, much more, having been reconciled, we shall be saved *by His life*" (ROMANS 5:10, EMPHASIS MINE).

Does it make sense that Jesus would *die* for our sin and then not provide a way for victory over sins after we are saved? We are saved from sin's power *by His life* as it is expressed through us. I'll never think of getting my spiritual battery charged again. When we abide in Christ, it is like turning a switch into the "on" position and allowing the full power of Jesus Christ to flow through us. When we choose to rest in His life, we experience victory. When we choose not to abide, we flip the switch to the "off" position and we fail.

Christ's life is the remedy for every temptation. It's the answer to Philip's vulnerability toward adultery. The life of Christ being expressed through him each day will save him from an adulterous lifestyle. He simply needs to choose to abide in Christ each moment. As long as he does that, Christ will effectively handle any temptation that may come along.

FLESH WILL ALWAYS BE FLESH

For some time after God revealed the truth of the exchanged life to me, I lived on an emotional mountaintop. Then the time came when my flesh reared its head again. I'm sorry to say that my flesh hasn't improved—it's just as ugly as it ever was. But please understand that it looks ugly only when I see it through the eyes of Christ. At times when I fail to abide in Him, it actually looks appealing. Let's face it: if temptation has no appeal, what's the big deal about being tempted? Yes, sometimes those flesh patterns do look enticing and I still yield to the flesh. There, I've said it. But don't be too quick to judge me—your flesh is no better than mine. Flesh won't improve through Christian maturity, spiritual warfare, or anything else. The only remedy for flesh is walking in the Spirit. I have found that when I rest in Christ's sufficiency, I experience victory; and when I don't, I experience defeat. It's that simple.

When Christians fail to abide in Christ, they assert their own independence. Sin came into the world when Adam and Eve chose to assert their independence from God by their disobedience. Christians who are not abiding in Him are walking in a state of continuous sin, regardless of their actions. This *attitude of independence* will eventually give birth to specific sins, which are the fruit of abiding in self. For that reason, it should come as no surprise that Christians sin when they don't abide in Christ. What else could possibly happen?

If I tell you that a man jumped off a ten-story building, would it occur to you to ask, "Did he fall?" That question would be ridiculous. Any man who jumps off a building will fall because of the consistency of the law of gravity. The only way he wouldn't fall is if a greater law took effect. For instance, if he were in a hang glider he wouldn't fall because the law of aerodynamics would supersede the law of gravity in that case. The law of gravity is not suspended, but it is overcome by a greater law. Flesh will always respond to the law of sin and death. But abiding in Christ causes us to experience the law of the Spirit of life in Christ Jesus, enabling us to soar above the temptations of the flesh.

We can take no credit when we triumph over the flesh, since the victory has been *given* to us by God. Could the Children of Israel take credit for the victory at Jericho when God knocked the walls flat? The only thing they did was to believe what God said about how He was going to give them the victory. They marched around the wall just as God told them to, in spite of the fact that their actions contradicted human logic. At the prescribed time, they shouted in victory, the wall fell flat, and God gave them the city. What would have happened if they had chosen their own battle plan instead of obeying the Lord? They would have been defeated, regardless of the ingenuity of their plan and the strength of their army.

We experience victory in the Christian life as we receive God's gift in faith. It might seem logical that victory would come by a fight, but fighting for victory is the surest way to experience defeat. God has determined to *give* it to those who will receive it by faith in His Son. As Charles Trumbull says:

> The great truth that so many earnest, surrendered Christians have even yet failed to see is that salvation is a twofold gift; freedom from the *penalty* of sin, and freedom from the *power* of sin. All Christians have received in Christ as their Savior their freedom from the penalty of their sins, and they have received this as an outright gift from God. But many Christians have not yet realized that they may, in the same way, and by the same kind of faith in the same God and Savior, receive now and here the freedom from the power of their sins which was won for them by their Savior on the cross and in His resurrection victory. Even though they know clearly that their own efforts have nothing to do with their salvation from the *penalty* of their sins, they are yet deceived by the Adversary into believing that somehow their own efforts must play a part in their present victory over the *power* of their sins. *Our efforts can not only never play any part in our victory over the power of sin, but they can and do effectually prevent such victory....* We are to use our will to accept the gift of victory; we are not to make an effort to win the victory.[3]

At times I experience a struggle against the law of sin and death within me. Because of an understanding of *truth*, I have learned to recognize that struggle as a red flag. God doesn't intend for us to struggle for the victory. As we rest in Him, we enjoy the victory of His life. It is impossible to struggle and rest at the same time! ❖

CHAPTER NOTES

1. Major Ian Thomas, *The Saving Life of Christ* (Grand Rapids: Zondervan, 1961), 85.

2. Major Ian Thomas, *The Mystery of Godliness* (Grand Rapids: Zondervan, 1964), 258–59.

3. Charles G. Trumbull, *Victory in Christ* (Fort Washington, PA: Christian Literature Crusade, 1969), 47–49.

How Do I Forgive Others?

by John Nieder and Thomas M Thompson

Chapter:
Where Do You Go To Forgive?

Book:
Forgive and Love Again

Look for your coupons for this and other
featured titles in the back of this book.

Forgive AND Love Again

Healing Wounded Relationships

John Nieder and
Thomas M. Thompson

Author's Bio

John Nieder is a Bible teacher whose
ministry spans over 20 years on radio and
television. Dr. Thomas M. Thompson is a
pastor who has served congregations
across America. Both Nieder and
Thompson are graduates of Dallas
Theological Seminary.

How Do I Forgive Others?
by John Nieder and Thomas M. Thompson

Your husband stomped out of the house this morning without saying a word. You know his job pressures are grinding on him. But you were sitting across the table from him, and he didn't even acknowledge your existence—and it hurt.

You know you should forgive him, and you're willing to do so. But what should you do? Should you call him at the office and say, "I forgive you for slashing me with your silence this morning"? Should you wait until he gets home to tell him? Where do you go to forgive?

Perhaps the offense was at the hands of your onetime fiancé. From the day you met your relationship seemed destined for marriage. All those years of waiting and praying and waiting and praying. Finally he came along. Your friends touted you as the perfect couple. And he was a Christian! Maybe that's why you dropped your guard and did what you promised yourself you would never do until you were married. You felt so secure in his love that you gave yourself to him.

But the wedding never happened. He left. One night, with little warning, he said it was over. He said goodbye. Your tears didn't matter. You stood there in disbelief and shock as he walked out the door. You felt used, cheated, abandoned.

The Holy Spirit has brought the incident to your mind and urged you to forgive. But he walked out years ago. He could be anywhere in the world; you have no idea where he is. Do you have to find him, face off, and say "I forgive you" to be healed? Where do you go to forgive?

Or maybe your father mistreated you for years, and the pain today is just as real as it was when it was actually happening. What are you going to do—especially now that he's dead? Will he continue to ruin your life from his grave? If you allow him to, he can. But since you can't go to him to tell him you forgive him, what can you do? Where do you go to forgive?

FORGIVE IN FRONT OF THE ONE
WHO HAS FORGIVEN YOU

The place you go to forgive is not to the person who has offended you. First of all, that person may be only a distant memory in your past. You wouldn't know where to find him if your life depended on it. Second, the offender may be dead. Obviously, you can't go to him to forgive. If God required you to forgive these offenders by confronting them face-to-face (which He doesn't), you'd be in deep trouble.

What about the person who is alive and near at hand—your spouse, your child, your parent, a friend? If you go to that person out of the blue and say, "I forgive you," you may lay a tremendous guilt trip on him, especially if he isn't aware of his offense. It's not your job to convict people of sin; that's God's job. So you don't go to that person to forgive, although you may go to him later in loving confrontation of his offensive behavior.

Where then do you go to forgive? There are well-meaning counselors who recommend that you sit across from an empty chair and let that chair represent the person who hurt you. Then you proceed to speak words of forgiveness toward the chair. This may be a helpful technique, but it misses a critical spiritual dimension for the believer.

For the Christian, forgiving someone is a sacred act done before God in response to His forgiveness of us and His command to forgive others. It is a Godward act in which we trust Him to deal with the offender and bring healing to our hearts.

While traveling from Ephesus to Macedonia, Paul wrote a letter to the church at Corinth. He gave them counsel on how to handle a situation which involved formal church discipline. Apparently a man had been punished and then repented. It was time to restore him and move on.

Paul entered into this case of discipline with them. Then he makes a fascinating statement: "If you forgive anyone, I also forgive him. And what I have forgiven— if there was anything to forgive— I have forgiven in the sight of Christ" (2 CORINTHIANS 2:10). Although Paul was miles away, he extended forgiveness to this man by expressing it to Jesus Christ. He agreed with the church's decision and communicated his agreement before the Lord.

Don't miss the significance of the phrase "in the sight of Christ." When we forgive, we talk to God, not to an empty chair. We go to God to forgive for several important reasons.

God was there when you were hurt. Whatever happened, whenever it happened, and wherever it happened, God was there. He saw your father hit you. He witnessed the assault. He heard the allegations. He was there, and in His unsearchable wisdom He allowed it to happen to you. And when you were offended, He was offended.

David expresses this truth in his touching psalm of repentance for his adultery with Bathsheba and the murder of her husband, Uriah: "Against you, you only, have I sinned and done what is evil in your sight, so that you are proved right when you speak and justified when you judge" (PSALM 51:4). God was there when David was in the bedroom with Bathsheba. He was there when David plotted Uriah's death. He saw and heard everything. David's sin against Bathsheba and Uriah was a sin against God.

When someone sins against us they also sin against God. When you sense the Holy Spirit prompting you to forgive, but it seems impossible to let go of your bitterness and pain over such a vicious act, remember that it hurts God so much more. Yet God was anxious to forgive us at a price you could not endure or even imagine: the price of His Son's death. You can go to Him because He understands the offense and the cost of forgiveness like no one else.

After delivering a message at a conference, I was being escorted through the crowd when a desperate woman grabbed my arm. With tears in her eyes, she asked me if we could talk. Although surrounded by people, she proceeded to tell me of how she had been abandoned by her parents.

I asked her what the Lord had communicated to her about their sin against her. She responded with a blank stare and started to stammer. She then admitted that she had never really taken this to the Lord. She had not sought His counsel and direction. She was willing to share this very private hurt with me, a stranger, in public, but she had never opened her heart to her God about the offense.

When you forgive, go to your Eyewitness. God was there.

God cares and responds. Even when it seems that no one cares, God does, and He promises to respond on your behalf. The apostle Paul discovered this time and again. He was beaten, battered, and even abandoned by his friends. His life and ministry were filled with heartache. Fortunately, Paul knew where to turn to forgive: "At my first defense, no one came to my support, but everyone deserted me. May it not be held against them. But the Lord stood at my side and gave me strength" (2 TIMOTHY 4:16-17).

What an example of forgiveness! In the heat of battle, Paul's colleagues left him to fight alone. How did he do it? Verse 17 gives us a clue: "But the Lord stood at my side and gave me strength." Paul's friends left; the Lord didn't. They didn't care; the Lord did. Paul turned to the Lord and forgave those who jumped ship. He released them and experienced God's personal presence and enabling power. God cares about your hurt more than you can ever imagine. Out of His great love for you He tells you to forgive in His presence and promises to stand by your side. His Word assures you that He is well aware of the harm you suffered and that justice will be carried out. He wants you to leave it in His hands.

God will judge the offender. When we are hurt by someone else, God views it as a three-way transaction. The one who inflicted the pain on us owes us, but he must also answer to God, who acts as our personal witness and judge. Similarly, God says He wants us to respond to Him rather than to the offender and that our response is to be one of forgiveness. So when we communicate forgiveness before God, the person no longer owes us, but he still owes God. When we forgive another we trust God to act as judge and jury over the offender.

"When did you become God?" When I was younger I often used this question in response to someone who was critical of me. In our fallen humanity we seem to enjoy casting doubt on each other's motives and questioning each other's lifestyles. This tendency to condemn others runs contrary to the very essence of forgiveness. When we claim the right to judge, it often causes us to fail to forgive others. We end up taking matters into our own hands.

Paul's response to the criticism he received teaches us a crucial lesson. He said he didn't care who judged him, whether it was an individual or a court of law. The reason? God is the only One who has the authority and the capability to truly judge us (1 CORINTHIANS 4:3-5).

Paul knew that God is our judge. God knows our motives better than we do. A day is coming when each of us will pass in review before God. This is what Paul had in mind in 2 Corinthians 5:10: "For we must all appear before the judgment seat of Christ, that each one may receive what is due him for the things done while in the body, whether good or bad."

When we refuse to forgive we judge others and assume the role that God has reserved for Himself alone. He knows what happened. He knows the motivating factors. He knows the person's heart.

It may be that the one who hurt you is as wrong as wrong can be. God's command is clear: "Do not take revenge, my friends, but leave room for God's wrath, for it is written: 'It is mine to avenge; I will repay,' says the Lord" (ROMANS 12:19). Retaliation is not a valid option. We are not to fight back. We should not return evil for evil. Instead we are to forgive and leave judgment to God. When we forgive we do so before God as an act of obedience and an expression of our trust in Him as judge.

God will bring good out of what happened. So often we casually quote Romans 8:28: "And we know that in all things God works for the good of those who love him, who have been called according to his purpose." Can we apply this passage to our lives when someone maligns us? Can God bring good out of a rotten divorce or an episode of infidelity? Does He really mean all things? Absolutely.

Young Joseph's hate-filled brothers tossed him into a pit, then sold him into slavery (GENESIS 37). Was God watching? Did God care about Joseph? Could God bring anything good out of what his brothers did to him? Yes. The rest of the story chronicles Joseph's rise from slavery to become second in command in Egypt. And he was eventually reunited with his brothers and father (GENESIS 39–47).

But after Jacob died, Joseph's brothers weren't sure if Joseph had really forgiven them or if he was just waiting until their father died to get revenge. They said among themselves, "What if Joseph holds a grudge against us and pays us back for all the wrongs we did to him?" (Genesis 50:15).

But Joseph's response proved that he had long since forgiven his brothers: "Don't be afraid. Am I in the place of God? You intended to harm me, but God intended it for good" (vv. 19-20). Joseph refused to stand in judgment of his brothers because he knew that this was the unique prerogative of God. His story beautifully reveals how God can bring good things out of bad experiences.

From start to finish, God is not only watching but He is working to bring good out of your personal pain and heartache. He is committed to turning it all around if you will just forgive and allow Him to do His perfect work. When we go before God to forgive, we are saying, "Lord, I trust You to bring good out of my grief and something productive out of my pain."

God reveals the need to forgive. Those of us who give our lives to the ministry of God's Word soon discover that we either learn to forgive or lose our spiritual sanity. The ministry is rewarding but also very painful. One of the biggest problems is a lack of loyalty. I have been knifed in the back more times than I care to remember.

On one occasion a young man—I'll call him Ben— waited until I left town to attack me. When I returned Ben refused to answer my repeated phone calls to make matters right. He avoided me and my invitations to get together with everyone involved. But at the same time he sought out anyone who would listen to his grievances. Ben talked to everyone else, but he wouldn't talk to me.

A close friend who knew the situation firsthand told me, "It's not worth the effort, John. Just forget about Ben and move on." So I did, or I thought I had until one day Ben's name was mentioned, and I found myself wanting to do to him what he had done to me: gossip, slander.

At that precise moment I sensed the Holy Spirit saying to me, "You haven't forgiven Ben, have you?" My desire to retaliate revealed my unforgiving heart. I confessed to God that I had not forgiven Ben for what he had done to me and my family. Forgiveness was the only way, and I knew it. I forgave him before God from my heart.

Just a few days later I saw Ben for the first time. I was totally at peace shaking his hand and inviting him to call so we could get together. He never called, but I did what God wanted me to do. It is no longer my concern. The matter rests between Ben and God.

As rocks pelted his body and his life ebbed away, Stephen gazed into heaven and saw Jesus Christ standing at the right hand of the Father. He cried out, "Lord, do not hold this sin against them" (ACTS 7:60). Beaten, bruised, and bloodied, Stephen went to God and forgave those who were taking his life. Stephen knew what it meant to forgive in God's presence.

Forgiving someone is a deeply personal and spiritual expression that God directs through His Word and the Holy Spirit. When we forgive, we go before Him. He shows us who we need to forgive, and then He gives us His power to forgive.

You don't need to come before the offender or sit across from an empty chair to forgive. All you need is a willing spirit that is ready to go into God's presence and say by faith, "Lord, I forgive Mom. I forgive Dad. I forgive my spouse. I forgive my friend. I forgive before You." Are you ready?

THE SACRED MOMENT OF FORGIVENESS

Forgiveness is the foundation of God's relationship with us. His love, His kindness, His guidance, His protection, His mercy, His joy, His justification, His adoption of us as His children, His activity of making us holy—they all come to us through the funnel of His forgiveness. Apart from His forgiveness we would never know these spiritual blessings. The moment you received God's forgiveness was a sacred moment.

God's Word repeatedly tells us that we can and must forgive those who wrong us in just the same way that God has forgiven us.

There is nothing casual or flippant about forgiveness. Just as God's forgiveness of us is sacred, the moments we spend before God forgiving others are sacred moments.

Isn't it time for you to enter into the sanctuary of God's presence for sacred moments of forgiveness? Are your hands full? Good. Bring your burdens with you, but be prepared to set them down. You have finally come to the right place to meet with the right Person about your hurts. You are carrying nothing He hasn't already seen. There are no surprises to Him.

Allow the following steps to guide you in your sacred moment of forgiveness.

Get alone with the Lord. Find a quiet place where you will not be interrupted. Take a long walk, or find a secluded place. Make this a holy experience alone with your God. Eliminate distractions so you can clearly hear from heaven. Give yourself plenty of time and space.

You may want to begin by getting on your knees. Get ready to give everything to Him, every contemptible offense and cutting word. Just tell Him, "Lord, I admit that I am a sinner just like those who have offended me. Thank You for forgiving my sins. I want to share in Your forgiving character. I want to know Your forgiving heart."

Remember that He has forgiven you. Take a few moments to look back to the cross. Remember Jesus Christ with nails in His hands and feet and a crown of thorns on His head. Think about the blood that was shed to cover your sins. Think about the debt you owed to God that was paid at Calvary. Thank Him for paying such an incredible price. Thank the Father for forgiving you. You might pray something like this: "Father in heaven, Your Son had to die so I could be forgiven. And You have forgiven all of my sins against You. I have hurt You in so many ways, yet You have forgiven me. Father, please help me extend to others the same forgiveness You have so freely given me. In Jesus' name I pray. Amen."

Ask the Holy Spirit to be your Counselor. Ask the Holy Spirit, the Counselor, to show you who you need to forgive. You may be surprised at who the Lord brings to your mind. It may be a person or incident that you have blocked out for years because of the magnitude of the pain. If you experience a great deal of trauma over this event, you may need a spiritually sensitive counselor to pray with you and to encourage you from God's Word as you deal with the hurts from the past.

Write each of the names and offenses that God brings to your mind on a separate sheet of paper. Keep writing as long as the Holy Spirit keeps bringing people and hurts to mind. He wants you to clean house with His able assistance.

Don't run from the pain; release it. Take a few moments to allow yourself to deal honestly with the emotional pain you experience as you remember and write. Forgiveness is a decision, but it's not a cold, hard decision devoid of feeling. In fact, honest feelings may be the best indication that the decision is real.

As the Holy Spirit brings someone to your mind, you may relive the painful experience simply by remembering it. Instead of burying the pain or reacting against it with bitterness or anger, surrender it, release it before God.

Take each person and offense before the Lord. Pray, "Lord, before You today I forgive *(the offender)* for *(the offense)*. I will not fight back or seek revenge. I am trusting You to act on my behalf. Heal my broken heart."

Destroy the record of wrongs done. Corrie ten Boom, the extraordinary Dutch Christian who was imprisoned for hiding Jews from the Nazis during World War II, discovered in a remarkable incident that she had not fully forgiven a wrong until she stopped holding on to it and cherishing her memory of it:

> I recall the time ... when some Christian friends whom I loved and trusted did something which hurt me....Many years later, after I had passed my eightieth birthday, an American friend came to visit me in Holland. As we sat in my little apartment in Baarn he asked me about those people from long ago who had taken advantage of me.
>
> "It is nothing," I said a little smugly. "It is all forgiven."
>
> "By you, yes," he said. "But what about them? Have they accepted your forgiveness?"

"They say there is nothing to forgive! They deny it ever happened. No matter what they say, though, I can prove they were wrong." I went eagerly to my desk. "See, I have it in black and white! I saved all their letters and I can show you where ..."

"Corrie!" My friend slipped his arm through mine and gently closed the drawer. "Aren't you the one whose sins are at the bottom of the sea? Yet are the sins of your friends etched in black and white?"

For an astonishing moment I could not find my voice. "Lord Jesus," I whispered at last, "who takes all my sins away, forgive me for preserving all these years the evidence against others! Give me grace to burn all the blacks and whites as a sweet-smelling sacrifice to your glory."

I did not go to sleep that night until I had gone through my desk and pulled out those letters—curling now with age—and fed them all into my little coal-burning grate. As the flames leaped and glowed, so did my heart. "Forgive us our trespasses," Jesus taught us to pray, "as we forgive those who trespass against us." In the ashes of those letters I was seeing yet another facet of His mercy.[1]

Just as Corrie ten Boom burned those incriminating letters she had treasured and kept within a moment's reach for so long, you must stop cultivating and nurturing your memory of the wrong you have suffered. Of course, you will always remember what happened; our memories cannot be erased like a videotape. But with the Lord's help you can refuse to keep tabs on the painful memory and the emotions that it awakens.

Love does not keep a record of wrongs done (1 CORINTHIANS 13:5). After you have listed and prayed about a particular person and the hurts he caused you, destroy that sheet of paper to symbolize and finalize your decision to release the offender from the moral obligation incurred by his actions. You have canceled the debt. You have agreed to accept the consequences of that person's actions. You will not retaliate or seek to do that person any harm.

As you work through these steps of forgiveness, your experience may well match that of Doris, a woman who recently shared with us how God enabled her to forgive in very difficult circumstances. She wrote what happened as she and her best friend walked through a park and around a beautiful little lake.

> The sun was shining brightly, the birds were chirping, and carefree people surrounded me as they enjoyed this gorgeous spring day. But I could not share any of their feelings. I was caught in a turmoil of emotions ranging from anger and bitterness to deep pain and sadness. I angrily stomped along, kicking pebbles out of my way, barely able to carry on our conversation. I was dealing with my husband's adultery—for the second time.

> The first time I quietly suffered through the hurt and quickly forgave him. I hurt immensely, but with the counsel, support, and prayers of my friend, I endured. I remember the Lord whispering to me at that time, "Seventy times seven!"—showing me His command to forgive, just as Jesus had instructed Peter. The Lord also led me to 2 Corinthians 2:7: "You ought to forgive and comfort him, so that he will not be overwhelmed by excessive sorrow."

> But this time was different. I was livid with anger. How could my husband do this to me again? How could he put me through this after I forgave him so graciously? What a fool I was! And then my emotions led me further into the past. Why me? Why did it *always* seem to be me who suffered? I remembered how my father died while I was still very young, and my mother became an alcoholic. I suffered through those feelings of aloneness and rejection, too. Why always me?

> As I allowed my bitter thoughts and feelings to pour forth to my friend, I was also able to listen to myself. That's all I heard—myself. I was completely focused on me. But I didn't care; I was entitled to it; I was tired of being the victim.

And then, ever so gently and quietly, the Holy Spirit spoke. So this is how Jesus must have felt. He didn't do anything wrong, yet He suffered horribly. 1 Peter 2:22,24 states, "He committed no sin, and no deceit was found in his mouth....He himself bore our sins in his body on the tree, so that we might die to sins and live for righteousness."

Suddenly, I felt some small measure of purpose in what I was going through. "So this is how Jesus must have felt—and even more." I thanked the Lord for that insight. I was humbled at the contrast between my own bitterness and what Jesus bore for me. My steps lightened and I felt a sense of comfort: "For we do not have a high priest who is unable to sympathize with our weaknesses" (HEBREWS 4:15).

My friend and I continued walking and talking and later stopped to pray. When we left the park, I was still hurting; I still felt some bitterness and anger; I knew that the journey ahead of me would not be easy. But I also knew that I would never be alone in my sorrow. Again the Lord brought to my mind that phrase "seventy times seven" and my need to obey and forgive.

I chose to forgive. My heart wasn't fully in it at first, but gradually the bitterness died out and love was replanted. Forgiveness is not just an emotion; it's a decision. Peter's words now have new meaning for me: "By his wounds you have been healed" (1 PETER 2:24).

BEYOND FORGIVENESS

In your heart you know you have done right. You have obeyed God. You have forgiven. You have accepted the cost. You have, in a very small measure to be sure, experienced the kind of suffering Christ bore when He paid the price for your sins on the cross.

Be prepared. Your decision to forgive will be challenged. Some people may look at you as one who has played the part of a fool.

Disruptive thoughts may tempt you to bring your decision up for further examination and severe questioning. Your emotional responses may not be positive right away. But be confident: In forgiving you have done the right thing.

As you move beyond forgiveness remember that the fruit of your righteous action will be peace, quietness, and confidence forever (ISAIAH 32:17).

There may be two other parties you need to consider. You may blame yourself or God for some of the pain and heartache you have suffered. You can forgive your parents, your spouse, your friends, and even nameless, faceless strangers for wrongs they inflicted on you. But if you don't learn to forgive yourself and don't cease blaming God, you will never be healed. ❖

CHAPTER NOTES
1. Corrie Ten Boom, *Tramp for the Lord* (Fort Washington, PA: Christian Literature Crusade, Inc., and Old Tappan, NJ: Fleming H. Rebell Company, 1974), 182-83.

How Do I Stay Connected To Christ?

by Bruce Wilkinson

Chapter:
Living in the Presence

Book:
Secrets of the Vine

Look for your coupons for this and other
featured titles in the back of this book.

Author's Bio

Dr. Bruce H. Wilkinson, author the the
No. 1 bestseller *The Prayer of Jabez*, is
the founder and president of Walk Thru the
Bible Ministries, and international organization dedicated to providing the finest biblical
teaching, tools, and training. His books
include *Experiencing Spiritual Breakthroughs*
and *First Hand Faith*. Bruce and his wife,
Darlene, live in Atlanta, Georgia, and have
three children.

How Do I Stay Connected to Christ?

by Bruce Wilkinson

After arriving home from a meeting with my friend, George, I made three simple commitments to the Lord for the next year. I would:

- get up at 5 A.M. every day to read my Bible;
- write a full page in a daily spiritual journal;
- learn to pray and seek Him until I found Him.

I still remember the first line of my first spiritual journal: "Dear God, I don't know what to say to You."

Day after day I would look at what I had written. On every page I saw the real reason my busy Christian life now left such a bland taste in my mouth—I'd become an expert at serving God but somehow remained a novice at being His friend.

But I stayed with it. By the middle of the second month, things started to shift. It was as if a great Presence walked into my room in those early morning hours and sat down near me. My rambling journal entries gradually became personal confessions to the Listener. His passion for me, His purposes for my life—not just for the *idea* of my life, but for that particular day, hour, and minute—began to rise up from the pages of my Bible.

That was more than fifteen years ago. The pleasures of abiding—and the extraordinary benefits—have redefined the scope and impact of God's work through me. I see fruit everywhere I turn. Yet not even one grape is a result of working harder.

I assure you that I possess no special knowledge in these matters—generations of seasoned disciples have traveled ahead of me down this road. Yet, as far as I can tell, the great majority of God's people today live ignorant of the promise and practice of abiding. As a result, they fail to reach the level of "much fruit" represented by that fourth, overflowing basket.

Maybe you're among that majority. You're not sure how an overflowing spiritual experience actually happens. And you might be asking, "How could merely abiding possibly propel me to the highest levels of fruitfulness?" My prayer is that in the next few pages you'll find answers.

◆

It was as if a great Presence walked into my room in those early morning hours and sat down near me.

◆

THE PERSON OF ABIDING

Abiding is all about the most important friendship of your life. Abiding doesn't measure how much you know about your faith or your Bible. In abiding, you seek, long for, thirst for, wait for, see, know, love, hear, and respond to … *a person*. More abiding means more of God in your life, more of Him in your activities, thoughts, and desires.

In our Western-style rush to do and perform for God, we often falter at the task of simply enjoying His company. Yet we were created to be dissatisfied and incomplete with less. In the words of the psalmist, "As the deer pants for the water brooks, so pants my soul for You, O God" (PSALM 42:1).

If our need for this relationship is so deep and constant, why do so few of us fervently pursue it? One of the primary reasons, I'm convinced, is that *we don't really believe God likes us*. Sure, we believe God loves us in a theological sense ("God loves everybody, right?"), but we don't feel particularly liked by Him. We're convinced that He remembers all the bad things we've done in the past and is quick to judge how we're doing now. We assume He's impatient, busy with more important things, and reluctant to spend time with us.

Why would you want to spend time with a person who felt that way about you?

If you were to list the qualities of your best friend, I expect you would note things like "She accepts me," "He always makes time for me," and "I always leave her presence feeling encouraged." What you appreciate in a best friend is precisely what God offers. He is trustworthy and patient. When He looks at you, He does not call to mind the sins you've asked Him to forgive. He sees only a beloved child, a worthy heir.

And this God—your Friend—wants to abide with you even more than you want to abide with Him. Jesus said, "As the Father loved Me, I also have loved you; abide in My love" (JOHN 15:9). Did you catch that? *Stay, luxuriate, find real love "in My love"!*

If we really abided in His love, we would come away feeling so nourished, so cherished, so liked, that we would rush back to Him whenever we could.

THE PRINCIPLES OF ABIDING

When you start with the Person of abiding and realize how much He loves you and wants to share His life with you, you have taken the most important step toward the practice of abiding.

◆

I am convinced that we don't believe God likes us.

◆

Think again about the meeting place of vine and branch. Why would Jesus give us a picture of a living thing whose life force—the sap—is mysteriously out of sight? One reason could be that in abiding, what happens on the surface doesn't count; what's happening inside does. Abiding begins with visible spiritual disciplines, such as Bible reading and prayer. Yet it may shock you to find out that *we can do these things for years without abiding.* After all, reading a book about a person isn't the same thing as knowing the person who wrote the book. The challenge in abiding is always to break through from dutiful activities to a living, flourishing relationship with God.

Annie, a mother of four, wrote to tell me about her recent breakthrough:

> I'm not just reading my Bible or making requests anymore. I listen for Him, meditate on His Word. I write down what I hear Him saying to me. I try to make this time as honest, deep, and intimate as possible. When I started out doing devotional times, it was like I was getting my time card stamped by heaven—"Yep, she was here. A whole ten minutes!" Lately, I've had to drag myself away.

I see two principles that will help you discover the kind of experience Annie describes. Both have to do with how you spend your time.

Principle 1: To break through to abiding, I must deepen the quality of my devoted time with God.

Notice that I didn't say "devotional time." That might imply that the purpose of your time with God is to have devotions. I use the word *devoted* in the biblical sense of something set apart for God. In Psalm 27, David expresses his desire for this kind of time with God:

> One thing I have desired of the LORD, That will I seek: That I may dwell in the house of the LORD All the days of my life, To behold the beauty of the LORD And to inquire in His temple. *(v. 4)*

All the how-tos that follow are intended to help you create and enjoy "set apart" times with the Person of God.

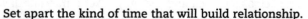

In abiding, what happens on the surface doesn't count; what's happening inside does.

Set apart the kind of time that will build relationship. Some Christians I know try to have their meaningful personal times with God just before bed, but I have yet to find a respected spiritual leader throughout history who had devotions at night. Unless you get up early, you're unlikely to break through to a deeper relationship with God. Set aside a significant time and a private place where you can read and write comfortably, think, study, talk to God out loud, and weep if you need to.

Savor God's Word to You. When you read your Bible, receive and savor it like food, like a treasure, like a love letter from God to you. Remember, you're reading in order to meet Someone. Ponder what you have read, and apply it to your present circumstances. Let it go down into the core of your being. And as you read, expect Him to commune with you. Paul advised, "Let the word of Christ dwell in you richly" *(COLOSSIANS 3:16)*.

Talk and listen to a Person. So often, when we turn to prayer, we treat God like He's some mystical force "out there." But God wants you to talk to Him like you would a friend. He wants to hear your requests, your worries, and your praise and thanks. Risk being honest, and expect His insight in return. Take time to be still before Him. Decide to seek the Lord until you find Him.

Keep a daily written record of what God is doing in your life. I recommend that you keep a spiritual journal—not a diary of your day, or an attempt at literature, but a living record of your very personal journey with God. Share with Him your disappointments, celebrations, and confusions. Ask Him for wisdom … and leave your request on the page until you receive guidance. Keep track of His answers. I believe that men in particular need a tool like journaling to bring a sense of reality to their relationship with our invisible God.

Remember, these simple practices are called disciplines because they take effort. But the reward is worth it!

◆

Unless you get up early, you're unlikely to break through to a deeper relationship with God.

◆

Principle 2: To break through to abiding I must broaden my devoted time—taking it from a morning appointment to an all-day attentiveness to His presence.

Too many of us leave God in the study or beside our favorite chair and go on with life. But the lessons of the vine show us that so *much more* is possible!

One day, in a library, I happened upon a lithograph of a legendary vineyard set on a rocky hillside high above Germany's Rhine Valley. The illustration showed vines that had been producing bountiful harvests for generations. An inset depicted one of the vines. It came out of the ground thick as an elephant's trunk. All along the row, enormous clusters of grapes hung down through the light canopy of leaves.

For years people wondered how these vines could flourish in such an inhospitable environment. An accompanying text explained: "The roots of the ancient plants have been traced to the distant river."

That ancient vineyard reminds me that I can always be "present" with God, no matter what is whirling around me. God invites each of us to be tapped into His purposes and power *all the time.*

Brother Lawrence, a seventeenth-century lay Christian who worked in a monastery kitchen, described his practice of abiding in God: "I do nothing else but abide in His holy presence, and I do this by simple attentiveness and an habitual, loving turning of my eyes on Him. This I call ... a wordless and secret conversation between the soul and God which no longer ends."

How could this work in a busy person's life? Annie shared her experience:

> I'm putting away groceries, and the kids are tearing through the house with the bags over their heads, screaming. I can be a little frazzled, but inside I'm saying, "Jesus, You are here with me, in me, around me. Thank You for food and for my noisy kids." I'm not always successful at this, but I try to take Jesus with me wherever I go. We keep each other constant company.

OVERCOMING BARRIERS TO ABIDING

If abiding is the key to unlimited abundance, why are there so few Annies? I believe the answer goes beyond laziness or indifference. Many have never been taught what it means to abide. Others are hindered by damaging misconceptions, such as the idea that God doesn't really like them. Here are two more misconceptions that keep good people from the riches of abiding.

Misconception 1: Abiding is based on feelings.

Communion with God is a relationship, not a sensation. That will come as a huge relief if you think you must have an emotional rush or sentimental feeling when you spend time with God. You won't always, and you don't need to.

We understand this in our marriages and other significant friendships. My love for Darlene is constant—but my feelings for her are far different during an argument than they are during a candlelight dinner. We don't measure the depth of our relationship by our feelings at any particular moment.

Abiding is an act of faith—a radical expression that you value God's unrestricted presence in your life more than any immediate sensation. If you think you must always have strong feelings in order to know you've been with God, you'll go away from your devoted times disappointed. Before long you'll say, "Abiding just didn't work for me."

♦

Communion with God is a relationship, not a sensation.

♦

Misconception 2: We can abide in Jesus without obeying Him.

Jesus told His friends in the vineyard, "If you keep My commandments, you will abide in My love" (JOHN 15:10). We might paraphrase what Jesus is saying like this: "If you want to abide with Me, you have to go where I'm going. When you go your own way, you're on your own."

Disobeying always creates a breach in your relationship with God. You can enjoy an emotional worship experience on Sunday but if you pursue a sinful lifestyle during the week, you will never succeed at abiding.

MORE FOR LESS

If you're at all like me, by now you're struggling with the basic math of abiding. It may sound a bit fishy, like one of those fast-food TV ads promising more beef for less bucks. You're wondering how working less *for* Him in order to spend more time *with* Him can add up to "much fruit" in your life.

One reason is that when you abide, God rewards you by supernaturally multiplying your efforts. I've experienced this firsthand more times than I can count. But there are other reasons why the third secret of the vineyard—*abiding more, doing less*—leads us to more results for God. These have to do with the benefits of abiding—what happens to us and through us when we consistently practice it.

Abiding helps us to sense the leading of the Lord. We learn to recognize God's "still small voice" (1 KINGS 19:12) and become familiar with His ways. Abiding helps us to accomplish more for Him because we are more in tune with His directives.

Abiding helps us to tap into all of God's spiritual riches. As we saw with the illustration of the vineyard in Germany, when we're abiding, we can draw deeply from God's resources. The disciples learned this principle, and it was evident as they healed and preached. In Acts 4:13 we read, "Now when they saw the boldness of Peter and John, and perceived that they were uneducated and untrained men, they marveled. And they realized that they had been with Jesus." When we abide, we are "with Jesus" and are filled with His Spirit and power.

◆

By the miracle of His life in us and with us, we will realize our greatest achievements.

◆

Abiding gives us the "rest" we need to bear a much greater yield. When we spend intimate time with our Savior, we are strengthened and refreshed to do His work.

Abiding carries with it a promise of answered prayer. Jesus said, "If you abide in Me, and My words abide in you, you will ask what you desire, and it shall be done for you. By this My Father is glorified, that you bear much fruit" (JOHN 15:7–8). Later, in verse 16, Jesus repeats the promise, and again it is directly connected to the disciples' mission of bearing fruit.

Nothing pleases God more than when we ask for what He wants to give. When we spend time with Him and allow His priorities, passions, and purposes to motivate us, we will ask for the things that are closest to His heart.

ONE FOR THE RECORD BOOKS

By the miracle of God's life in you and with you, you will see fruit of such quantity and size in your life that you will be amazed, and you will know that *you had nothing to do with it.*

Undoubtedly the most startling symbol of abundance in the Old Testament is this snapshot of what the spies found in the Promised Land: "They came to the Valley of Eschol, and there cut down a branch with *one cluster of grapes; they carried it between two of them on a pole*" (NUMBERS 13:23, EMPHASIS ADDED). Have you ever heard of such an astounding harvest?

My friend, keep that snapshot of supernatural abundance in your mind because it is the portrait of fruitfulness that God has in store for you! ❖

What About the Bible?

by Bruce Bickel and Stan Jantz

Chapter:
The Bible: The Deeper You Go

Book:
Knowing the Bible 101

Look for your coupons for this and other featured titles in the back of this book.

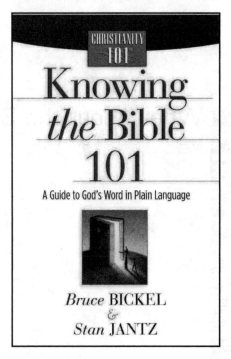

Author's Bio

Bruce Bickel is an attorney who specializes in estate planning and trust law. He is also a corporate motivational speaker whose ministry involvements include preaching and speaking at Christian conferences. Stan Jantz is a marketing consultant and a partner in a community-building software company. Stan and Bruce are coauthors of over 40 books including *What Ticks God Off*, *God is in the Small Stuff* and *Bruce and Stan Search for the Meaning of Life*. As a writing team, their goal is to present God's truth in a correct, clear and casual manner.

What About the Bible?

by Bruce Bickel and Stan Jantz

What's Ahead
- Read to Live
- Why Study the Bible?
- How Do You Interpret the Bible?
- Watch Out for Twisted Scripture
- Get Alone—and Get a Group
- Begin to Build a Bible Study Library
- Which Bible Is Right for You?
- You Have All the Help You Need

The Bible requires an activity that must take place before we can enjoy its benefits. It's called *reading*. Because God chose written language as the primary method of communicating His message to us, the Bible is, first of all, meant to be read.

We know that for some people this may be a new idea. After all, throughout history, the Bible has had a number of uses:

- The Bible looks great on a coffee table, especially when the pastor comes for a visit.
- On several documented occasions, a Bible stuffed into the breast pocket of a military jacket prevented a bullet from inflicting mortal harm to a soldier.
- Without the Bible, people in a courtroom would have to swear on a copy of Webster's dictionary.

READ TO LIVE

The Bible is nothing more than a symbol or a prop for many people. It will become meaningful to you under one condition and one condition only: You have to *read* it. And we're not talking about reading it only on special occasions or religious holidays. If you want to experience God and enjoy spiritual results, you need to develop the reading habit.

Here's yet another way to think of it: There's never a day when you don't read your mail. You don't leave it unopened and say, "Someday, when I have time, I'm going to read my mail." You at least open your mail before the end of the day.

If your earthly mail, which is filled with so much meaningless trivia and bad news, has such a hold on your life, how much more should you be eager to read your heavenly mail each day?

Although we're going to spend quite a bit of time in this chapter talking about how to study the Bible, studying should never be a substitute for reading. Here's why. Reading is subjective. Reading is a personal thing between you and the author. Reading is intimate.

Remember, the Bible is God's message to *you*. In effect, it's a collection of letters God has written to you—and He wants you to read them.

◆

Fifteen Minutes a Day

If you started reading the Bible aloud, you could probably read every verse in 80 hours or less. Think about this: You could read the Bible through in two weeks if you spent eight hours a day. You could read the Bible through in a year in just 15 minutes a day.

◆

WHY STUDY THE BIBLE?

Let's face it, studying is not the most popular activity in the world. Somehow we've come to view studying as something difficult and unpleasant. True, work is involved. But at its core, studying the Bible will produce such joy in your life that you will be eager to do it on a regular basis.

In fact, that's what the word *study* actually means: "to be eager, or diligent." Once you've gotten into the habit of reading, you need to take the next step and develop a habit of systematic study. You want to be *eager* to learn more about God's Word.

Look at the benefits:

1. You will please God.
There is a direct correlation between your eagerness to study and God's approval.

> Work hard so God can approve you. Be a good worker,
> one who does not need to be ashamed and who
> correctly explains the word of truth *(2 Timothy 2:15)*.

2. You will learn how to live and grow as a Christian.

Just as a baby needs and craves his mother's milk, Christians
(especially new Christians) must drink in the spiritual nourishment
provided by God's Word.

> You must crave pure spiritual milk so that you can
> grow into the fullness of your salvation. Cry out for this
> nourishment as a baby cries for milk *(1 Peter 2:2)*.

◆

Your Letter from Home

Read the Bible not as a newspaper, but as a home letter. If a cluster
of heavenly fruit hangs within reach, gather it. If a promise lies upon the
page as a blank check, cash it. If a prayer is recorded, make it yours and
launch it as a feathered arrow from the bow of your desire. If an example
of holiness gleams before you, ask God to do as much for you. If the truth
is revealed to you, ask God to make it shine through your whole life.
—F.B. Meyer

◆

3. You will develop spiritual discernment.

The only way to know if others are speaking the truth is
to know the truth yourself. When the apostle Paul stopped at
a church in Berea, he found believers there studying diligently.

> And the people of Berea were more open-minded than
> those in Thessalonica, and they listened eagerly to
> Paul's message. They searched the Scriptures day after
> day to check up on Paul and Silas, to see if they were
> really teaching the truth *(Acts 17:11)*.

4. You will be able to answer the questions of others. Studying the Bible will help you give clear answers to those who ask you about your faith.

> And if you are asked about your Christian hope, always
> be ready to explain it *(1 Peter 3:15)*.

HOW DO YOU INTERPRET THE BIBLE?

The most valuable thing you can do as you read and study the Bible is to *bring out the meaning*. This is also known as *interpretation*. When you interpret something, you make it plain and understandable. Remember what we said in the last chapter about the value of writing something down? There's no mistaking your words. Your *meaning*, however, is a different matter. Any written document—a letter, a novel, a contract—needs to be interpreted if it is to be understood.

The goal of interpreting the Bible should be to apply the meaning of what you learn to your life. As James says, it doesn't do much good to hear (or read, or study) God's message if you don't do anything about it.

> And remember, it is a message to obey, not just to listen to. If you don't obey, you are only fooling yourself (*JAMES 1:22*).

◆

Scripture is like a pair of spectacles which dispels the darkness and gives us a clear view of God.
—John Calvin

◆

A Few Basic Principles of Interpretation

R. C. Sproul lists three important principles for making the Bible plain and understandable.

1. Interpret the Bible by the Bible. "What is obscure in one part of Scripture may be made clear in another," writes Sproul. "To interpret Scripture by Scripture means that we must not set one passage of Scripture against another passage." This also means that you always read Bible verses and passages *in context*.

Context is a lot like *character*. Just like it's tempting to jump on a rumor about someone even if it's totally out of character, it's tempting to take something in the Bible out of context. In both cases, all that does is make you feel better, even if you're wrong. Here's a guideline:

> When it comes to *people*, consider the *character*.
> When it comes to *Scripture*, consider the *context*.

2. Interpret the Bible literally. What this means is that you should interpret the Bible *as it is written*. Don't read into it something that isn't there, and don't skip over something that is. Because the Bible speaks honestly about the human condition, we sometimes get offended by what we read in the Bible. We would rather *deny* what the Bible says than *deal* with what the Bible says.

◆

Sweet to the Taste

King David was so in love with God's Word that he could literally taste it: "How sweet are your words to my taste; they are sweeter than honey" (Psalm 119:103). The prophet Jeremiah wrote that the Word of God sustained his life (Jeremiah 15:16).

Sound crazy? Not in the least. In addition to merely reading the Bible regularly (like we would the newspaper), we can really take it in—and let it change our lives. Try these three ways:

• Study—Make an effort to learn God's Word (2 Timothy 2:15).
• Meditate—Think deeply about God's Word (Psalm 1:2).
• Memorize—Be ready to recall God's Word (Psalm 119:11).

◆

3. Interpret the Bible objectively. It's easy to interpret the Bible subjectively, according to our own viewpoints and desires. This is where people can get into serious disagreements, both with the Bible and with each other. As you read and study the Bible, focus on what it says rather than on what you already believe. As one Bible scholar wrote: "One must first ask what a given Scripture was intended to mean to the people for whom it was originally written. Only then is the interpreter free to ask what meaning it has for Christians today."

Avoid the temptation to stamp your own impressions or feelings on Scripture before you discover the objective truth it contains. Let's say Bruce made a statement regarding an area of law in which he was an authority. But Stan disagreed—not because he knew the law, but because he didn't "feel" it applied to him. Stan's viewpoint would be subjective (and probably wrong), which would prompt Bruce to say, "It's your right as an American to feel that way, but you are wrong."

This doesn't mean that you shouldn't come to your own conclusions about what the Bible means. You aren't obligated to follow someone else's viewpoint. However, your own "private interpretation" will only be meaningful with the guidance of the Holy Spirit combined with your own diligent study. Remember that the Bible bears the authority of God. Trust God's Word to mean what it says.

By following these principles, you will become a person who "correctly explains the word of truth" *(2 TIMOTHY 2:15)*.

◆

Good Form

Interpreting the Bible literally doesn't mean that you read each Bible passage the same way. It's important to know what kind of literary form you are reading. The Bible contains historical narratives (or stories), poetry, parables, prophecies, and teaching.

◆

WATCH OUT FOR TWISTED SCRIPTURE

The reason it's so important to handle Scripture correctly is that it's the only way God has chosen to speak *directly* to us. That's not to say that God doesn't speak to you *indirectly*. He can and does—through your circumstances, through wise people, and through your own inner sensitivity to the Holy Spirit.

But when you interpret Scripture to fit your own desires and preconceived ideas, you just might change it from truth to error. When you change the Bible's objective truth to fit your life rather than changing your life to fit the Bible, you run the risk of "twisting Scripture."

◆

Cults at Your Door

The difference between a cult and a religion is that the major teachings of a cult come out of someone's false interpretation of the Bible whereas a religion is defined more broadly as any system of faith and worship. The major cults in the world today (these are the ones you will probably encounter) are Jehovah's Witnesses, Mormonism, Christian Science, and the Unification Church. Interpreting the Bible literally doesn't mean that you read each Bible passage the same way. It's important to know what kind of literary form you are reading. The Bible contains historical narratives (or stories), poetry, parables, prophecies, and teaching.

◆

How to Spot Twisted Scripture

"Scripture twisting" refers to what happens when people interpret the Bible to suit their own false beliefs. The apostle Paul confronted members of the Galatian church, who were following a "different way."

> I am shocked that you are turning away so soon from God, who in his love and mercy called you to share the eternal life he gives through Christ. You are already following a different way that pretends to be the Good News but is not the Good News at all. You are being fooled by those who twist and change the truth concerning Christ (GALATIANS 1:6-7).

Sometimes entire belief systems will come from people who "change the truth." If such people organize and begin teaching others their beliefs, we can correctly call them a "cult." Josh McDowell defines a cult as "a perversion, a distortion of biblical Christianity." At its core, a cult "rejects the historic teachings of the Christian Church."

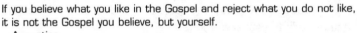

If you believe what you like in the Gospel and reject what you do not like, it is not the Gospel you believe, but yourself.
—Augustine

How to Spot a Counterfeit

Think about counterfeit money. A good counterfeit bill is one that looks exactly like the real thing. Do you know how the experts learn to tell the phony bills from the genuine article? They don't study the counterfeit bills (there are too many variations to keep track). They study the real thing (there is only one). Bank tellers are great at spotting counterfeit money because they *handle* the real bills all day long.

Do you think Satan and his demons know the Bible? Absolutely. Better than you do. We sometimes refer to Satan as the "prince of darkness," and that he is. But he's also known as the "angel of light." Satan and his servants work by sneaking up on you with something that looks like the truth. But it's a lie.

> These people are false apostles. They have fooled you
> by disguising themselves as apostles of Christ. But I am
> not surprised! Even Satan can disguise himself as an
> angel of light. So it is no wonder his servants can also
> do it by pretending to be godly ministers. In the end
> they will get every bit of punishment their wicked
> deeds deserve (2 CORINTHIANS 11:13-15).

If you want to get good at spotting false teachings—if you want to develop your spiritual discernment—then spend time with the real deal. Learn to correctly handle the Word of Truth (2 TIMOTHY 2:15). Then, like the Bereans who checked out Paul, you will be able to see if the people you hear or the books you read are "really teaching the truth" (ACTS 17:11).

◆

The devil can cite Scripture for his purpose.
—William Shakespeare

◆

GET ALONE—AND GET A GROUP

Studying the Bible on your own is an important and practical way to approach Bible study. You can set your own schedule and read and study in your own room.

What counts to God is your *heart*. This prayer of King David should be our prayer every time we approach God's Word:

> Create in me a clean heart, O God. Renew a right spirit
> within me (PSALM 51:10).

◆

What About Bible Difficulties and Weird Stuff?

There are things about God and the Bible that will take time to understand (we'll talk about some Bible "difficulties" as we get into the Bible books). Be confident in knowing that as you carefully study God's Word, He will be faithful to reveal answers to you through the Holy Spirit (1 Corinthians 2:12-16). But don't expect to grow in your understanding of Scripture if you don't spend any time with it.

On the other hand, don't expect to know everything about God and the Bible. You can't. God is simply too vast for you to know everything. Trust God that He will show you what you need to know when you need to know it.

◆

As you study alone, you could do one of the following:
- ◆ Follow a self-study guide through a particular Bible book.
- ◆ Explore a topic using various Bible-study resources.
- ◆ Study groups of Bible books, such as the Gospels.

What If You Just Don't Get It?

Just because you pray for guidance and study hard doesn't mean you are going to understand everything in the Bible. Since the Bible is God's Word, and because there are things about God that are a mystery, it is inevitable that there will be things in Scripture that you don't understand. This doesn't make them wrong, and it doesn't mean that God has made a mistake.

Think of it this way. God is an infinite being. We are mere finite mortals. Likewise, God's Word is eternal *(ISAIAH 40:8)*, and our minds, even when we fix our minds on heavenly and eternal things, are still limited.

Rather than concentrate on what we don't know, we need to value and obey those things God has revealed to us, especially the truths in His Word.

> There are secret things that belong to the LORD our God, but the revealed things belong to us and our descendants forever, so that we may obey these words of the law *(DEUTERONOMY 29:29)*.

◆

Do's and Dont's of Group Bible Studies

Do study on your own before you meet with your group.
Don't show up without first doing your homework, depending on the Lord to "speak to you" with profound truth. God gets the credit for too many dumb ideas.
Do feel free to disagree with someone else's interpretation of a particular verse or Bible passage.
Don't intimidate or make other people feel inferior. Disagree in love and with diplomacy. And don't dominate the conversation when you're in a group. Remember, your own voice sounds better to you than to other people.
Do be honest as you share your questions or confusion.
Don't go for "shock value." Be sensitive to your group as you open up.

◆

The Advantages of a Group

In addition to studying on your own, we advise that you also participate in a *group* Bible study on a regular basis. It could be once a month or once a week. Again, the goal should be consistency.

When you're a part of a group Bible study, you have the advantage of learning and gaining insights from other people. Getting together with others who are eager to study God's Word can create a kind of *synergism* (the whole is greater than the sum of the individual parts). Plus, you can be an encouragement to others, and there may be times when you need encouragement yourself.

Ways to Get Involved in a Group Bible Study

◆ Meet with an existing organization, such as Bible Study Fellowship or a Sunday school class.

◆ Help organize a home Bible study where you meet with friends in various home locations.

◆ Volunteer to *disciple* someone else one-to-one (a disciple is a *learner*). There are some excellent materials available for this, most notably the "Operation Timothy" study guides.

◆ You may want to be discipled yourself. Seek out someone who knows more about the Bible than you do and whose life demonstrates the kind of Christlike qualities you want in your own life.

◆

Seekers Wanted

Does everyone in a group Bible study need to be a Christian? That's up to you, but our suggestion is that you include seekers who really want to learn what the Bible has to say. In this way a Bible study can be a means of telling others about the good news of the Bible.

◆

BEGIN TO BUILD A BIBLE STUDY LIBRARY

The more you study the Bible, the more you will want to use some Bible study resources. At the end of each chapter of this book, we give you a short bibliography of recommended books and other resources.

Right now we want to give you some *categories* of Bible study resources that you will want to begin adding to your personal library. These are listed in a kind of priority order. The best place to purchase these types of materials is at your local Christian retail store. You can also find these materials in your church library.

Bible concordance. A concordance lists the words found in the Bible and tells you which verses in the Bible contain each word. An *exhaustive* concordance will list every word (except *and, a, an,* and *the*) and then give you the original Hebrew (if the word is found in the Old Testament) or Greek (if the word is found in the New Testament) meaning of the word. The original meanings of words can provide amazing insight into your Bible study. The concordance found at the end of some Bibles will simply tell you where to find certain key words.

Bible dictionary. Like a Webster's dictionary, a Bible dictionary will give meanings and, in some cases, the history of significant Bible words, people, and places.

Bible handbook. Books of this type provide a basic overview of the Bible and a book-by-book synopsis of all 66 books.

Bible commentary. You can get commentaries for each book of the Bible, but we suggest you start by adding a single-volume Bible commentary to your library. It can help you with the background of the Bible, as well as provide insights when you study a particular word, verse, passage, chapter, or book in the Bible.

WHICH BIBLE IS RIGHT FOR YOU?

Choosing a Bible to read and study can be confusing. You'll find dozens of different Bible translations (or versions) available in English. Which one is the best? Actually, there is no "best" Bible, although there may be a Bible that's best for you. Don't be concerned that you are going to end up with a "bad" Bible translation. "Translating" simply means changing from one language to another. Where different Bible versions may differ is in the *method* used to translate them.

Here are some examples of popular Bibles that were translated according to three different methods:

Word for word. This approach, technically called literal, or *complete equivalence*, translates each word of the Hebrew and Greek as closely as possible in order to keep the meaning and structure of the original language. These translations are generally more difficult to read because they often use long sentences and complicated grammar.

> King James Version (KJV)
> New King James Version (NKJV)
> New American Standard Bible (NASB)
> New Revised Standard Version (NRSV)

Thought for thought. This approach, technically called *dynamic equivalence*, focuses more on ideas than word-for-word translation. The emphasis in these Bibles is on translating the Hebrew and Greek into contemporary English "idioms," or concepts, while keeping the original meaning.

> Today's English Version (TEV)
> New International Version (NIV)
> Contemporary English Version (CEV)
> New Living Translation (NLT)

Paraphrase. This approach simplifies or expands the author's words to make the Bible easier to understand. A paraphrase is not a translation in the literal sense.

> The Living Bible
> The Message

◆

God used the scriptural Gospel to bring me to saving faith in Jesus Christ. He has also convinced me that the Scriptures are utterly true, inerrant, if you will; they are the "swaddling clothes in which Christ is laid." Some will call this conviction hopelessly naÔve or a refusal to look at the findings of twentieth-century science. So be it. If the scientist is our authority, ask him if dead men rise.

—Karl Barth, twentieth-century theologian

◆

Take a Test Drive

With a car, there's no substitute for getting behind the wheel. When it comes to a Bible, a test drive involves reading it for yourself. Have some favorite verses picked out in advance so that you can read them in different translations when you get to the Christian bookstore. For example, here's Psalm 1:1 in three different translations:

> *Blessed is the man that walketh not in the counsel of the ungodly, nor standeth in the way of sinners, nor sitteth in the seat of the scornful*—Kings James Version.

> *Blessed is the man who does not walk in the counsel of the wicked or stand in the way of sinners or sit in the seat of mockers*—New International Version.

> *Oh, the joys of those who do not follow the advice of the wicked, or stand around with sinners, or join in with scoffers*—New Living Translation.

Once you've decided which Bible translation you want, you will need to select your *options*. Here's a handy checklist:

- ◆ Text Only
- ◆ Cross-References
- ◆ Concordance
- ◆ Study Notes
- ◆ Hardback
- ◆ Leather Cover
- ◆ Small Print
- ◆ Medium Print
- ◆ Large Print

Keep in mind that your options will affect the size of your Bible.

Fortunately, the Bible publishers have come up with some wonderful Bible packages which provide practical features helpful in your Bible study. Our personal favorite is the *Life Application Bible* (a type of study Bible which includes thousands of helpful notes, references, and personal applications) in the *New Living Translation* (the translation we are using in this book). Most study Bibles are available in a variety of translations.

YOU HAVE ALL THE HELP YOU NEED

There's no question that the Bible has a lot of words (773,692 in the King James Version). But it doesn't have to be intimidating. God wants to talk to you through His Word, regardless of where you are in your spiritual journey:

- ◆ searching but skeptical
- ◆ exploring with an open mind
- ◆ interested but ignorant
- ◆ eager for more

And all you have to do is begin reading with a sincere desire to learn.

When you begin to search for God through His Word, He will meet you where you are. He has promised...

> "If you look for me in earnest, you will find me when you seek me. I will be found by you," says the LORD (JEREMIAH 29:13-14).

◆

What's That Again?

1. Because reading is a personal thing between you and the author, reading the Bible should be your first priority.
2. Studying the Bible offers many benefits, not the least of which is that it pleases God.
3. When you interpret the Bible, you bring out the meaning.
4. When people interpret the Bible to suit their own false beliefs, they are engaging in Scripture twisting.
5. Satan and his followers are very good at creating counterfeit beliefs.
6. Group Bible studies give you the advantage of learning and gaining insights from other people.
7. There is no "best" Bible, but there is probably a Bible which is best for you.

◆

DIG DEEPER

Here are some great books that explain how to read and study the Bible:

Living by the Book by Howard Hendricks and William Hendricks. With wit and wisdom, legendary Bible teacher Howard Hendricks and his son, William, tell you how to study the Bible so it will affect your life.

How to Read the Bible for All Its Worth by Gordon Fee and Douglas Stuart. This very popular book is a step-by-step guide to understanding the Bible.

How to Study Your Bible by Kay Arthur. The founder and president of Precept Ministries shows you how to study the Bible inductively, which means directly interacting with God's Word.

735 Baffling Bible Questions Answered by Larry Richards.
If you've got questions about the Bible, Dr. Richards
has the answers. A great resource.

Unmasking the Cults by Alan W. Gomes. An inexpensive
booklet which gives you the characteristics of a cult. ❖

QUESTIONS FOR REFLECTION AND DISCUSSION

1. You've read the benefits of reading the Bible. What influences
    keep you from reading and studying the Bible on a regular
    basis? What can you do to overcome them?
2. How can R.C. Sproul's three principles of interpretation help
    you get more out of your Bible reading? Give one benefit for
    each principle.
3. Have you ever "twisted" Scripture to suit your own false
    beliefs? Have you ever twisted Scripture to justify your own
    wrong behavior? What happened, and how did you straighten
    out?
4. List three things you can do—starting immediately—to
    correctly handle the Word of truth (hint: quick fixes and magic
    formulas won't work).
5. Does anything in the Bible really bother you? What is it? (Don't
    be afraid to be honest. God isn't going to hit you with a bolt of
    lightning.) What are three practical things you can do deal
    with your dilemma?
6. Can people who disagree with each other's interpretation of
    a particular Bible verse or passage still get along? Is "agreeing
    to disagree" always enough when interpretations differ?
7. Review the two different methods of Bible translation (word
    for word, thought for thought) and Bible paraphrasing. Is your
    Bible a paraphrase, a word-for-word translation, or a thought-
    for-thought translation? How did you happen to choose your
    Bible? Is reading and studying from more than one Bible
    translation a good idea? Why or why not?

MOVING ON...

We hope that you're getting the idea that the Bible is a very personal thing between you and God. The more you read and study the Bible, the more you're going to know about God. And the more you know about God, the more you're going to love Him.

What is Heaven?

by Anne Graham Lotz

Chapter:
The Home of Your Dreams

Book:
Heaven: My Father's House

Look for your coupons for this and other featured titles in the back of this book.

Author's Bio

Anne Graham Lotz has passionately carried the gospel throughout the world in venues ranging from downtown arenas to death-row prison cells, church sanctuaries to university lecture-halls. She is the founder of AnGeL Ministries, a nonprofit organization that is holding Just Give Me Jesus revivals in arenas throughout the United States. Anne's previous books, *The Vision of His Glory*, *God's Story*, and *Just Give Me Jesus* were each awarded the ECPA Gold Medallion Award for excellence. She is the second daughter of Billy and Ruth Graham.

What is Heaven?
by Anne Graham Lotz

My Father's House is the home you have always wanted.

"No eye has seen, no ear has heard, no mind has conceived
what God has prepared for those who love him,"—
but God has revealed it to us by his Spirit.
—1 Corinthians 2:9–10

What is the home of your dreams? If you are ...
an Eskimo living in an ice hut,
a Chinese living in a bamboo hut,
an African living in a mud hut,
a homeless person living in a newspaper hut,
a Bedouin living in a tent,
an Indian living in a teepee,
a royal living in a palace,
a tenant living in a project,
a slum dweller living in a shanty,
a president living in the White House,
a celebrity living in a penthouse,
a peasant living in a farmhouse,
a city dweller living in a rowhouse,
an orphan living in a foster house,
a criminal living in a prison house,
a soldier living in a guardhouse,
a beggar with no house at all ...
it doesn't matter! We all have dreams of what home
should be like.

Do you dream of a home you can never go back to, or a home
you can never have?

Do you dream of a home with love and laughter and loyalty,
with family and fun and freedom?

Do you dream of a home where you are accepted, encouraged, and challenged, forgiven, understood, and comforted?

Do you dream of a home that never was, or a home that never will be?

When did your home begin to unravel? Have you been blindsided by divorce or death or disease or depression or a thousand and one other difficulties that have turned your dreams into a nightmare?

There is hope! The home you've always wanted, the home you continue to long for with all your heart, is the home God is preparing for you! As John continued to gaze at the vision of the glory of Jesus Christ that God revealed to him, he must have stood in awed wonder of a "new heaven and a new earth" (REVELATION 21:1). What he saw was confirmed by the words of the One Who was seated on the throne: "I am making everything new!" (REVELATION 21:5). Imagine it: One day, in the dream home of My Father's House, *everything* will be brand-new!

NO SEPARATION

Following the terrorist attack on the World Trade Center in New York City and the Pentagon in Washington, D.C., our nation was gripped by the heartrending sight of thousands of individuals wandering the streets of lower Manhattan carrying pictures of their friends and family members who were missing. A fence lining one of the nearby parks became a memorial wall as hundreds of pictures were posted with detailed descriptions of what the missing loved ones were wearing, of where they worked, of when they were last seen—all in the hopes that those missing persons might be found. As the days dragged into weeks, it became apparent that there would be no more survivors. Just when our nation thought there were no more tears to weep, we wept uncontrollably as a seemingly endless stream of memorial services was begun and the separation between friends and loved ones was finalized. Each heart-wrenching, tearful good-bye made me long for My Father's House.

John reassured us that there will be no separation in Heaven when he said, "There was no longer any sea" *(Revelation 21:1)*. Now, I love the sea. Every summer, I spend as much time there as I am able. I love to see the vast expanse of sky and water. I love to hear the waves crashing on the shore. I love to walk along the beach and feel the sand beneath my feet and the breeze blowing gently in my face. But the sea separates families and friends and entire continents from each other! In Heaven, there will be *nothing* that separates us from each other or from God. Ever!

> No hard feelings or hurt feelings,
> No misunderstandings or critical spirits,
> No divorce or death,
> No piles of rubble or prisons of debris,
> No business trips or military call-ups,
> No sickness or weakness,
> No dangers or hardships,
> No fires or famines or floods,
> No wars or refugee camps or ethnic cleansing,
> No racial or political or religious prejudice,
> No religions or polls or denominations,
> No class systems or economic sanctions or human slavery,
> *Nothing* will ever separate us in My Father's House.

We will enjoy perfect health and harmony and unity and unbroken times together! There will not even be the natural separation between night and day because, "The city does not need the sun or the moon to shine on it, for the glory of God gives it light, and the Lamb is its lamp" *(Revelation 21:23)*. Our heavenly home will glow and radiate with light from within—the light of God Himself and the glorious radiance of His presence.

I have been in some of the great cities of the world at night. I have looked out after sunset from Victoria Peak in Hong Kong during the Chinese New Year, and I have seen the lights transform the hills surrounding the harbor into a virtual fairyland. I have seen the lights of Capetown, South Africa, wrapped around Table Mountain at night forming a vast, jewel-studded skirt. I have seen Paris from Montmartre after dinner, stretched out for miles in an endless sea of light with the lighted outline of the Eiffel Tower beckoning like a finger to those who love beauty.

But even in those great cities with their millions of lights, there are still pockets of darkness. In our heavenly home, there will be no darkness at all. No one will ever stumble or be lost or unable to find his or her way. Jesus said, "I am the light of the world,"[1] and He also said we "are the light of the world."[2] The sole light in Heaven will be the light that comes directly from God through Jesus Christ, and that light will be reflected in the life of each one of His children! The entire city will be saturated with the glory and light of life, truth, righteousness, goodness, love, and peace. Your hope is sure! John said that he was instructed, "Write this down, for these words are trustworthy and true" (REVELATION 21:5). You and I can look forward with confident hope—our heavenly home will be perfect!

NO SCARS

Because Heaven is perfect, there will be nothing to mar its beauty. My husband, Danny, and I bought the house we live in when it was twenty years old, and we have been living in it now for thirty years. Because it is about fifty years old, there are some stains I will never be able to remove, some cracks in the tile that can never be repaired, some wear and tear that gives the house a slightly frayed, worn-out look. It's just scarred by age. When I visit some of my friends in their brand-new homes, I look longingly at the fresh, unmarked woodwork and painted walls; the fresh, unstained carpet; the fresh, glistening tile and appliances; the fresh, unscratched windowpanes. It's all fresh! New! Unscarred, unsoiled, and unworn by age!

Planet earth is, at the very least, thousands of years old. Some think it may be millions or billions of years old. And it is showing signs of age. It is getting frayed and worn out. It is being polluted, gouged, stripped, burned, and poisoned, and much of the damage has been willfully and selfishly inflicted by man. But some of the scars are simply due to the wear and tear of age. It was not created to last forever!

In contrast, our heavenly home is going to be brand-new. Not just restored, but created fresh. John emphasized this again and again when he described "a *new* heaven and a *new* earth," and a "*new* Jerusalem," and once again the clear directive came from the One Who was seated on the throne, saying, "'I am making everything new!' Then He said, 'Write this down, for these words are trustworthy and true.'" God Himself was verifying that all His promises are true.

What scars of sin or stains of guilt do you bear in your life? On your emotions? On your personality? On your relationships? On your memories? Like planet earth, do you feel abused and gouged and worn out and burned by other people? Does your life show the signs of wear and tear inflicted willfully and selfishly by those who have had authority over you? Have you ever longed to be able to start your life over again? Maybe you can even identify with the following testimony of a woman who spoke with me several years ago.

After presenting a message to a large convention, this woman came up to me and briefly told me her story. She described being raised in a family where her father and brothers repeatedly abused her sexually. She was so humiliated, angry, and bitter, she grew up to live a very immoral lifestyle. When she finally married and had a family, she abused her own children. One day she heard that God loved her and had sent His Son, Jesus Christ, to die in order to cleanse her of her sin. She responded by asking God to forgive and cleanse her for Jesus' sake, and she said she knew He had answered her prayer. "But," she softly cried, "I just can't seem to forget. What can I do about the memories?"

What could I say? There was nothing I could do except put my arms around her and tell her that one day there will be no more scars. God will wipe all tears away and erase all memories of such sin and abuse. *Everything*—including our heart, mind, emotions, psyche, and memories, past, present, and future—will be made new.

However, until then God does give us encouragement. His reassurance is illustrated by this true story that took place years ago in the Highlands of Scotland. A group of fishermen sat around a table in a small pub, telling their "fish stories." As one of the men flung out his arms to more vividly describe the fish that got away, he accidentally hit the tray of drinks that the young barmaid was bringing to the table. The tray and the drinks sailed through the air, crash-landing against the newly whitewashed wall. As the sound of smashed glass and splashing beer permeated the room, the pub became silent as all eyes turned to the ugly brown stain that was forming on the wall.

Before anyone could recover from the startling interruption, a guest who had been sitting quietly by himself in the corner jumped up, pulled a piece of charcoal from his pocket, and began to quickly sketch around the ugly brown stain. To the amazement of everyone present, right before their eyes the stain was transformed into a magnificent stag with antlers outstretched, racing across a highland meadow. Then the guest signed his impromptu work of art. His name was Sir Edwin Landseer, Great Britain's foremost wildlife artist.

God transforms lives as Sir Landseer transformed the ugly mess on that pub wall. What ugly brown stain does your life bear? Like the woman at the convention, were you abused as a child? Have you abused someone else's child? Or your own? Have you been raped? Have you been the victim of a violent crime? Have you had an abortion? Or performed one? Have you committed adultery? Or seduced someone else to do so? Is there a nasty addiction in your life to drugs? alcohol? pornography?

Regardless of what the stain is, submit it to God. You must be willing to turn away from any and all sin. Period. Then God excels in transforming ugly brown stains into beauty marks when we surrender them to Him. He will bring peace and freedom to you and glory to Himself. And when we get to Heaven there will be no more scars and no more suffering of any kind, including the kind that inflicted the wound that has scarred your life.

NO SUFFERING

Heaven will not only *look* fresh and new, it will *feel* fresh and new! John gives us, not just a vision of Heaven's fresh beauty, but a "feel" of Heaven's serenity, which permeates the atmosphere because God is there: "And I heard a loud voice from the throne saying, 'Now the dwelling of God is with men, and he will live with them. They will be his people, and God himself will be with them and be their God. He will wipe every tear from their eyes. There will be no more death or mourning or crying or pain, for the old order of things has passed away'" (REVELATION 21:3–4).

In what way are you suffering? Are you suffering ...

> Physically?
> Emotionally?
> Mentally?
> Financially?
> Materially?
> Relationally?
> Socially?
> Spiritually?

One day, God Himself will take your face in His hands and gently wipe away your tears as He reassures you there will be no more suffering in My Father's House. No more ...

> pain
> or hospitals
> or death
> or funerals
> or grief,
> or walkers
> or canes
> or wheelchairs.

There will be no more ...

> suicide bombers or fiery infernos,
> broken homes or broken hearts,
> broken lives or broken dreams.

There will be no more ...

> mental retardation or physical handicaps,
> muscular dystrophy or multiple sclerosis,
> blindness or lameness, deafness or sickness.

There will be no more ...

> Parkinson's disease or heart disease, diabetes or arthritis,
> cataracts or paralysis.

No more ...

> cancer or strokes or AIDS.

No more ...

> guns in schools
> or car bombs
> or terrorists
> or missiles
> or air strikes.

No more war!

You can look forward with hope, because one day there will be no more separation, no more scars, and no more suffering in My Father's House. It's the home of your dreams! ❖

CHAPTER NOTES
1. John 8:12
2. Matthew 5:14

How Do I Find Peace?
by Charles Stanley

Chapter:
Five Essential Beliefs for a Peaceful Heart

Book:
Finding Peace

Look for your coupons for this and other featured titles in the back of this book.

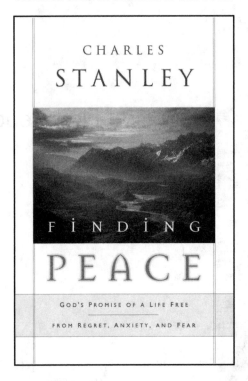

Author's Bio

Dr. Charles F. Stanley is pastor of the 15,000-member First Baptist Church in Atlanta, Georgia, and is president and CEO of In Touch® Ministries. He has twice been elected president of the Southern Baptist Convention and is well-known internationally through his IN TOUCH radio and television ministry. His many bestselling books include *Walking Wisely*, *When Tragedy Strikes*, *Charles Stanley's Handbook for Christian Living*, *A Touch of His Power*, *Our Unmet Needs*, *Enter His Gates*, and *The Source of My Strength*.

Excerpted from *Finding Peace* ©2003 by Charles F. Stanley. Used by permission of Thomas Nelson Publishers. All rights reserved.

How Do I Find Peace?
by Charles Stanley

Do you think Saddam Hussein or Osama bin Laden or any other person on this earth is in control of your safety and well-being? If so, you are sorely mistaken. If you are a Christian, then God alone is in charge of your life. He is your security.

"But what about the events of September 11, 2001?" you may ask. "Was God in control?"

My answer is, "Absolutely!" God has never been out of control over His creation for one fraction of a second since the beginning of time. Could God have prevented what happened? Certainly. Did God *allow* what happened? Yes. Did He have a purpose for allowing this to happen to our nation? Without a doubt.

◆

God has never been out of control over His creation for one fraction of a second since the beginning of time.

◆

We may not completely understand God's purposes, but we can be assured of this—God is *still* in control. He hasn't lost one measure of His power or might. He is just as omnipotent, omniscient, omnipresent, and all loving today as He was the day before September 11, 2001.

The godly response to tragedies such as those that occurred 9/11 are not the questions "Why did this happen?" or "Why did God allow this?" The godly response is to ask, "God, what do you want me to learn in response to this?"

If you continue to ask why, you will get bogged down, because why questions can never be answered fully. If you begin to ask, "what now?" or "how shall I respond?" you will find yourself moving forward with direction, purpose, and new energy. You will also have much greater peace.

Understanding the ways of God always leads to an understanding that God will act in a way that brings about eternal blessings for

His children. It is what we *believe* that makes it possible to ask the right questions in the face of a tragedy.

Through the years I have discovered five essential beliefs for a peaceful heart. I challenge you to take a long, hard look at what *you* believe about God. Your peace is determined by the degree to which these truths are embedded in your soul.

ESSENTIAL BELIEF #1: GOD IS ABSOLUTELY SOVEREIGN

Recognizing and accepting the truth that God is sovereign over absolutely everything is vital for your inner peace. God is absolutely sovereign—which means that nothing related to you is beyond His watchful eye and loving care.

So many people live with a nagging concern: "What will happen? Suppose this happens? Suppose that happens?" I've met a large number of people in just the last two years who tell me that they have a gnawing fear deep within—they wonder what will happen if they get on an airplane, open their mail, go into a high-rise building, or are bitten by a disease-carrying mosquito or tick. Others have confessed to me that they have a daily fear of sending their children to school. Still others have admitted they have a fearful dread of opening the business section of their newspaper—they feel an ongoing pressure inside them about the stock market and the current business climate.

If you have any of these concerns, I encourage you to carefully read Psalm 91—one of the outstanding passages in the Bible—as it speaks about God's control over all the affairs of life. It reads:

> He who dwells in the secret place of the Most High
> Shall abide under the shadow of the Almighty.
> I will say of the Lord, "He is my refuge and my fortress;
> My God, in Him I will trust."
> Surely He shall deliver you from the snare of the fowler
> And from the perilous pestilence.
> He shall cover you with His feathers,
> And under His wings you shall take refuge;
> His truth shall be your shield and buckler.

You shall not be afraid of the terror by night,
Nor of the arrow that flies by day,
Nor of the pestilence that walks in darkness,
Nor of the destruction that lays waste at noonday.
A thousand may fall at your side,
And ten thousand at your right hand;
But it shall not come near you.
Only with your eyes shall you look,
And see the reward of the wicked.
Because you have made the Lord, who is my refuge,
Even the Most High, your dwelling place,
No evil shall befall you,
Nor shall any plague come near your dwelling;
For He shall give His angels charge over you,
To keep you in all your ways.
In their hands they shall bear you up,
Lest you dash your foot against a stone.
You shall tread upon the lion and the cobra,
The young lion and the serpent you shall trample
underfoot.
"Because he has set his love upon Me, therefore
I will deliver him;
I will set him on high, because he has known My name.
He shall call upon Me, and I will answer him;
I will be with him in trouble;
I will deliver him and honor him.
With long life I will satisfy him,
And show him My salvation."

God is your protector. He is the One who preserves your life from hour to hour, day to day, year to year. He is in charge of keeping you alive on this earth until the split second that He desires for you to be in eternity with Him. No matter what happens to you, God has a plan to bless you on this earth and reward you in eternity. Everything you experience, even those things that you might label "bad," God can and will turn to eternal good if you will only trust Him to be your sovereign Lord.

A friend recently received very upsetting news in the mail. The realty company that had handled the sale of a house he owned was being sued by the couple who had purchased the house. The buyers were claiming fraud, and the implication was that my friend had been deceitful in what he had failed to disclose about the condition of the home at the time of the sale, as well as negligent in making repairs. While my friend was not named in the lawsuit against the realty company, he nonetheless was shocked at the allegations made against the real-estate agent and, indirectly, against him. For a few moments, he felt uneasy, sick at heart, and confused as to what course of action to take. His peace was momentarily shattered.

He told me, "Then as I finished reading the text of this legal document for the second time, I remembered you saying in a sermon, 'God is in control. He's always in control.' So I prayed, 'Lord, You are in control. This letter isn't any surprise to You. You know my heart. You know that I dealt honestly and in a straight-forward way with this couple. You know that I disclosed everything that I knew to be a problem with the property I sold. You know that I did my best to comply with all the rules and regulations stipulated by both the realty company and the property inspectors. You know how much money I spent on the required repairs, and that I went above and beyond what was required legally, both in disclosure and in fixing up the property for this family. I ask You right now to help me know what to do and how to respond, including whether I should do anything at all. Show me how to pray for this couple. Show me how to pray for the real-estate agent.'"

"What happened?" I asked.

He said, "I immediately had peace fill my heart. I knew without any doubt that I wasn't to do anything but pray for the couple that had purchased the house. I had a deep knowing that this couple had needs that were far deeper and more eternal in importance than the superficial property-upkeep needs that were outlined in the long letter they had written to the realty company. They were troubled, overwhelmed, in a panic, seeking to blame others, and were perhaps undercapitalized for the purchase they had made. So I set myself to praying that God would meet their needs and turn their hearts. I knew that if they continued to pursue this lawsuit, they were going to find themselves even more frustrated, more hurt, and that they very likely would not receive more than a small portion of the compensation they were seeking. As best I could tell from other property transactions I've been through, this sale had been handled in a quality manner.

"I don't know what will ultimately happen in this case," this friend concluded, "but I do know this. God is in control. He knows my heart, my motives, and all that has happened. He will protect me. And I also believe He will fulfill His purposes in the lives of this couple and the lives of all who are involved with this case at the realty company."

"Do you know why you have this confidence and peace?" I asked.

"Sure," he said with a smile. "You're just testing me, aren't you? I have peace because God said He would work all things together for good to those who are the called according to His purpose. I was led by God to sell this property. I sold it in a godly manner and with a clear conscience in all aspects of the sale. God will be true to His word. All things will work together for good."

He was absolutely right.

ESSENTIAL BELIEF #2:
GOD IS YOUR PROVIDER

From cover to cover, the Bible has a clear message that God is the One who provides for all your needs. No need is too massive, too problematic, or too severe for Jesus to meet it! The Bible tells us: "Those who seek the Lord shall not lack any good thing" (PSALM 34:10).

It is not part of God's plan for you to lie awake at night, tossing and turning and wondering, *How am I going to pay my bills if I lose my job? What am I going to do when I retire if the stock market continues to decline? How am I going to provide for my family if my company goes through bankruptcy?* or any other concern that you may have.

The need you have may not be a need for food, water, or clothing. It may be a need for emotional healing, spiritual deliverance, a new opportunity for employment, reconciliation of a broken relationship, or any one of a host of other internal or relational needs. Friend, God is able to meet that need! He is the God who provides for His people all things that are required for a full, satisfying, and purposeful life.

Jesus said,

> I am the door of the sheep. All who ever came before me are thieves and robbers, but the sheep did not hear them. I am the door. If anyone enters by Me, he will be saved, and will go in and out and find pasture. The thief does not come except to steal, and to kill, and to destroy. I have come that they may have life, and that they may have it more abundantly. (JOHN 10:7–10)

Jesus was referring to the fact that in Bible times, shepherds slept with their sheep when the sheep spent the night in outdoor pens that were made of rocks. The shepherd would lie in the open doorway that allowed the sheep to enter the pen. With his very life, the shepherd would protect the sheep from any predators or thieves. Note that Jesus said that we are not only saved because Jesus stands between us and the enemy who seeks to steal, kill, and destroy us, but that Jesus, as our Shepherd, allows us to "find pasture." That little two-word phrase means that a sheep has all of its needs for survival met fully.

Not only does Jesus provide eternal life when we accept Him as our Savior, but He also came to provide us an abundant life. An abundant life is a life filled to overflowing with every good blessing so we can accomplish all the Lord has called us to do and to be in our lives.

If you lose your job, God has another job for you. As you trust Him to lead you and to open the doors for you, that new job will be a better opportunity.

If you have been relying on one source of income to provide the money you need to pay your bills and that source of income changes, God has countless other means of providing for you.

Never forget that God

◆ sent manna to feed more than two million Israelites who were wandering in a wilderness—in fact, He sent manna for decades to meet their need for food (EXODUS 16:35).

- brought forth water out of solid rock to give life-giving refreshment to His people *(Exodus 17:6)*.
- sent ravens with food to feed His prophet Elijah even in a time of terrible drought and famine *(1 Kings 17:4–6)*.
- multiplied a boy's sack lunch of bread and fish to feed thousands of people *(Matthew 14:14–21)*.
- provided a daily supply of oil and flour for the prophet Elijah and a single mother—in fact, this supply lasted for years until a time of famine came to an end *(1 Kings 17:10–16)*.
- multiplied a supply of oil for a widow after the death of her husband so she could support herself and her sons *(2 Kings 4:1–7)*.

The examples of provision in the Bible are too numerous to recount fully. If you doubt God's ability to provide for you, remind yourself of the many methods He has used to provide for His people. Remember as you read about His provision that God is the same today as He was in Bible times. His nature as your Provider is unwavering. His resources are unlimited. His love for you is infinite. And His power to provide is absolute.

You cannot have peace and at the same time doubt that God will provide for you. Settle the issue once and for all in your heart and mind. God is your Provider. He will meet your needs as you learn to trust and obey Him.

Trust God in all financial matters! Do you believe God is in control of your finances? Are you certain that you are handling your finances the way God wants you to handle them?

If you can answer yes to those questions, then you need to put down your worries and get on with the business at hand—continue to use your money and manage your finances in a godly way. Focus your work at those things that God has put in your path to do, and help others to the best of your ability. God has ways and means of providing for you that you haven't even dreamed about.

◆

You cannot have peace and at the same time doubt that God will provide for you. Settle the issue once and for all in your heart and mind. God is your Provider.

◆

Ask yourself "Who is in control of my material resources?" If you think you are in control, you're wrong. You certainly have a responsibility to be a good steward, or manager, of the resources God has given to you ... but you aren't in control of your income or the material substance that comes your way. Everything you have today is a gift from God to you. He is the One who has given you the energy, vitality, health, ideas, and opportunities that have led to your "possessing" all that you have. Surely as He has provided for you all your life, He will continue to provide for you as you trust Him, obey Him, and seek to do His will.

If the stock market is the governing force for your material resources, you are in trouble. If your financial future is based upon your own human ability to "figure out" the wisest investments, you are in trouble. It is only as God gives you wisdom that you can make sound financial choices in today's marketplace. Ask God to guide you. Ask Him to reveal to you if there is anything about the way you are presently handling your material resources that should be changed.

If you don't have peace in a particular area of your finances or possessions, ask God to reveal to you where you should be investing your finances. He will reveal ways in which you should be handling your resources so you can experience His peace.

I recently heard about a woman who suddenly had no peace about living in the home she had occupied for more than fifty years. She had a great urgency to be out of her house, not just for an afternoon, but to sell it and move. She put her house on the market, and to her amazement, the real-estate agent she contacted told her that her house was worth far more than she thought. Furthermore, she learned that a temple was going to be built only about a half mile from her home. Apparently, members of this religion wanted to live close to this temple and they were the ones who were driving the prices so high. She realized even as the real-estate agent gave her this information that most of her neighborhood would likely be filled with families who had a membership in that temple in a relatively short time. This loomed as a problem for this dear woman. She was single, mature in age, and felt concern about being alienated from her longtime neighbors and friends.

Now, as soon as her daughter and son-in-law heard that she was willing to move, they invited her to come live with them. They had wanted this for years, but hadn't pushed the issue since she had been so adamant about keeping her house and living in it until the day she died. She accepted their invitation, and within two months, she had sold her home and moved. For the next ten years of her life, she lived in great comfort and peace, receiving the love and tender attention of her daughter, son-in-law, and four grandchildren.

Was God in charge of this woman's financial matters? Did He provide for her? Exceedingly and abundantly more than she could ever have asked or imagined (EPHESIANS 3:20)!

ESSENTIAL BELIEF #3:
GOD MADE YOU THE WAY YOU ARE FOR A PURPOSE

There are many things about your life in which you have no control. Accept those things as part of the way God made you. A friend of mine recently said, "God gave me fair skin. My skin seems to turn red even when I think about being out in the sun. I'd love to have a nice dark tan, but it's just not the way God made me. So ... I put on sunscreen, wear my straw hat, wear loose, long-sleeved clothing, and go to sunny places anyway. Just because God didn't create me with the ability to tan doesn't mean He does not want me to enjoy a tropical island!" This woman has accepted the way God made her.

Another friend said to me years ago, "I don't know why God made me so short and gave me such dark hair and dark skin. I'm by far the shortest person in my family, and my skin and hair are darker than the skin and hair of any of my brothers and sisters. But the way God designed me sure makes my work as a missionary in Mexico easier." I laughed and said, "God saw you working as a missionary in Mexico long before your birth. Don't you realize that's why He made you the way He did?"

Your race, culture, language, nationality, sex, and many attributes of your physical being are God's "choices." God also gave you certain talents and aptitudes that make it easier for you to acquire and perfect certain skills. He gave you a degree of intelligence to develop through study and to apply to practical matters. He gave you a basic personality—even from birth some babies seem more outgoing and others seem more passive. At the time you accepted Jesus Christ as your Savior, God gave you certain spiritual gifts to use in ministry to others. The way in which you express those gifts is uniquely linked to the talents He has given you and the skills He has helped you develop.

◆

You are a unique and very special creation of God, designed for a particular purpose on this earth that God has had in mind from eternity past. Accept who God made you to be!

◆

All these traits and factors taken as a whole make you a unique person on this earth. Nobody who has ever lived before you has been just like you. Nobody alive on the earth today is just like you, not even a sibling who is your twin. Nobody who will ever live will be just like you, including your children. You are a unique and very special creation of God, designed for a particular purpose on this earth that God has had in mind from eternity past. Accept who God made you to be!

I've met people who are very upset with the ministry gifts God has given to them. A man once said to me, "God gave me a gift of mercy. Some people think I'm a wimp. I wish He had given me a gift of exhortation." To want a ministry gift other than the one God has given you is to say three things: "God, you made a mistake," "God, I don't like who You have called me to be," and "God, I'm not going to use this gift You've given me to the maximum of my ability." A person who doesn't value and appreciate his or her own ministry gift is a person who isn't eager to volunteer that gift or be willing to use the talent even when asked.

I've also met people who are very upset with the physical features God has given to them. Some people hate one aspect of their appearance to the point that they despise their whole being.

Others don't like their appearance so much that they withdraw, isolating themselves from other people. Still others hate one aspect of their appearances so much that they seem bent on destroying all aspects of their appearances—they let themselves go completely.

I'm not opposed to the use of makeup, hair stylists, or even plastic surgery. But I am deeply concerned about people who dislike their appearance so much that they turn away from God because they blame Him for the way He made them. Some go to extreme measures in improving their appearance to the point where they spend virtually all their money and much of their time on improving their image. Some withdraw from serving God openly and willingly because they are too preoccupied with what they perceive to be their less-than-attractive appearance, physical handicap or limitation, or physical weakness. They are missing out on much of the joy God desires for them to experience in life. They certainly don't have peace deep within their hearts.

Change what you can change

If you look at yourself in the mirror and conclude, "I'd like my appearance better if I lost twenty pounds," then lose those pounds. Don't moan and groan about how many fat cells God gave you. Make some decisions about how to drain those cells of their fat. On the other hand, don't look at yourself in the mirror and conclude, "I'd sure like to be six inches taller." That wish isn't going to come true no matter what you do!

What do you say when you look at yourself in the morning? Is it, "Yech!" or do you laugh and say, "Well, there are some improvements I could make here," or do you say, "Hmmm. Not bad!" Each of us should get to the point at which we say, "I'm getting better every day!"

God expects us to change whatever it takes to be our best at whatever we do. He wants us to look our best, dress our best, speak our best, act our best, try our best, give our best, and work to the best of our ability and energy. It is important to understand that the term *best* is related to your own potential, not a term of comparison with others. Your best has nothing to do with another person's best. Furthermore, your best today is not likely to be your best tomorrow. We all can improve certain aspects of our lives, and continue to improve them every day for the rest of our lives.

You will live up to the image that you have of yourself. Your actions will follow your imagination every time. If you see yourself as a failure, you will act like a failure, and in the end, you will fail.

If you see yourself as ugly, you will do very little to improve your appearance, and in the end, you will sink to the worst image you have of yourself.

If you see yourself as stupid, you won't study or learn to develop skills, you won't seek opportunities in which to apply what you do know, and you will remain as uneducated, inept, or undeveloped tomorrow as you are today.

The person you see yourself to be will in the end be the person you become.

Never stop growing in character

One area in which God always challenges us to grow and change is in our character. The Bible tells us that God is at work in every believer's life to conform that person into the character likeness of Christ Jesus. The character that God desires for us to manifest bears the hallmark qualities of love, joy, peace, longsuffering, kindness, goodness, faithfulness, gentleness, and self-control (GALATIANS 5:22–23).

Everyone can always be more loving. Everyone can always have still greater joy, be more at peace, have greater patience, show more kindness, reflect more goodness, walk in greater faithfulness. They can express themselves with greater gentleness, and manifest more self-control. No matter how mature the believer, there's always room for growth in these areas. And there are always opportunities to display these traits in new situations, environments, and relationships.

Your flesh, your mind, your outer material possessions are not the most important aspects of the real you. True importance of you is bound up in your character.

You can't have enough money, you can't have enough friends, you can't take enough drugs or enough alcohol, you can't go enough places or have enough experiences, you can't lose enough weight or gain enough muscle, you can't wear expensive enough clothing and jewelry or drive a fancy enough car to ever compensate for a poor character.

Reject lies you may have been told

I've discovered through the years that a very high percentage of people with a poor self-image acquired that self-image because of what someone said or did to them in their childhoods. In nearly all cases, somebody lied to them and they bought into the lie. Somebody told them, "You can't do that," "You'll never amount to anything," "You're not wanted," "You're not worthy," "You can't be successful," "You can't learn that," or "You can't become that." The truth is, somebody fed them an opinion that was not rooted in what God has said ... and they believed the lie. They acted according to the lie. They "lived out" the failure that somebody predicted for their life.

Sometimes people who don't like themselves voice deep criticism of self, and at other times they try to gloss over what they don't like with little jokes. I've heard people of all ages say such things as, "There's nobody who cares anyway" or "I'm just stupid" or "Mama always said I'd fail at this" or "Dad was never there for me."

Those statements, while they may be rooted in fact, also are clues to a person's emotional well-being and self-image. Anyone who says, "nobody cares," very likely believes the reason is: "there's no value in loving me." The person who says, "I'm just stupid," is voicing a belief that he is incapable of learning or is in-adequate intellectually. The person who says, "Mama always said ... ," is a person who has believed that he is unqualified for success. The person who says, "Dad was never there for me" is a person who internalized the belief that he was unworthy of Dad's love and attention. These are all signs that point to the conclusion: "I'm not lovable." That's a lie! God says you are lovable!

Take stock of what you have been told about yourself. Were you told the truth? If you have in any way been taught a lie about yourself—which is something contrary to what God says about you—then it is up to you to reject what you have been told and believe what God's Word says about you. You are lovable. You are worthy. You are intelligent and talented. God has created you to succeed.

Accept the truth others speak to you

Other people have been told a truth about themselves that they have refused to believe. Thousands of young women across our nation believe they are overweight and are struggling with anorexia nervosa, bulimia, and other eating disorders—many have refused to believe parents, teachers, doctors, and close friends who have told them repeatedly that they are not overweight. They have refused to accept the truth about themselves.

If someone says to you, "You look fantastic today," don't dismiss his or her comment. Accept in that person's eyes that you do look fantastic!

If someone says to you, "You're really smart" or "You're really creative," don't dismiss their compliment with self-deprecating remarks or a comment that sweeps aside their assessment of you. Agree with the person! You are smart to some degree, in some ways. You are creative to some degree, in some ways. And the person who gives you that compliment is trying to express appreciation for who you are. Accept the compliment and that you are being appreciated!

At times a person will respond to a compliment with a "thank you," but the minute he walks away, he says to himself, "He doesn't really mean that. He's just saying that. I wish he wouldn't say things like that." If you find yourself thinking such thoughts after you receive a compliment, take note. There's something about yourself that you aren't valuing or appreciating.

A surgeon once told me about a patient of his who was in a terrible automobile accident. The victim was a beautiful teenage girl. The accident horribly mangled her face. After several years and several surgeries, everybody who saw that young woman thought she was even more beautiful than she had been before the accident. But the girl herself still saw a mangled, disfigured face when she looked in the mirror. She refused to believe the truth that others frequently spoke to her. She discounted every compliment and actually became angry when a person said, "You're very beautiful."

This surgeon said, "It wasn't until a total stranger at church spoke to her one day that she began to change her self-image. This person was praying with her and she said, 'The Lord has just spoken to my heart that I'm to tell you something.' The young woman said, 'What is it?' The woman praying with her said, 'The Lord wants you to know that He thinks you are beautiful and He wants you to start thinking about yourself the way He thinks about you.' That young woman began to weep. She didn't stop crying for hours. Believing the truth about herself was a hard thing for her to accept, but once she did, she was able to let go of the bitterness and anger she had held on to in the aftermath of her accident. Believing the truth brought about a healing deep inside her, even though the injuries to her face had healed long before."

Do you have the courage to lay down the lies you have been told and to receive God's truth about your life? Do you have the courage to walk in that truth?

Accept who God created you to be. Change what you know you can change, need to change, or God is asking you to change. Trade in the lies of others for God's truth about you. Be willing to continue to yield to the conforming work of the Holy Spirit and to develop the character He desires for you to develop.

And friend, you will have greater peace deep within.

ESSENTIAL BELIEF #4:
GOD HAS A PLACE WHERE YOU TRULY BELONG

A person who feels unwanted, rejected, or continually lonely is not a person who has peace deep within. Feeling that we belong to someone or to a group of people who love us is vital for our inner peace.

Everybody on earth wants to be loved and to love someone. When you feel as if you are connected to someone who appreciates you, values you, and loves you, you have feelings of deep tranquillity and calm.

God tells us plainly that we are to have fellowship with other believers in the church. The Bible clearly tells us that we are not to forsake the assembling of ourselves together *(Hebrews 10:25)*. Why? Because every person in the body of Christ has been given a unique personality, set of abilities and skills, at least one ministry gift, and natural talents. God expects each of us to share these unique attributes with other believers in a loving, generous way so needs within any particular body of believers will be met and the gospel will be extended to those outside the church. We need one another in the church. We are part of one another.

At the church I pastor, we have members who represent more than fifty nations. What a warm fellowship we have!

You may not go to a church as large or diverse, but in a sense, you do belong to such a church—as believers in Christ, we are all part of the same body of Christ that encompasses the entire world. The Holy Spirit connects you to believers everywhere. The apostle Paul wrote, "There is neither Jew nor Greek, there is neither slave nor free, there is neither male nor female; for you are all one in Christ Jesus. And if you are Christ's, then you are Abraham's seed, and heirs according to the promise" *(Galatians 3:28–29)*. Paul wrote to the Ephesians, "There is one body and one Spirit, just as you were called in one hope of your calling; one Lord, one faith, one baptism; one God and Father of all, who is above all, and through all, and in you all" *(Ephesians 4:4–6)*.

◆

As believers in Christ, we are all part of the same Body of Christ that encompasses the entire world. The Holy Spirit connects you to believers everywhere.

◆

Jesus prayed for His disciples and us on the night before His crucifixion:

> I do not pray for these alone, but also for those who will believe in Me through their word; that they all may be one, as You, Father, are in Me, and I in You; that they also may be one in Us, that the world may believe that You sent Me. And the glory which You gave Me I have given them, that they may be one just as We are one:

I in them, and You in Me; that they may be made
perfect in one, and that the world may know that You
have sent Me, and have loved them as you have loved
Me. *(JOHN 17:20–23)*

Jesus' prayer was that we might have a strong sense of
belonging to God, and that we might have a strong sense of
belonging to one another, to the extent that we have a "oneness"
in belief, fellowship, communication, faith, and purpose.

Every person has a lonely moment now and then. Do I ever get
lonely? Yes. But I know what to do when I'm lonely. I work on my
relationship with the Lord Jesus Christ. And I reach out to call
friends and invite them to come over or go someplace with me.
No person needs to accept loneliness as a fact of his or her life.
Nor does God desire for loneliness to be the general state of being
for any person. Deep loneliness and peace cannot coexist.

Jesus always called His people to be in association with one
another. He sent out His disciples two by two *(LUKE 10:1)*. He said He
would be present wherever "two or three are gathered together in
My name" *(MATTHEW 18:20)*. He said that if "two of you agree on earth
concerning anything that they ask," He would do it *(MATTHEW 18:19)*.

A person who lives as an island is a person who has opted for
an isolated, lonely, out-of-touch-with-others existence. No person
can live that way long before deep unrest invades his heart.

Trust God to help you gain a strong sense of belonging to Him,
and to provide for you a "family" of fellow believers to whom you
can belong.

As you grow, then, in friendships, reach out to others.
genuinely and generously give to others. Give your time. Give
words of sincere affection. Give a listening ear. Give comfort. Give
encouragement. Love others with the love of the Lord flowing
through you to them.

Become a loyal and faithful member of your church. Find
a place where you feel you truly "belong" and nurture those who
are in that community with you. Even as you bond together with
other believers, reach out to those who don't believe to encourage
them to join your group and be part of your warm fellowship.

ESSENTIAL BELIEF #5:
GOD HAS A PLAN FOR YOUR FULFILLMENT

For real inner peace, a person needs to know that he or she is competent, able, capable, and skilled at doing something. The "something" may be a task that the world as a whole considers to be a menial chore or service. Nonetheless, if you can do that task, and you know that you do it well, you are competent!

Many years ago I had lunch with a group of people at a restaurant that is part of a popular chain. We were sitting at a table that gave us a view of the short-order cooks in the kitchen area. One of the women in the group, whom I knew to be a gourmet cook, said as she watched the cooks at work, "I love to cook and I'm a good cook, but I'll tell you one thing, I could never do what those guys do."

I said, "What do you mean?"

She said, "I could never juggle that many orders, fix that many kinds of food, hear new orders coming in from several waitresses, prepare an order all in a matter of minutes, and figure out how to keep the grill cleaned and French fries in the fryer all along the way."

There's a wonderful sense of peace that comes when you know you are capable of putting in a good performance or doing a good job. That's true if you are a concert violinist about to walk onto the stage for a performance ... a baseball player about to step out of the dugout to the batter's box ... a mom who is diapering a baby while keeping a watchful eye on a busy two-year-old child ... a lawyer about to make an opening statement before a jury ... a teacher preparing to greet a class on the first day of school ... a surgeon about to walk into a surgical suite ... or a short-order beginning to prepare a cheeseburger.

Reject nagging self-doubts

Those who don't feel competent have a feeling that they might be about to fail. They often say to themselves, "I don't really know how to do this and I'm about to be found out," "What if I hurt somebody because I'm just not good enough at this?" or

"I shouldn't be here doing this." Those nagging self-doubts destroy inner peace.

God's desire is for every person to become skilled at using the talents and aptitudes he or she was given from birth. He also greatly desires each to use the ministry gift received at the time of their salvation. The turning of talents and gifts into skills is part of our responsibility. It sometimes takes education or the acquiring of specific knowledge in order to become competent. It sometimes takes the learning of repetitive tasks. It always takes practice. Nobody is fully competent at any activity the first time he or she tries that activity—that was true for you as a toddler learning to walk and feed yourself as much as it is true for a business intern learning to trade stocks or a young preacher about to enter the pulpit for the first time. You may be good as a rookie, but if you are honest with yourself, you'll recognize you aren't an expert the first time out in the application of any skill.

Continue to learn and practice

God's desire is that we continue to develop in our talents, aptitudes, and ministry gifts every day of our lives. We should never stop practicing or stop learning, no matter how experienced and skilled we may become. I'm told that the truly great concert pianists still practice playing scales on a routine basis. Top athletes still work out and practice "basic drills" during training camps and warm-up sessions, no matter how many years they've been in the professional ranks.

My favorite hobby is taking photographs, developing the film, and printing photos in my darkroom. I've taken literally tens of thousands of photographs in my life. I've also attended seminars and availed myself of expert instruction on a number of occasions. I routinely read magazines and instructional materials that describe new darkroom techniques or tell about new camera and film products. I'm a much better photographer than I was thirty years ago, but I also firmly believe that I'm not as good a photographer as I'm going to be ten years from now! I intend to keep learning and keep improving every year for the rest of my life.

God will not lead you to "become" something without aiding you to become the "best" you can possibly be in that area. He will not give you a talent and then fail to give you opportunities for discovering, using, developing, practicing, and perfecting it.

Trust God to help you learn and grow

Please do not misunderstand me on this matter of competency—there's nothing wrong with feeling a certain amount of incompetence or inadequacy. Incompetence and inadequacy are two different things:

◆ Incompetence says, "I can't do this because I'm lacking something."

◆ Inadequacy says, "I can't do this in my own strength."

The apostle Paul wrote, "Not that we are sufficient of ourselves to think of anything as being from ourselves, but our sufficiency is from God" (2 CORINTHIANS 3:5).

The very fact that you are capable of continuing to learn and develop tells you that you will never be fully competent at anything. Each of us will always have plenty of room for growth, and that's part of God's design for us. We also will never be fully adequate because we will always have a need for God to do in us, for us, and through us what He alone can do. God is the author and finisher of our lives; not only of our faith, but of all aspects of the potential He has built into us.

◆

The very fact that you are capable of continuing to learn and develop tells you that you will never be fully competent at anything. Each of us will always have plenty of room for growth, and that's part of God's design for us.

◆

As a pastor, I know that it is the Lord who "completes" what I preach—I often receive reports of how He has caused a person to hear something I have preached with greater emphasis or greater impact than I put into the sermon. The Lord has a way of personalizing His Word, including the preached word, for every person who hears it. He does this so the person will apply the message to his or her own heart and life, and respond in the way the Father desires. Truly, the sufficiency of any sermon lies in what God does with it after it leaves a preacher's lips.

The same thing is true for your job, no matter what that job is. You can teach to the best of your ability, but it is the Lord who will complete the learning process in a student's mind and heart. You can perform a surgical procedure to the best of your ability, but it is the Lord who will complete the healing process in a patient's life. You can plant seeds and then water, fertilize, and cultivate a field, but it is the Lord who turns seeds into a harvest.

Don't ever lock yourself into saying, "I can't, I can't, I can't," when you feel less than fully competent. Instead say, "By the grace of God and with the help of God, I can do this. The Lord is my sufficiency. He is living inside me, and He will make me adequate for whatever task He calls me to accomplish. He will give me the insights, knowledge, direction, strength, energy, vitality, focus, associations, contacts, and all other things that are necessary!"

Anytime you feel inadequate, go to God and say, "I feel inadequate. I'm trusting You to be my adequacy."

If you feel ignorant, trust God to be your source of wisdom.

If you feel weak or exhausted, trust God to be your strength.

If you feel yourself totally without adequate resources, trust God to provide what you need.

The apostle Paul said, "I can do all things through Christ who strengthens me" (PHILIPPIANS 4:13). He also wrote how the Lord had spoken to him and said, "My grace is sufficient for you, for My strength is made perfect in weakness." Paul's response was, "Therefore most gladly I will rather boast in my infirmities, that the power of Christ may rest upon me ... For when I am weak, then I am strong" (2 CORINTHIANS 12:9–10).

Paul knew that in every area where he was weak, Christ would more than make up for his weakness, and the result would be far more strength than he could ever have apart from Christ. The same is true for you and me. When we rely on Jesus Christ to be our sufficiency, He steps in and makes us "more" than anything we could ever be in our own strength, intellect, or ability. If we are willing to trust Him and rely upon Him, He will take what we offer—doing our best and giving our best—and enhance it with His own presence, power, wisdom, and creative spirit. He will produce more than would otherwise be physically, naturally, or materially possible.

All of us face things in our lives that we have never done before. Any new venture—whether it is going away to college, getting married, having a baby, starting a new job or launching a business, changing a career, embarking on an outreach ministry—will challenge your competence. If you wait until you "get it all together" before you try something you've never done before, you'll never step out to try anything. It takes faith to start something—and part of our expression of faith is our saying within ourselves, "I may be inadequate in myself ... but with Christ dwelling in me and executing His will, plan, and purpose in me, I am adequate!"

A person who feels he or she is a "failure" does not have peace. A person who feels as if he is on thin ice, is in over his head, or has taken on more than he can carry, does not have peace.

Believe God when He says that He loves you. Trust Him to help you fulfill anything He leads you to undertake.

Never Discredit Your Purpose

Finally, when God reveals His purpose to you, never discount that purpose. Never say to others, "I'm just a ..."

Every form of honest, morally sound, godly work is worthy of reward, worthy of your doing it to the best of your ability, and worthy of respect.

WHY SUCH AN EMPHASIS ON WHAT YOU BELIEVE ABOUT GOD?

Why am I placing such great importance on what you believe about God and His relationship to you?

Because if you truly believe God is not sovereign ...

If you don't believe God desires to provide fully for you—materially, physically, emotionally, spiritually ...

If you don't believe God considers you to be worthy and lovable …

If you don't believe God cares about your loneliness …

If you don't believe God has a plan for your fulfillment and deep satisfaction …

You are never going to trust God to do what He wants to do for you. You are never going to trust Him to give you peace. You are never going to put yourself in a position to receive all the blessings He desires to pour out upon you.

Just as it is critically important that you not lay down your peace, it is just as critical that you pick up, embrace fully, and become firmly committed to right beliefs about God and His relationship with you.

If you are a person who holds to relative truth, if you are a person who quickly compromises your beliefs or who has no real convictions, you are not going to have deep peace. You can't have deep peace. You will always be in some kind of flux on the inside, moving from emotion to emotion and from opinion to opinion, never really reaching a place where you have "settled the matter" in your mind and heart about the most important issues of life.

Face your life today. Do you have deep tranquillity? Do you genuinely value who you are, why you are on the earth, and the traits God has given you? Do you like the person God created you to be? Do you believe God has a plan and purpose for you? Do you believe He has a "place" where you can belong and be loved?

If not, ask the Lord to help you address the inner conflict you feel. His desire is that you might experience serenity in your heart so you can truly enjoy your life, your relationships with other people, and your relationship with Him. He wants to bind up the fragmentation, connect the pieces of your life, and calm the agitation you feel within. He desires to give you peace and end the turmoil in your own heart. ❖

If you have trusted Jesus Christ as your savior as a result of reading this book, or if it has helped you in your spiritual journey, we would like to know. E-mail us at info@fcsdirect.familychristian.com. We invite you to visit your favorite Family Christian Store for books, Bibles, music, gifts and so much more! We have everything you need to help deepen your faith.

CHRISTIANITY FOR SKEPTICS
by Steve Kumar

Does God exist? Why is there evil? Is the Bible for real? This book presents the scholarly, analytical arguments of Christians and non-Christians whose conclusions all support a basis for belief.

Item#895791

THE CASE FOR CHRIST

by Lee Strobel

Using his skills as a former investigative journalist, Lee Strobel digs deep into the evidence for Christ from the fields of science, philosophy, and history.

Item#854320

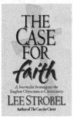
THE CASE FOR FAITH
by Lee Strobel

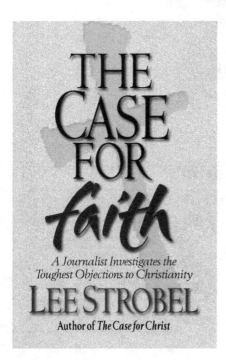

In this follow up to The Case for Christ, Lee Strobel speaks directly to those who may be feeling attracted to Jesus but who are faced with formidable intellectual barriers standing squarely in their path.

Item#896362

HOW GOOD IS GOOD ENOUGH?

by Andy Stanley

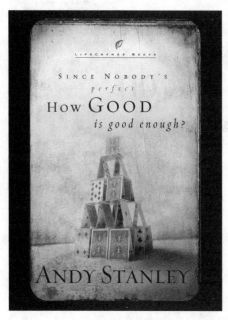

How good do you have to be to get to heaven? Pastor Andy Stanley tackles that troublesome question, leading both believers and skeptics to a grateful awareness of God's grace and mercy.

Item#951461

SIMPLY JESUS
by Joseph M. Stowell

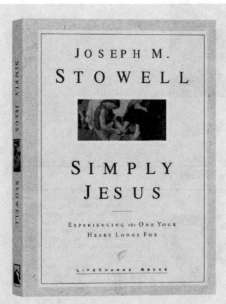

Only you can make the choice to just know Jesus or enter into an experience with Him. This book contains dramatic stories and surprising insights on how believers can experience significant life-change as they encounter Christ.

Item#914502

THE RAGAMUFFIN GOSPEL
by Brennan Manning

As Christians, we often beat ourselves up over our shortcomings, but this book reminds us that even as "ragamuffins," the Father beckons us to Him with a furious love that burns brightly for His children.

Item#888670

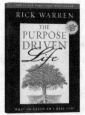
THE PURPOSE DRIVEN LIFE
by Rick Warren

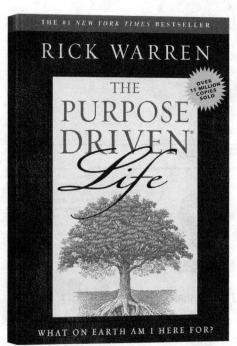

Why am I here? What is my purpose? More than fifteen million people have gotten answers from Rick Warren's *New York Times* bestseller which describes step-by-step God's perfect plan for each life.

Item#838487

WHO MADE GOD?

by Ravi Zacharias

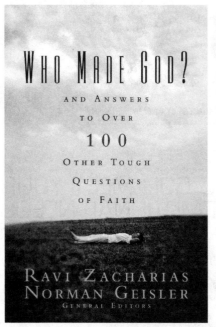

Authors answer 100 commonly asked questions about Christianity and the presence of evil on earth. Part two of the book delves into other faiths, including Islam, Mormonism, Hinduism, and Buddhism.

Item#949888

LETTING GOD MEET YOUR EMOTIONAL NEEDS
by Cindi McMenamin

Women long to be loved, to be known, to be understood. But only the Creator of women can truly meet those needs at their deepest level. Learn where true love, acceptance, and security lie in this book.

Item#940332

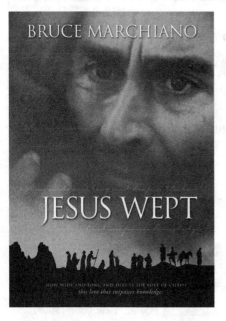

JESUS WEPT
by Bruce Marchiano

John 11:35. It is the shortest verse in the entire Bible. "Jesus wept." What power there is in those two words and what comfort we can all take as we deal with the human tragedy in our lives.

Item#958504

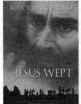

THE POWER OF PRAYING TOGETHER

by Stormie Omartian

Discover how to tap into the power of group prayer, find unity in prayer, and cover the world with God's power. Link your hearts with others before The Lord and open yourself up to amazing strength.

Item#949911

GRACE WALK
by Steve McVey

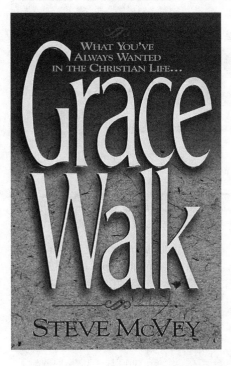

Nothing you have ever done, nothing you could ever do, will match the incomparable joy of letting Jesus live His life through you. This book helps you develop and enjoy a deep relationship with God.

Item#843074

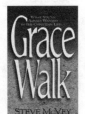

FORGIVE AND LOVE AGAIN
by John Nieder & Thomas M. Thompson

A warm and compassionate bestseller containing life-changing insights to help us forgive. Find freedom from the past and peace that comes from God by learning to truly forgive from the heart.

Item#949950

SECRETS OF THE VINE

by Bruce Wilkinson

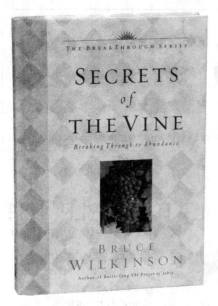

In his powerful follow up to *The Prayer of Jabez*, Dr. Bruce Wilkinson explores John 15 to show readers how to make maximum impact for God. Learn three life-changing truths that will lead you to new joy and effectiveness in His kingdom.

Item#905575

KNOWING THE BIBLE 101
by Bruce Bickel and Stan Jantz

A must have for readers who have been planning to get serious about Bible study. The perfect resource for longtime believers, new Christians, Bible study leaders, and even seekers who want to read the Bible for the first time.

Item#949938

HEAVEN, MY FATHER'S HOUSE

by Anne Graham Lotz

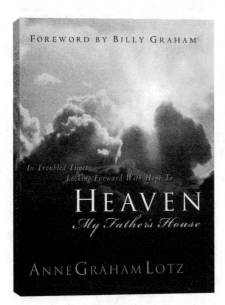

Amid the turbulence of today's terror-besieged world, we cling to the hope of a heavenly home where we will be welcomed into eternal peace and safety. Do not fear death, but be filled with hope and joy.

Item#923832

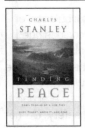
FINDING PEACE
by Charles Stanley

Living without God's peace in our lives is a path leading to nowhere. This book shows us how to reverse course and open our hearts to Him. Learn to combat regret, anxiety, and fear by breaking down obstacles that block peace with the Lord.

Item#950053